CHAUCER STUDIES II

CHAUCER'S LANGUAGE AND THE PHILOSOPHERS' TRADITION

CHAUCER STUDIES

I MUSIC IN THE AGE OF CHAUCER
Nigel Wilkins

III ESSAYS ON TROILUS AND CRISEYDE
Edited by Mary Salu

In preparation

Chaucer's Boccaccio:
Sources and Analogues of *Troilus* and the Knight's and Franklin's Tales
Edited and Translated by Nicholas Haveley

The Sound of Chaucer's Poetry
Eric Stanley

Sources and Analogues of Chaucer's Dream Poetry
Edited and Translated by B. A. Windeatt

CHAUCER'S LANGUAGE
AND THE
PHILOSOPHERS'
TRADITION

J. D. BURNLEY

Lo here, the forme of olde clerkis speche
In poetrie

D. S. BREWER · ROWMAN & LITTLEFIELD

First published 1979 by D. S. Brewer Ltd,
240 Hills Road, Cambridge and PO Box 24, Ipswich IP1 1JJ
and Rowman and Littlefield Inc, 81 Adams Drive,
Totowa, New Jersey N.J. 07512, USA

British Library Cataloguing in Publication Data
Burnley, J D
   Chaucer's language and the philosophers'
   tradition. – (Chaucer studies; 2).
   1. Chaucer, Geoffrey – Language
   I. Title   II. Series
   821'.1   PR1940

ISBN 0-85991-051-2

To my parents

Photoset by Rowland Phototypesetting Limited,
Bury St. Edmunds, Suffolk
Printed in Great Britain by St. Edmundsbury Press Limited,
Haverhill, Suffolk

Contents

ACKNOWLEDGEMENTS

I am happy to acknowledge here the generosity of the University of Sheffield in providing financial assistance towards the publication of this study.

The debts I owe to colleagues and students in London, Lancaster, and Sheffield are too compendious to recite, so that I hope they will forgive me if I do not attempt to specify them. No doubt the subjects of past discussions will be recognizable in the chapters of this book. I would, however, like to record my gratitude to Professor G. V. Smithers whose undergraduate lectures first drew my attention to the possibilities of lexical analysis exploited here. I am grateful also to Professor Norman Blake for his encouragement to present my ideas in book form and his continuing interest in the project. Finally I should like to thank Miss Sandra Harrison for cheerfully and speedily typing the greater part of my manuscript.

Abbreviations

CHAUCER

CT.	*The Canterbury Tales*
BD.	*The Book of the Duchess*
HF.	*The House of Fame*
AA.	*Anelida and Arcite*
PF.	*The Parliament of Fowls*
Bo.	*Boece*
TC.	*Troilus and Criseyde*
LGW.	*The Legend of Good Women*
ABC	*An ABC*
Pity	*The Complaint unto Pity*
Lady	*A Complaint to his Lady*
Mars	*The Complaint of Mars*
Stedfastnesse	*Lak of Stedfastnesse*
W. Unc.	*Against Women Unconstant*
Complaint	*A Balade of Complaint*
RR.	*The Romaunt of the Rose*

All the above are cited from:
The Works of Geoffrey Chaucer, edited by F. N. Robinson, Second
Edition (London, 1957)

Tusc. Disp.	*Tuscalan Disputations*, with an English translation by J. E. King, Loeb Classical Library (London, 1971)
Sir Gawain	*Sir Gawain and the Green Knight*, edited by J. R. R. Tolkien and E. V. Gordon, Second Edition, revised by Norman Davis (Oxford, 1968)
ST.	St. Thomas Aquinas, *Summa Theologiae*, 60 vols, with facing translation by members of the English-speaking Dominican Provinces (London, 1964–6)
PL.	*Patrologiae Cursus Completus*, Series Latina, 221 vols, edited by J.-P. Migne (Paris, 1844–80)

A.I.D.E.L.A.	Association internationale d' éditeurs de linguistique appliquée
E.E.T.S.	Early English Text Society
ELH.	*English Literary History*
JEGPh.	*Journal of English and Germanic Philology*
M.E.D.	*Middle English Dictionary*
M.H.R.A.	Modern Humanities Research Association
MLN.	*Modern Language Notes*
MLR.	*Modern Language Review*
MP.	*Modern Philology*
PMLA.	*Publications of the Modern Language Association of America*
S.A.T.F.	Société des Anciens Textes Francais
SP.	*Studies in Philology*
UTQ.	*University of Toronto Quarterly*

Introduction

THIS BOOK IS about language. It is also about ideas. But, more particularly, it is about the inter-relation of the two. Such an approach, relating language structures to conceptual structures, is an unfamiliar introduction to the works of Chaucer, so that it seems desirable to begin by stating some of the linguistic assumptions upon which it is based. Thereafter, although my chapters are based upon the interpretation of linguistic usage, it should be possible to proceed without undue reference to distracting technical terminology. Linguistic analysis is not considered as an end in itself, but only as an indispensable precursor to a fuller literary understanding.

To say that language is structured is perhaps the most familiar cliché that can be expressed about it. What is usually implied by this is that the relations between the elements which make up any linguistic utterance can be shown to be predictable by relatively stable specifications known as 'rules.' The stability of these rules for constructing utterances is of course necessary for the language to fulfil that other cliché of its characterization, its primary purpose of communication within society. Structure does not exist at the concrete level of the utterance itself; rather, its items are defined by relationships existing at the level of the abstract patterns underlying the utterance. The actual words uttered can, for example, be grouped together into classes according to the circumstances of their occurrence, and it is the relationship between these classes, not between the words themselves, which is specified by the rules of grammar. For example, the word *Smith* can be shown to contrast with words like *red, every, go, swift,* in terms of the place which each can occupy in the sentence pattern. Furthermore, although words like *smith, sky*, and *corn* will apparently correspond to *Smith* in some details of both their form and occurrence, they may be separated into different classes – proper noun, count noun, or mass noun – by such factors as whether or not their occurrence may be preceded directly by a definite or indefinite article, whether they may take a plural inflexion, and so on.

In a much simplified form, the above examples illustrate what the linguist habitually thinks of when he speaks of the grammatical structure of language. But, whilst this book depends for its existence upon a kind of structuring in language, the structure with which we shall be concerned is neither one of grammar nor phonology, but the less precisely definable one of usage.[1] To avoid confusion with the more usual technical sense of the word 'structure' – which is best reserved for grammar, phonology, and some approaches to semantics – I shall, in this introductory discussion, substitute for it the term 'architecture.'[2] In a very general way, the architecture of a language belongs to its semantic function, but is related to neither grammatical semantics nor the logical analysis of lexical meaning; indeed its study may be better termed 'general stylistics' than 'semantics.'[3] Any historical language is partially composed of sub-systems of usage whose terms may be of similar significance, or refer to the same external objects, yet will still be perceived by any competent speaker to belong to distinct sub-systems. For example, the words *first* and *primary* may have the same significance, but are recognizable as belonging to different levels of formality, whilst *refuse disposal operative* and *bin-man* may have the same referent, but belong to markedly different registers. The relationships between such stylistic variants have a stability which makes them significant to anyone familiar with modern English.[4] Of even greater stability, and especially in the written mode of the language, we recognize associations between such formal patterns as habitually co-occurring groups of words (collocational sets), repeated verbal strategies or more condensed idioms, and finely differentiated semantic patterns (lexical fields). Such formal features are associated in the language architecture with ideas or events which are, or have been, important in the culture in which the language is used. Consequently they occur habitually in linguistic utterances. In the succeeding pages of this book we shall be considering such features of usage related to moral and psychological themes important to the world of Chaucer.

An exhaustive treatment of the architecture of any language is, by definition, impossible, since, as a system of stylistically-differentiated items and procedures, it depends upon associations whose stability cannot be objectively tested: prediction of the existence of such an association for any given speaker of the language is a matter of probability rather than certainty. Consider, for example, the phonaesthetic pattern in which, according to Firth, the sequence /sn/, occurring initially, connotes pejoration in English.[5] Subjectively, many will agree with this observation, and they may be able to produce a list of words to support their feeling. But there are also those who would deny such an association, and produce counter-examples like *snug* or *snowdrop* to support their contention. Such limiting cases aside, it must be admitted, however, that mastery of the stable architecture of a language is a sign of the fullest competence in that language, for it is in the appropriate observance, or in the deliberate breach, of architectural norms that language reaches its greatest communicative efficacy.[6] Indeed, by heeding consciously the architecture of a language, at the same time as unconsciously decoding its structure, the listener is likely not only to know more subtly what a speaker is telling him, but may also perceive revealing details which the speaker has not consciously included in his message, some of which, indeed, he may have been happy to conceal.

Now, since we are accustomed to regard poetry as language used with maximum significance, it is among the writings of poets that we might expect to find the most adroit use of language architecture. Conversely, we must assume that mastery of language architecture is a *sine qua non* of the subtle, yet valid, interpretation of poetry. But from this assumption a critical problem arises. If the understanding of any utterance is considered to be the process of attributing meaning to a text, if the presupposition also exists that poetic texts involve complexity of meaning, and if linguistic competence is to be assessed by the ability to attribute meanings of greater subtlety, then how are we to distinguish between valid literary interpretation and the heinous crime of 'reading in?' Clearly, there is no definitive answer to this problem, but an interim answer is offered by a scholarly consensus upon what meanings are possible. Such a consensus can be achieved by the adoption of two unspoken assumptions, one of which logically precedes the other: firstly, that a poem is in some sense a communication between a poet and his audience; and secondly, upon a prior consensus on the nature, knowledge, and language skills of that audience. If we accept these conditions the problem of the validity of interpretation becomes more manageable, since the only interpretations which can be considered valid are those which correspond with the assumed nature of the audience. Historical criticism should aim to offer the fullest interpretation which coincides with the narrowest specification of the abilities of the poem's audience at its date of composition. Clearly, therefore, a knowledge of contemporary language architecture is as crucial as literary-historical and cultural knowledge in arriving at a valid interpretation of a poem on historical lines.[7] The aim of this book, then, is not to provide any particular interpretation of Chaucerian works, even though the direction which such an interpretation would take may

3

occasionally be obvious; it is rather to furnish a small part of the general blueprint with which any interpretation of Chaucer's poetic achievement must coincide if it is to be valid. It investigates a portion of the architecture of the language used by Chaucer and his London contemporaries, gives some indication of how it could be exploited by them, and traces some of the ways in which that architecture came into existence.

The complexity of a language's architecture, unlike that of its grammatical structure, depends fairly directly upon the complexity of the culture in which it is used. Complexity is greatly increased by the existence of a written tradition, since written language facilitates communication between sub-cultures which may be geographically remote, thereby introducing dialectal sub-systems into the sum of usages. Furthermore, a written tradition telescopes time as well as distance, so that the language preserves usages from earlier stages of its development, gaining a diachronic perspective. One need only look at the great historical dictionaries to see how the size and variety of the lexicon of literary languages is the product of a chronological process of the accumulation of documents. A similar process is at work in the creation of the diction of a literary tradition. In this respect, the Middle English of Chaucer's time occupies a peculiarly interesting position, since throughout the twelfth and thirteenth centuries, when the intellectual foundations of western medieval civilization had been laid, English had been regarded as a third-rate language, hardly to be considered for the composition of serious literature. In the twelfth century documents written in English are hard to find at all, whilst for more than a hundred and fifty years after the Conquest, the first language of those with power and prestige was French: English, they used only for utilitarian purposes.

Since it did not participate in matters of much intellectual complexity, and since it scarcely possessed a written tradition by the year 1300, we should reasonably expect the architecture of Middle English to be a very simple one. This, indeed, is the traditional view which H. S. Bennett applied to the language of Chaucer when he claimed that the latter could not draw from his words those 'peripheral overtones' of meaning which the modern reader associates with poetic practice:

> Chaucer wrote in an age when words were still limited in their associations. Often, indeed, no word was available which would express Chaucer's exact meaning, and he had to coin a word, or more generally to take one over from a Latin or French source.

Chaucer's words, we are told, 'have a clear-cut and limited meaning' and lack the 'overtones and associations which now cling about certain words and phrases.'[8] The implication of such remarks is that, lacking connotations, Chaucer's language also lacks a significant architecture to be exploited by the poet and appreciated by his audience. The development of this book will, I hope, illustrate the limits of the truth of such remarks, but it will be necessary to state in advance the assumptions about the linguistic situation in Chaucer's England which cause me to question the complete acceptability of such a view.

Before the first quarter of the fifteenth century, and indeed, it is arguable, long after then, it is a fallacy to equate the language of Englishmen too definitively with the English language. English culture in the Middle Ages was not monolingual, but was served by Latin and French as well as by the descendant of the vernaculars used in England before the Conquest. The situation was a highly complex one in which stages of bilingualism and diglossia co-existed or succeeded one another, and in which developments in the spoken language were often out of step with skills in the written forms of the languages involved.[9] There is no space to trace such developments in detail, but certain essential points must be made. It is an axiom of modern sociolinguistic theory that no speaker of a language is limited to only one style of speech. Furthermore, if he has some bilingual competence, his switches from one style to another may correspond to what the monolingual perceives as switches from one language to another. This is as much as to say that, in a bilingual culture, the linguistic architecture extends beyond the bounds of traditional language groupings. In Middle English the switch between historically different languages was frequent for anyone involved in the more elaborate concerns of the society, and we should not think of such switching as representing competence in two quite discrete languages. Well into the fourteenth century French remained the language of instruction in the schools, and since we know that students tended to lapse into their English mother tongue in informal discussion, it is inevitable that such conversations would contain a large number of Franco-Latin technical phrases embedded in English contexts.[10] Some such background as this probably lies behind the host of legal, scientific, and philosophical terms which find their way into English in both courtly and religious literature.

The tradition of devotional literature in English, and no doubt sermons based upon it, is important as the only English literary tradition which can plausibly be claimed to exhibit continuity from pre-Conquest times.[11] It is a tradition of writings produced by clerks for lay people, and it reflects the bilingual skills of the clerks in the introduction of many words and phrases from French at their earliest recorded occurrence. But more than this, one can trace the introduction of some of the complexes of ideas which these words represented. The author of the *Ancrene Wisse* (c. 1225) is among the first English authors to refer to the ideals of courtly love and love service; less surprisingly, his work contains one of the earliest references to the theological concept of charity, which he glosses as *luue*.

Other devotional works reveal the development of the familiar architecture surrounding the word. In the *Ormulum* (c.1200), the extension from affect to effect, from charitable feeling to the act of alms-giving, is found, and the word *kariteþ* is found collocating with *allmess werrkess*. The traditional conceptual opposition between charity and envy is attested by 1300, whilst the familiar definition of charity as love of God beyond wife, child, and all earthly things, occurs in a devotional manuscript dated about 1225. These examples of conceptual relationships, collocational habits and verbal strategies are here limited to the usage of one word, but they are enough to indicate how contact between English and French had begun to lend greater complexity to the architecture of the language even before the close of the thirteenth century.

By the end of that century the wind of social change was blowing briskly through England. Competence in spoken French had seriously declined, so that even great lords were often less happy in French than in English, whilst, in the course of the fourteenth century, this decline was extended to the written language also. At the same time a new wealthy class was being created by commerce in urban centres like London, so that towards the end of the century Langland can testify ironically to the substance of the burgesses and their consequent allure for mendicant friars:

> Noþer in cote noþer in caytyf hous. was crist y-bore,
> Bote in a burgeises hous. þe beste of alle þe toune.
> (C-text, xv, 90–1)

Such men of substance, aware of the prestige of French literature but incapable of enjoying it fully, perhaps provided the audience for a new and more sophisticated secular literature of entertainment in English. The Old French *lais*, a literature of notable refinement originally associated exclusively with Anglo-Norman aristocratic circles, began to be translated and imitated in English, and, in London, romances of some literary pretension began to be produced. *King Alisaunder*, for example, has an author who can consult Latin as well as French source material, and can brandish French technical terms of astrology, masonry and the law. Furthermore, he can effectively use contemporary epistolary formulae (6675) or employ epic decorative devices drawn from the Old French literary tradition.[12] The attempt made by this author to create the illusion of an English secular literary tradition was not a piecemeal one, but a constructive effort to imitate the literary prestige of French. He is well aware of the dignity of tradition, and assures his readers of the seriousness of his work:

> þis is nouȝth romaunce of skof,
> Ac storye ymade of maistres wyse,
> Of þis werlde of mest pryse.
> (Bodleian MS., 668–70)

6

Such claims of learned authority are a sign that popularized learning was about to be introduced into English, bringing with it the phrasings and conceptual patterns of its Franco-Latin ancestry. By the end of the fourteenth century the process was complete, and in an English poem which achieved great and widespread popularity Langland was able to recommend a respect for learning to ordinary men:

> *For-thi ich consaile alle cristene. clergie to honoure.*
>
> (C-text, xv, 43)

Since Jespersen published his famous chart of French borrowing showing the pace of borrowing to have been at its height during the lifetime of Chaucer, it has usually been interpreted by historians of English as reflecting the decline in competence in written French, and the consequent tendency for English to fulfil roles previously discharged by that language. Such an explanation often involves the assumption that the available English vocabulary had lexical gaps or uncertainties which, for functional reasons, had to be remedied by the appropriation of foreign words and phrases. Whilst there is some truth in this mechanistic conception, it is far from the whole truth. A sociolinguistic, or, with literary reference, stylistic, explanation is often preferable. In literature, borrowing is largely for the purpose of capturing the social and literary prestige of French culture. Indeed the word 'borrowing' itself, which implies a deficit, is an unfortunate one for this process, for it would often be truer to say that French words and phrases were imported into English by those who were capable of recognizing their worth, the proprieties of their use, and of utilizing them.[14] That the principles of French style were well understood by those who introduced them could be demonstrated by the independence of the author's treatment of his source in adaptations like *King Alisaunder,* and indeed has been clearly demonstrated with regard to Chaucer's employment of the 'style curial' in *Melibee.*[15] The competence of such men as Chaucer and Gower in literary French cannot be questioned: their adoptions include not only the topics of early romance, but also the concerns of contemporary poets like Machaut, Froissart, Deschamps, and Granson. The courtliness which Gower and Chaucer found in these poets, and which they clearly understood, demanded urbanity, and urbanity presumes that a man be witty and well-informed of the learning of his day. It was therefore inevitable that a tradition modelled upon that of French courtly literature would include in its diction a massive reinforcement of those words, phrases, and verbal strategies of *clergie* which were already present in the English language from earlier times.[16] In poetry of Chaucer's time we find a characteristic extension of the use of the word *charite* from its theological and moral

7

registers into the courtly discussion of secular love, and this is matched by the adoption of the terms of *curteisie* into homiletic discourse.

Enough has been said to illustrate how, long before Chaucer's time, a process had already commenced by which the allegedly simple architecture of Middle English gained in complexity. During the lifetime of Chaucer, English was being used in a wide variety of more specialized fields, and in the linguistic registers associated with these any attempt to fix lexical boundaries between English and French languages would have seemed arbitrary. The verbal repertoire of an educated man included words and phrases which were indeed of French, Latin and native origin, but switching between these forms, at least in the written language, was commonplace.[17] For authors like Gower and Chaucer, culture, whether courtly or scholastic, was international and multi-lingual; the linguistic boundaries which trouble modern critics did not constrain their consciousness, and the connotations and associations of the words they used extended into the literary traditions of French and Latin. We have the evidence of Gower's poetry to illustrate how for him the labels French, Latin, and English, were as much a question of stylistic register as discrete language systems. When he wished to imitate the verses of the *trouvères*, he adopted the verse form of the *balade*, and echoed the sensibility of the French diction proper to the form.[18] In a Latin chronicle, he could adopt the phrasing and conceptual patterns of partisan chronicle style. The architecture of the linguistic competence of men such as this can scarcely have been a simple one.

The concept of architecture, however, only has validity as a tool of historical interpretation if the recognized system of usage extends throughout a reasonably large population of language users. If we are to place the poetry of Chaucer in a historical situation in which the complex architecture we have presumed can be used for poetical effect, we must presuppose the existence of an audience whose language use shows a comparable complexity. Chaucer must be an isolated genius only in his exploitation of what the language had to offer him, and not in his unique possession of such linguistic competence. It is therefore no accident that it was in London that Chaucer and Gower created their poetry, for it was only in the capital that English, at this date, could expect to find an audience with the requisite qualifications. The researches of Eilert Ekwall have shown that the large immigration into London in the first decades of the fourteenth century consisted of a disproportionately high number of men with legal and clerical training.[19] There is no need to assume that this circumstance changed during Chaucer's lifetime. Among the hopeful clerks seeking opportunities for their talent, there must have been those grounded in moral philosophy, political and administrative theory, even those with a taste for classical literature. It is among men of

8

this class, among their fellow civil servants and lawyers, among the educated gentlemen on the fringes of the court, and perhaps merchants who had been to school, that we should look for the audience of Chaucer and Gower's poetry.[20] Although writing in London, and a contemporary of these authors, Langland is not of their milieu, and his language reveals it. One may find there the phrasal echo of the Fathers, or traces of lexical patterning owed to the earlier *rapprochement* between French and English in devotional works, but systems deriving from French courtly literature, and ultimately from the literary devices, or political and ethical theory of the ancient world, are greatly attenuated. In this, Langland has more in common with the provincial *Gawain*-poet, whose lexical usage, although reflecting general conceptions of courtliness and exploiting them for poetic effect, also has a theological and even exegetical bias which makes Chaucer and Gower seem markedly secular authors; philosophers rather than theologians. Both Gower and Chaucer are concerned with secular ethics, and are the inheritors of ethical traditions descending by grace of the twelfth-century *ethici* from the rational philosophy of the classical past. At the same time they are aware of the more affective values of Christian teaching, and of the potential conflict between the two. The ensuing complexity of thought and language will be revealed in the development of this book, and we shall see something of how both Chaucer and Gower are at times the victims of their inheritance, as it controls their patterns of thought, whilst, at times, they make of it their poetic tool. It will come as little surprise to find that Chaucer escapes the tyranny of imposed architectural norms more frequently and more adroitly than his friend and contemporary, John Gower.

9

CHAPTER ONE

The Tyrant

EARLY IN 1391, John Gower took the important decision to modify his most recent work, a lengthy poem in English which he had only recently completed, and which he says he had begun at the instigation of the king himself. His altered epilogue to the *Confessio Amantis* omitted a commendation of Richard and substituted in its place a prayer for England. Within a couple of years the prologue of the poem was to be altered too. The account given of Richard commissioning it was excised and replaced by a general lament for the times, a conventional injunction to learn from previous ages, and a re-dedication of the poem to Henry Bolingbroke, who, as Duke of Lancaster, was later to depose and destroy the king. At about the same time as he made his alterations to the *Confessio Amantis*, Gower also returned to his long Latin poem, the *Vox Clamantis*, and altered some passages in its sixth book. Again, the substitutions were to the disadvantage of the king. The sixth book had been written about 1380, and had originally contained enthusiastic praise of King Richard, which, in the course of events, had come to seem embarrassing. In the new version a plea to reform his rule and bring about a fair administration of justice is found in place of an uncritical paean in praise of the young king; and accusations replace excuses on the king's behalf.

It is clear that Gower's attitude to his sovereign had changed, but the extent of the change does not become obvious until after the latter's deposition. For in 1400 the Latin colophon in which he describes the content of his major works is altered for the third and final time.[1] The *Vox Clamantis*, which had originally been described as containing an account of the 'sensational happenings' (*mirabili eventu*) of King Richard's reign, was now said to tell of the 'manifold misfortunes' (*variis infortunis*) of the reign:

> whence not only the nobles and commons of the realm underwent torments, but also the most cruel king himself, falling through his own faults from on high, was finally cast into the pit of his own making.

> Vnde non solum regni proceres et communes tormenta passi sunt, set et ipse crudelissimus rex suis ex demeritis ab alto corruens in foueam quam fecit finaliter proiectus est.

Richard is now identified as *crudelissimus rex*, a man cast down not by the wheel of Fortune but by the results of his own misrule. This is the theme expanded in the *Cronica Tripertita* which Gower added as a sequel to the *Vox Clamantis*. Here the accusations of cruelty are repeated and extended far beyond the simple condemnation *crudelissimus rex*. At the very beginning, Gower virtually takes as his text the sentence 'Rex induratum cor semper habet,' and he elaborates this theme throughout. Richard's heart was hardened, he tells us, so that he showed no pity (*tota regis pietate remota.* 314. 20; *parcere nescit.* 330. 16). Far from sparing his enemies, he raged against them (*sevit rex . . . nil pietas.* 321. 36); he even fulminates against Christ (*in Cristum sevit.* 326. 237). He is overwhelmed by the vice of Ire and indiscriminately executes the innocent (*rex iratus.* 325. 209). In victory over his opponents, no magnanimity is found, and indeed he is even accused of forbidding a decent burial to the Duke of Gloucester (323. 108). His good counsellor, Thomas of Arundel, attempted to restrain him from these excesses, but he was unable to deflect the king from his vindictive rage (*ab ira flectere regem.* 327. 253).

The epithets directed at Richard range from *crudelis* and *iratus*, as we have seen above, through *scelus* and *sceleratus*, to *ferus, ferox, pestifer, pomposus, fervens*, and references are made to his *furor* and *feritas*. By contrast, Henry is distinguished not so much by the range of epithets applied to him as by the monotonous repetition of a single one, *pius*. Whilst Richard is assailed by a verbal onslaught connoting cruelty, criminality, and furious madness, Henry is mild and majestic, gentle and understanding: *Henricus mitis et imperialis.* 341. 458; *probus Henricus, pietatis semper amicus.* 341. 452). The relationship between the two kings is well-represented in a Latin gloss:

> Note here the goodness of the most blessed King Henry and the wickedness with which, according to common report, the cruel Richard tyrannically harassed his kingdom as long as he could.

Nota hic secundum commune dictum de pietate serenissimi regis Henrici, necnon de impietate qua crudelissimus Ricardus regnum, dum potuit, tirannice vexavit.

(Latin Works, p. 342)

It is a relationship crystallized in the verbal opposition between *crudelitas* and *pietas*. Richard's rule was tyranny; as another gloss puts it, he is *rex tyrannus*, and Henry is his direct antithesis.

One cannot help but feel the pathos as well as the circularity of the situation. Towards the end of his life, on the verge of blindness, Gower closes with a harsh judgement upon the reign which he had once greeted so enthusiastically; but as he closes this chapter he opens another, looking just as expectantly for better things from Henry IV. To those who would accuse him of mere time-serving, of that *variaunce* and *envye* which both he and Chaucer deplored, he left an answer in his *explicit*:

> Here ends the Chronicle, which is to be heeded with a watchful heart by kings present and future.
>
> Explicit Cronica presentibus que futuris vigili corde
> Regibus commemoranda.

The *Cronica*, then, whatever the uses to which it might be put, was not admitted to be propaganda on behalf of the Lancastrian cause; rather it was a warning and an example from which Henry IV, just as much as later kings, might profit. The desire to counsel kings had always been strong in Gower, and indeed his *Confessio Amantis* contains a lengthy section upon the supposed instruction offered by Aristotle to Alexander.[2]

When Richard had ascended the throne, he might reasonably have been thought heaven-sent for instruction by the philosophic poet, for he was no more than a boy. He began his reign with credit, gaining popularity by his handling of the Peasant's Revolt; he promised well for the future. Any earlier foibles, men were happy to ascribe to the shortcomings of the counsel he received. There was therefore ample opportunity for those who wished to offer advice in literary form to the young king, and Gower responded to the opportunity more directly than any other poet of the period:

> *Richard by name the Secounde,*
> *In whom hath evere yit be founde*
> *Justice medled with pite,*
> *Largesce forth with charite.*
> *In his persone it mai be schewed*
> *What is a king to be wel thewed,*

Touchinge of pite namely:
For he yit nevere unpitously
Ayein the liges of his lond,
For no defaute which he fond,
Thurgh cruelte vengaunce soghte.

(*CA*. VIII, 2987*–97*)

The above passage, which contrasts so markedly with the account of Richard given in the *Cronica Tripertita*, is perhaps best understood as neither sycophantic praise nor a recitation of unvarnished fact. It is rather in the spirit of encouragement offered by a schoolmaster to his pupil; Gower hopes that by representing Richard in a familiar, idealized rôle he will indeed correspond to those ideals.[3] Yet, as he repeated his platitudinous praise, Gower must have been increasingly aware how far Richard was falling short of the rôle allotted him, so that in 1391 he began to alter his public estimation of Richard, and by 1400 his re-appraisal culminated in the stark condemnation of the phrase, *rex tyrannus*.

Those who would accuse Gower of being a turncoat, the betrayer of his earlier patron, must take into account these signs of a change in his attitude spread over ten years, but more important than this is the nature of his conception of the function of the king. Gower did not reach his published assessments of King Richard as the result of painstaking and factual analysis of all his political actions, nor even by subtle insight into the character of the man himself. Rather, his conception of the rôles open to a king was moulded by an awareness of the examples of the past in the same way as his own chronicle was intended to offer a present example for the future. For him, the complexities of historical events were to be selected and modified so as to fit into recurrent and mutually confirming patterns. Historical rôles repeated themselves, and were instantly recognizable for what they were. Kings were either strong or weak, upholding the law so that a man may bear a bag of gold across their kingdom without fear of theft, and repelling foreign aggression, or weak, timorous and presiding over chaos.[4] Real personalities were dissolved and became reconstructed as exemplary figures: the 'just king', the 'useless king' or the 'tyrant'. So pervasive was this tendency in literature to conform actuality to received patterns that we find the rhetorician John of Garlande advising his audience that the subject matter upon which the description of a king is to be based is of two dichotomous kinds:

What to invent pertains to persons, examples and etymologies. With persons there is always a pair of alternatives; as with kings: to rule the kingdom well, or to tear the kingdom to pieces like a tyrant.

Contingit quid inuenire in personis, in exemplis, in ethimologiis. In personis duo, ut in regibus: bene regnum regere, vel regnum tirannide dilacerare.[5]

14

To Gower, accustomed to viewing the rôle of the monarch in such un-equivocal and restricted terms, Richard also would be likely to conform to a pattern. At some point, the nature of his behaviour and the state of the country must have precluded him from remaining an ideal in Gower's eyes, and in the ten years from 1391 to 1400 he was transferred from one exemplary company to the other, to be replaced in the traditional ideal-ising rôle by Henry of Lancaster.

Now, as Gower's 'invention' of the character of Richard changed, it is probable that his conception of his relationship to the king also under-went a parallel modification – and it is important here to note that we are discussing Gower's conception of the relationship rather than any actual one. In fact this conception has no closer identity with reality than the two pictures he paints of the king's character. But, as a moral philosopher, whose concern was with the 'commune profit,' Gower would begin to see himself no longer as the philosophic instructor of a young prince, as an Aristotle to Richard's Alexander, but rather he would begin to share the rôle that he allots also to Arundel who, by his moral teaching, endeav-oured 'to deflect the king from his fury'. No longer an Aristotle, he might well see himself instead as a Seneca restraining the madness of his own contemporary Nero.[6] Indeed, the conception of government which Gower possessed, and which is revealed in his written representations of Richard, indicates that he saw Richard's career as an exemplary fall, a contemporary tragedy brought about not by Fortune but by moral insuf-ficiency. Such a conception of history, which enabled present rulers to jostle figures from the legendary past in exemplary fellowship, also enabled Chaucer's Monk to make use of the contemporary story of Barnabò Visconti in the same set of *de casibus* tragedies as that which contains the story of Seneca and Nero:

> *In yowthe a maister hadde this emperour*
> *To teche hym letterure and curteisye,*
> *For of moralitee he was the flour,*
> *As in his tyme, but if bookes lye;*
> *And whil this maister hadde of hym maistrye,*
> *He maked hym so konnyng and so sowple*
> *That longe tyme it was er tirannye*
> *Or any vice dorste on hym uncowple.*

> *This Seneca, of which that I devyse,*
> *By cause Nero hadde of hym swich drede,*
> *For he fro vices wolde hym ay chastise*
> *Discreetly, as by word and nat be dede, –*
> *'Sire,' wolde he seyn, "an emperour moot nede*
> *Be vertuous and hate tirannye –'.*[7]
> (*CT*. VII, 2495–2508)

15

It is this rôle of restraint that Gower deserted finally in 1400 and unleashed his severest condemnations of tyranny. It is tempting to see in the vigour of the attack the pent-up energy of a disappointed instructor, but the truth of the matter is that we do not know what Gower the gentleman of Kent who died at St. Mary's priory in 1408 really thought of his king, nor even whether he was in a position to have an informed opinion. All the parts in the story, and much of the language in which they are described, have been predetermined by the literary milieu in which Gower lived. Richard, Henry, Gower himself, and the relationships between them, have been recast into pre-existing literary moulds.

The concourse of Latin epithets which Gower directed against his former 'pupil'; and indeed the patterns of thought which conditioned his perception of him, had become established in literary usage as the result of a very lengthy tradition. Nearly a thousand years before Gower, the same words and thought-patterns had sprung to the pen of Bishop Isidore of Seville as he composed his *Etymologiae*:

> when it is enquired what the difference may be between a king and a tyrant, what both may be is defined by applying the *differentia*, that 'a king is moderate and temperate, whereas a tyrant is cruel.'

> cum quaeritur quid inter regem sit et tyrannum, adiecta differentia, quid uterque sit definitur, ut 'rex modestus et temperatus, tyrannus vero crudelis.'

> (I, xxxi)

Isidore's purpose in the *Etymologiae* was to collect and preserve the philosophical fruits of the ancient world against the onset of the barbarians, and his gleanings became one of the most influential encyclopaedias of the medieval period. His words on the tyrant are brief, but their formulaic nature, and the fact that, in the circumstances, he thought them worth recording indicate that they belong to a tradition of thought of secure and established value. Indeed that tradition is a long one, and to discover the origins of the topic of the tyrant would involve us in an enquiry into the confrontation of the city-state and its ruler in the late Hellenic twilight. Fortunately, our investigation need not be pressed so far, for Greek was little known in western Europe before the renaissance, and knowledge of the ancient world depended upon Latin intermediaries.

Instead of Greece, we must return to Rome in Augustan times to witness the adoption of a body of popular Hellenistic ideas and themes concerned with the good life, compiled eclectically from a variety of philosophical sources, but known from its greatest indebtedness, as the Cynico-Stoic diatribe.[8] This body of ethical material was erected into a philosophical system by Sextius Niger during the Augustan efforts to rekindle in public life an awareness of the virtues of Republican times, but the tradition was drawn upon by most ethical writers in late Antiquity. Church fathers like Clement of Alexandria, St. John Chrysostom, and even Tertullian, forgot their distrust of pagan thought and found matter to their purpose in this less-schematized body of material. But from our point of view the most important beneficiary of this tradition was Seneca, for it is in Seneca that we find the direct link between this ethical and governmental tradition and fourteenth-century England.

Chaucer and his contemporaries read Ovid, Virgil, Cicero and Seneca, and drew moral inspiration from them all. But if Cicero could be understood as a moralist, he was also, *par excellence*, the authority upon rhetoric and style. By the same token, Seneca was considered pre-eminent among these instructive ancients as a moral philosopher. His dramatic works were scarcely known, but his moral letters and his essays, *De Beneficiis*, *De Ira*, and especially *De Clementia*, were widely read throughout the Middle Ages.[9] This last work, which had been dedicated to the Emperor Nero, confirmed Seneca in his rôle of moral guide and counsellor, the restraint of a tyrant. Seneca's treatment of his subject can be divided into two halves, the first of which is a political treatise, a *miroir de prince*, and the second an ethical and moral investigation of the virtue of *clementia*. It is this second approach which was particularly associated with Seneca, and when the French poet Eustache Deschamps wished to compliment Chaucer on his poetic achievement, he congratulated him upon his grasp of ethical doctrines by nominating him a second Seneca.[10] The literary man's concern with psychology and morality means that the literary figure of the tyrant stands somewhat apart from that figure as he emerges from *miroir de prince* literature, in which a more legalistic and political approach predominates. Although he may be a usurper, or consider himself above the law, such aspects of tyranny are not usually the focus of attention in the literary representation of the tyrant, so that Seneca's psychological analyses are often more pertinent to fourteenth-century literature than later, more technical, writings.[11]

In the ethical tradition upon which Seneca drew the figure of the tyrant looms large. Within that tradition, he is seen not primarily as the product of a particular political situation, but rather as a psychological symbol. The approach to the figure of the tyrant is predominantly that of moral psychology: he is considered to be a sympton of the disorder of the body politic. This latter phrase makes explicit an analogy between the constitution of the state and that of the individual. Just as the state may be oppressed by a tyrant, so the individual personality may be oppressed by fierce and unrestrained passions. Furthermore, the tyrannous king, in the midst of his depradations upon others, is himself the victim of the disorder of his own psyche. The association between violent passions and tyranny became proverbial ('as many cruel masters as passions'), and

Seneca sums up this idea in a description of the state of the man who is subject to anger: 'Such is the tyranny under which that man must live who surrenders to the bondage of any passion' (*De Ira*, I, x, 2). By contrast, whilst the tyrant is constantly racked by anger or insatiable desire, the philosopher lives in order and peace imposed upon his personality by the exercise of rational control. Hence this tradition, which is primarily concerned with the individual soul, frequently uses political metaphor in order to investigate it. A series of associations arise in which the well-ordered state, the personality of the wise man, and the just king, are all ranged against the tyrant.

Within the Cynico-Stoic diatribe a number of passions are especially associated with the tyrant: ambition, debauchery, irascibility, avarice, and cruelty are the most important. But in order to discover a clear statement of the ideas which formed Gower's attitude to Richard II we must examine in some detail the discussion of tyranny in two works, both of which were widely used and recommended through the medieval period, and both of which exhibit the same peculiar blend of governmental theory and moral psychology that animates the fourteenth-century exhortations to princes. These works are Seneca's *De Clementia*, and the earlier work of Cicero, *De Officiis*. Cicero briefly discusses tyranny (II, vii, 23–4) and it quickly becomes clear that, for him, the defining qualities of a tyrant's behaviour are captured by those words which we have seen Gower repeatedly using of Richard: *saevitia* and *crudelitas*. Seneca agrees that the tyrant takes pleasure in cruelty, and the same words recur:

> tyrannis saevitia cordi est (I, xii, 1)

> Non decet regem saeva nec inexorabilis ira (I, v, 6)

> Quid interest inter tyrannum ac regem . . . nisi quod tyranni in voluptatem saeviunt, reges non nisi ex causa necessitate? (I, xi, 4)[12]

In his treatise on Ire, Seneca also collocates words connoting ideas of cruelty, anger and madness, the vices of the tyrant which disturb the philosophical calm which his Stoic viewpoint demanded:

> Quantum est effugere maximum malum, iram, et cum illa rabiem, saevitiam, crudelitatem, furorem, alios comites eius adfectus (II, xii, 6)[13]

Although in *De Ira* Seneca's usage corresponds with that of Cicero and the majority of writers on this subject, in *De Clementia* there are peculiarities in his usage. He gives the Latin word *rex* an unusual moral prestige, by making it denote a beneficient ruler, and contrasting it with *tyrannus*.[14] More significantly, he departs from the common usage by failing to apply the word *crudelis* to tyrants. There is a good reason for this, since he redefines *crudelitas* to contrast with *saevitia*. The former is now considered to be rational and justifiable harshness, and no longer, in Seneca's estimation, a vice; the latter is vicious and unreasonable oppression. This distinction, made upon rational grounds, does not greatly affect the general usage concerning tyrants – they are still more often 'cruel' than anything else – but as a definition it is referred to not infrequently by medieval authors.

Although Gower's Latin does not preserve this distinction when describing Richard II, a comparison between his range of epithets for the tyrant and those of Seneca and Boethius is ample testimony to the stability of usage within this Latin tradition.[15]

Seneca: *tyrannus (crudelis) saevitia ira   feritas*
Boethius: *tyrannus *crudelis saevus   ira   –   ferox furor rabies* torvus*
Gower: *tyrannus crudelis   saevire iratus feritas ferox furor*

This stability of usage is partially reflected by the English works of Chaucer. In his translation of Boethius, the adaptation of the Latin expression to a vernacular had already been accomplished for him by the French translation of Jean de Meun which he used alongside the Latin. However, he did not slavishly follow Jean's choice of word at every occurrence, and his ability to vary Jean's rendering by the use of another French-derived term is perhaps better evidence of his familiarity with the field of appropriate epithets than mere copying would have been. In Chaucer's usage, the words associated with tyrants, then, are often of Latin origin, borrowed through French: *tyrant, cruel,* and *ire* are frequently collocated. The native-derived form, *wood,* which is equally as closely associated with tyrants as any of these, is an interesting exception. It combines within its semantic range the senses of madness, irrationality, and furious anger, and therefore occupies in Chaucer's usage a function discharged in the Latin by the words *furibundus, furor, rabies, saevitia,* and sometimes *ira.*[17] The fourteenth-century English vocabulary of tyranny (*tyrant, cruel, irous, wood*), although much more restricted than that of Latin, and usually less precisely defined, is no less firmly associated with the traditional image of the tyrant.

Of course the conception of the tyrant, and its evocation in fourteenth-century vernacular writings, does not depend simply upon the occurrence in a text of one or more of these words. A man may be called *wood* without necessarily evoking the image of the tyrant. A tyrant is defined not only by the epithets hurled at him, but by his deeds and by the situation in general. The perpetuation of the tyrant image as a potent literary device depended upon the continuation of a social situation of a markedly hierarchical kind. The author of a recent book on Seneca sees the appearance of *De Clementia* as a consequence of the political circumstances of the Roman Empire in which the greater judicial powers of the emperor tended to supplant legally prescribed penalties.[18] Such a situation, where the power of the individual exceeded that of centralized justice, had been perpetuated in early feudal Europe at the time when European conceptions of the tyrant were being crystallized. For, in the feudal system, every man's lord was in addition his judge, and could be held responsible for his good behaviour by the higher level of the hierarchy. The lord, therefore, administered justice to his vassal and exacted punishment, and although he may be directed by custom or the king's law, his powers were in reality very extensive. In such circumstances a breach of the law which affected the lord's interests might present a difficult situation with respect to impartial justice; indeed it is very common to find that medieval writers fail to distinguish between the notions of justice and vengeance. The Middle English verb *wreken*, whose primary sense is 'to avenge', is normally used also for the execution of a legal penalty. Since vengeance and justice were often equated by the social and political system, the equity of punishment tended to be based, as it is in Seneca's *De Clementia*, upon the criterion of reasonableness or rationality. The question 'Is the sentence just?' tends to be asked in the form 'Is the sentence reasonable?'. The concept of vengeance has no pejorative associations so long as the act of revenge can be rationally justified. Although kings were traditionally expected to be severe in their administration of justice, and many amply fulfilled this expectation, a rational assessment of a crime and its perpetrator need not lead inexorably to punishment. Prudence might indicate that the malefactor could be reformed by gentle treatment, or that mercy might sooner restore civil peace than rigour; the feudal judge, therefore, might determine upon harshness or clemency with equal rationality, according to his understanding of the circumstances. Either attitude is to be admired. But if the process of his judgement derives not from rational concern for the common good but from the promptings of uncontrolled passions, such as desire for vengeance, avarice, or pleasure in inflicting suffering, then his actions are not those of the just judge, and the man is a tyrant. In the judicial situation, then, which is the situation in which we most commonly encounter the tyrant figure, one crucial distinction of the tyrant is the irrationality of his behaviour, his subjection to his own lusts and desires.

In the *Tale of Melibee*, a ruler is guided in judicial and policy decisions by reason in the form of his allegorically-named wife, Prudence. She denounces Ire, that typical vice of the tyrant, and the scope of her denunciation is a very general one. It extends beyond the restricted case of the man in power, and, employing the traditional equation between the individual soul and the nature of the tyrant, she extends it to the individual's control over himself:

First, he that axeth conseil of hymself, certes he moste been
withouten ire, for manye causes. The firste is this: he that hath greet
ire and wratthe in hymself, he weneth alwey that he may do thyng that
he may nat do. And secoundely, he that is irous and wrooth, he may
nat wel deme.

(CT. VII, 1123–5)

Ire befuddles judgement in any man, and leads to tyrannical injustice in
the powerful. Although the vices of tyranny are found in men of all
stations of life, so that psychologically they may be considered identical,
and can be metaphorically regarded as tyrants, the proper application of
the word *tyrant* is to men of power: 'Whan myght is joyned unto crueltee,/
Allas, to depe wol the venym wade!' (*CT*. VII, 2493–4). In the *Manciple's
Tale* the psychological and behavioural characteristics of tyranny are
found in a domestic relationship. Here again tyranny, with its reckless
impetuosity, is seen to be the enemy of prudence. A husband laments the
hasty murder of a loyal wife, slain as the result of too ready acceptance of a
false accusation:

> *O deere wyf! o gemme of lustiheed!*
> *That were to me so sad and eek so trewe,*
> *Now listow deed, with face pale of hewe,*
> *Ful giltelees, that dorste I swere, ywys!*
> *O rakel hand to doon so foule amys!*
> *O trouble wit, or ire recchelees,*
> *That unavysed smyteth gilteles!*

(CT. IX, 274–80)

Ire leads to precipitate action, allowing no time for reflection, and is
frequently responsible for the murder of the innocent. The persecution of
the innocent is therefore a characteristic of the tyrant throughout the
history of the tradition. Gower accuses Richard of it:

> With burning eagerness, the irous king laid hold upon him;
> although the accused man was guiltless, he soon died of grief.

> Quem rex iratus, quamvis sine labe reatus,/Tangit in ardore, subito
> perit ille dolore.

The action is typical and the language is formulaic. Gower's formula for
representing the tyrannous persecution of the innocent (*sine labe*) has its
echo in Chaucer's English in the phrases *withouten gilt* or *giltelees*.
Although these are not a direct translation of the Latin phrase, they fulfill
a similar function within the verbal representation of the image of the
tyrant.

In Christian history, the outstanding example of the persecution of the
innocents is that by Herod. Consequently, in popular plays he is repre-

sented as an archetypal tyrant, raging with a vindictive fury close to madness.[19] The famous stage direction in the Coventry play of the massacre of the innocents gives something of the flavour of this:

Here Erode ragis in the pagond and in the strete also.

Chaucer's Pardoner, adapting his examples to his theme, ascribes Herod's murder of John the Baptist to a fury inspired by drunkenness:

> *Herodes, whoso wel the stories soghte,*
> *Whan he of wyn was repleet at his feeste,*
> *Right at his owene table he yaf his heeste*
> *To sleen the Baptist John, ful gilteless.*
>
> (*CT*. VI, 488–91)

Although the context is one of the condemnation of drunkenness, and is not strictly concerned with tyranny, the evocation of the figure of the irous tyrant in this passage perhaps sparks off the allusion to Seneca in the next line. The allusion is to the moral epistles rather than the *De Clementia*, but Chaucer is well aware of the relationship of Seneca to Nero, and the latter rivals Herod as the archetype of tyranny. Many were those to whom a line in the *Nun's Priest's Tale* could be applied: 'Withouten gilt this Nero hath hem slayn.'

Occasionally the victim is allowed to reply to the sentence passed upon him by the tyrant, and in these cases the moral strength of the accused, calm and rational, is made to contrast significantly with the conduct of the tyrant:

> *'Yowre princes erren, as youre nobleye dooth,'*
> *Quod tho Cecile, 'and with a wood sentence*
> *Ye make us gilty, and it is nat sooth.*
> *For ye, that knowen wel oure innocence,*
> *For as muche as we doon a reverence*
> *To Crist, and for we bere a Cristen name,*
> *Ye putte on us a cryme, and eek a blame.'*
>
> (*CT*. VIII, 449–55)

The scene is one of the persecution of innocent Christians by pagan tyrants, a favourite one in the works of the fathers and in saints' legends, and indeed an idealisation of much of the early history of the Church. In this passage, Cecile emerges as an exemplary characterization almost as markedly as the figure of the tyrant. She is the idealized virgin martyr; a blend of patience based on faith, and rational self-control, she contrasts with the *wood sentence* of her accusers. Such dignity of conduct by the accused innocent inevitably inspires pathos. At the end of the *Physician's Tale* of Virginia there comes an emotional outburst from Harry Baily; his pity is such that he temporarily loses his poise as leader of the pilgrimage:

22

'Myn herte is lost for pitee of this mayde,' he declares. In this he reveals himself to be psychologically remote from the tyrant, for in medieval portrayals a feature of the tyrant is that he is *hard* and *daungerous*. We may recall that the allegations that he possessed an *induratum cor* and showed no mercy formed the most repetitive part of Gower's condemnation of Richard. Now, this concentration upon hardness of heart, the failure to feel sympathy with the sufferings of others, is not a feature of the Senecan conception of the tyrant, since this was based upon subjection to irrational passions, and Seneca despised pity as irrational. Whilst he was willing to recommend *clementia* as preferable to *crudelitas* wherever possible, Seneca's conception of equity was thoroughly dependent on reason. The Christian middle ages, however, placed a different value upon emotion, and particularly upon pity and compassion. To the Christian all men were descended from Adam and Eve, and most were members of the same Church. In the words of St. Paul:

> there should be no schism in the body; but the members should have the same care one for another.
> And whether one member suffer, all the members suffer with it; or one member be honoured, all the members rejoice with it.
> Now ye are the body of Christ, and members in particular.
>
> (I *Cor.* XII, 25–7)

The doctrine of the mystical body of the Church, and that of charity, meant that it was considered both natural and commendable that Christians should share in the joyous expectation of salvation, and sorrow together at the misdemeanours of fellow Christians. This belief that even the wicked merit the compassion of their neighbours is found in Boethius when he argues that prosecutors, rather than attempt to deflect judges from rational justice by appeals to compassion, should offer their pity to the criminals whom they accuse, and whose vicious state is more a cause of pity than any physical suffering which may be imposed upon them, or which they had caused their victims.

In medieval writings, then, emotional communion, which the Stoics despised, was restored to respectability. Pity and clemency, which had been kept apart by insistence on the rational nature of the latter, became indistinct. Medieval writers in philosophical discourse certainly return to the original distinction, and it seems to have left traces in usage, but in fourteenth-century English *pitee* and *mercy* are often used synonymously; but it is an essential feature of the tyrant that he shows neither. Gower depicts the homicide as the psychological twin of the tyrant:

> *Be so thei have or swerd or knif*
> *Here dedly wraththe forto wreke,*
> *Of Pite list hem noght to speke;*
> *Non other reson thei ne fonge,*

23

> *Bot that thei ben of mihtes stronge.*
> *Bot war hem wel in other place,*
> *Where every man behoveth grace,*
> *Bot ther I trowe it schal hem faile,*
> *To whom no merci mihte availe,*
> *Bot wroghten upon tiraundie,*
> *That no pite ne mihte hem plie.*
>   (*CA*. III. 1108–18)

Both the tyrant and the homicide, in the Christian dispensation, can look forward to a judgement in which the extent of their own compassion will be the measure of that which God will show to them.

In fourteenth-century writings, then, the tyrant is irous, lacks reason and prudence, often rages madly, and entirely lacks compassion. Almost as a curiosity, we can add one other distinguishing feature of the tyrant which is met with quite widely. In this epitome, the tyrant, as an employer, withholds or cheats his servants of their just rewards. The concept of the just reward for labour is defended in *Piers Plowman* by Conscience who distinguishes two kinds of income: among those which are justifiable is:

> That laborers and lowe [lewede] folk taken of hire maistres
> It is no manere Mede but a mesurable hire.
>   (B-text, III, 255–6)

Chaucer's Parson evidently holds a similar opinion, for he adds the retention of just wages to a picture of tyrannical lordship. In fact, he adapts a biblical text (Proverbs xxviii, 15) by adding the retention of wages to it, yet still ascribing the whole to Solomon, the spirit of whose views he presumably thought he was echoing:

> Leon rorynge and bere hongry been like to the crueel lordshipes in withholdynge or abreggynge of the shepe (or the hyre), or of the wages of servauntz, or elles in usure, or in withdrawynge of the almesse of povre folk.
>   (*CT*. x, 568)

The addition to the biblical text suggests that this form of oppression was especially acutely felt by moralists of the time, and indeed Langland too mentions it, seeing it as one of the sins of omission of the slothful man:

> And my seruauntȝ som tyme: hir salarie is bihynde;
> Ruþe is to here þe rekenyng whan we shul rede acountes:
> So wiþ wikked wil and wraþe my werkmen I paye.
>   (B-text, V, 1426–8)

By contrast, the author of the *Ancrene Wisse* ascribed the same omission to avarice, and in doing so was perhaps closer to the traditional conception of the vices of the tyrant.[20]

When in the *Friar's Tale* a rapacious summoner meets a bailiff whom he regards as a brother in crime, they fall in conversation. The excuses given by the bailiff for his corruption sound plausible enough for anyone in his office. But they turn out to be ironic, for he is an agent of the devil sent into this world to seek a due toll of souls. The master of whom he complains in his companionly way turns out to be what the author of a fourteenth-century sermon refers to as 'that cruel terraunt', the Devil:

> '*As I shal tellen thee a feithful tale,*
> *My wages been ful streite and ful smale.*
> *My lord is hard to me and daungerous,*
> *And myn office is ful laborous,*
> *And therfore by extorcions I lyve.*'
> *(CT.* III, 1425–9)

With this representation of the devil as a stinting master the outline of the fourteenth-century image of the tyrant is complete.[21] We have found that, as well as a political phenomenon, he is a psychological and moral symbol of great antiquity: his chief psychological constituents are lack of rational control and consequently furious passions, and most notably ire. Furthermore, he feels no compassion for his fellow man, so that in terms of behaviour he is marked by his reckless persecution of the innocent, one peculiar manifestation of which is his reluctance to pay just rewards. Later chapters of this book will be concerned with filling in the details of this outline, and recording the variations of this basic theme of the tyrant. It will be useful, therefore, with the image of the tyrant and his antithesis the just ruler in mind, before it becomes necessary to invoke any metaphorical extensions, to examine the behaviour of Theseus in the *Knight's Tale*.

The first scene which attracts attention in the light of our concept of the tyrant is that in which the 'conquerour' Theseus, returning from his wars with the Amazons, is met by a group of lamenting women clad in black. The leader of the group presents a petition for *mercy and socour* in the following terms:

> '*Have mercy on oure wo and oure distresse!*
> *Some drope of pitee, thurgh thy gentillesse,*
> *Upon us wrecched wommen lat thou falle.*'
> *(CT.* I, 919–21)

The women have been waiting in the temple of the goddess Clementia for this opportunity to ask for Theseus's help. The cause of their distress is the tyrant Creon:

Fulfild of ire and iniquitee,
He, for despit and for his tirannye,
To do the dede bodyes vileynye
Of alle oure lordes whiche that been yslawe,
Hath alle the bodyes on an heep ydrawe,
And wol nat suffren hem, by noon assent,
Neither to been yburyed nor ybrent,
But maketh houndes ete hem in despit.

(CT. I, 940–47)

Now, although the particular manifestation of tyranny exemplified in this passage descends from the classical sources of the tale, contempt for the dead still seems to be recognized as an aspect of tyranny in Chaucer's time, for one of the accusations levelled at Richard by Gower is that he failed to accord proper burial to the body of one of his victims. Among the Church fathers, also, Lactantius identifies this as a feature of tyranny.[22]

Theseus is moved by the petition of the ladies. This is not a judicial situation but Theseus is impelled by an emotion which can be rationally justified since it leads to a beneficial end: the removal of a tyrant:

Upon the tiraunt Creon hem to wreke,
That al the peple of Grece sholde speke
How Creon was of Theseus yserved
As he that hadde his deeth ful wel deserved.

(CT. I, 961–64)

Thus, within this short scene we have an exemplary tyrant, Creon, overthrown by the action of a powerful king for apparently altruistic reasons. The action arises not from politics but from *pitee*, from the compassion which Theseus feels for the ladies' suffering.[23]

The second scene which we must consider is that in which Palamon and Arcite are surprised in single combat by Theseus and his hunting party. It is at once clear that they are in breach of the law, and breaking the peace, but Palamon also reveals that they are transgressors against Theseus's personal rulings; one who is an escapee from prison, and the other who has illegally returned from exile. The situation, therefore, is a judicial one. Palamon admits their guilt and that they deserve death:

And as thou art a rightful lord and juge,
Ne yif us neither mercy ne refuge,
But sle me first, for seinte charitee!
But sle my felawe eek as wel as me.

(CT. I, 1719–22)

Despite his rather curious evocation of charity, Palamon is in fact admitting guilt and calling upon Theseus to play the part of the just (*rightful*) judge, unmitigated by clemency. Theseus is ready to agree. But once

26

again the ladies intervene. Again they cry for mercy, and not without effect:

> And though he first for ire quook and sterte,
> He hath considered shortly, in a clause,
> The trespas of hem bothe, and eek the cause,
> And although that his ire hir gilt accused,
> Yet in his resoun he hem bothe excused,
> As thus: he thoghte wel that every man
> Wol helpe hymself in love, if that he kan,
> And eek delivere hymself out of prisoun.
> And eek his herte hadde compassioun
> Of wommen, for they wepen evere in oon;
> And in his gentil herte he seyde, 'Fy
> Upon a lord that wol have no mercy,
> But been a leon, both in word and dede,
> To hem that been in repentaunce and drede,
> As wel as to a proud despitous man
> That wol mayntene that he first bigan.
> That lord hath litel of discrecioun,
> That in swich cas kan no divisioun,
> But weyeth pride and humblesse after oon.'
>
> (CT. I, 1762–81)

This lengthy passage, of a markedly analytical nature, clearly represents the thought processes to be recommended to a prudent ruler in such circumstances. Theseus is an ideal, an example of the anti-type of the tyrant. His natural reactions of anger and desire for vengeance are modified by compassion operating in unison with careful rational consideration of the circumstances of the crime. He finds grounds for mercy, and in Seneca's terms, decides upon *clementia* rather than *severitas* or *crudelitas*. Although emotion has a part in his decision, it is controlled and subjected to rational scrutiny. Indeed the decision has a distinctly moralistic evocation of the notion of contrition being the rational justification for offering mercy; an idea which finds an echo in the Parson's treatise on confession.[24] As a result of these scenes, Theseus emerges as a prudent ruler, a man of discretion and compassion. Whether or not this appearance develops an ironic dimension when seen in the context of his committal of Palamon and Arcite to 'perpetual prison', or of his only partly justificatory final speech, is beyond the scope of this book. It must suffice to say that the usage and ideas of the narrator of the tale present Theseus as an ideal ruler, and that duplicity in his motivation is more easily argued than proved.[25]

We may summarise this chapter by repeating the discovery that within the works of Chaucer, and many of his contemporaries, there is echoed a conception of the tyrant and his antithesis. This conception is of very long development and shows some evolutionary features typical of the middle ages, but, through the essential Latinity of medieval culture, authors still had recourse to its early sources in the writings of Seneca, Boethius, Cicero and others. Essential to the conception was the contest of reason and certain emotions aroused in a lord's relationship with his inferiors. The tyrant is defined by certain typical aspects of behaviour and also by his association with a vocabulary which above all contains the words: *tiraunt, cruel, wood, ire, hard, daungerous,* and perhaps *wraththe,* together with phrases like *sleen giltelees.* The image of the tyrant, which is a moral and psychological symbol of disorder, extends far beyond the political sphere and the lord-vassal relationship. We have already seen the idea extended to include the devil as a tyrannous master, and a husband is perceived as a tyrant in the *Manciple's Tale.* Indeed, the majority of Chaucer's uses of the tyrant image are of this transferred kind, and an examination of some of these will form the subject of the next chapter.

CHAPTER TWO

The Image of the Tyrant

AT THE BEGINNING of the *Parliament of Fowls* Chaucer is in the *persona* of the bookish, inexperienced writer who is fascinated by the ways of love but does not feel them upon his own pulses. Contemplation of the vagaries of love leaves his mind reeling, stunned by its inability to grapple with the complexity of the problems associated with love, which, at length, are to provide him with the subject matter of his poem. Yet, even as he portrays himself as numbed by these difficulties, his handling of his material belies him, revealing an agile and creative intellect at work. The opening of the *Parliament of Fowls* is a subtle texture of verbal and conceptual devices employed with a very knowing skill. The fact that love is to be his subject is at first concealed, then combined with the narrator's literary and philosophical problems, when he refers to his own dilemma by the use of an image beloved of courtly writers to refer to their success or failure in a lady's esteem: he does not know whether he is floating or sinking.[1] Yet, he says, he reads books and has discovered from them something of the nature of love. Personification becomes explicit as he moulds his gleanings about love into the outline of a familiar image:

> *For al be that I knowe nat Love in dede,*
> *Ne wot how that he quiteth folk here hyre,*
> *Yit happeth me ful ofte in bokes reede*
> *Of his myrakles and his crewel yre.*
> *There rede I wel he wol be lord and syre;*
> *I dar nat seyn, his strokes been so sore,*
> *But 'God save swich a lord!' – I can na moore.*
>
> (*PF.* 8–14)

The situation is clear. Love is envisaged as a lord who demands dominion, refuses to countenance any criticism, and repays lack of loyalty by cruel punishment. The phrase *crewel yre* is significant, and Chaucer's decision to represent the uncertain rewards of the lover's service by reference to a lord whose payment of his servants is unpredictable is sufficient to clinch the matter. Taken together, these items spell out quite unambiguously the traditional image of the tyrant. The god of love is envisaged as a tyrant, or to put it in less personal terms, love is a mastering passion constraining lovers for no certain reward. This somewhat moralistic judgement of love might have been directly stated, but much less interestingly. More to the point, Chaucer was a poet, and a court poet, and the mere statement that love is uncertain, that sometimes it brings suffering with it, would have seemed mawkish and trivial. As it is, the familiar injustice of love, which strains the credulity of Troilus at the end of *Troilus and Criseyde*, is wittily realised by the use of the traditional literary *topoi* of the tyrant. However, Chaucer's use of the literary extension of the tyrant image to refer to love is less straightforward than we have acknowledged. His attitude to the God of Love is not simply one of respect, but is unmistakably one of mock-awe. That a contemporary love-poet should see Love as a tyrant is not particularly disconcerting, but that something close to scorn should infect his tone is more surprising. Love is a *would-be* lord and master, and there is an implication that he physically beats his servants (*his strokes been so sore*). Moreover, the phrase *quiteth . . .hyre* hardly seems appropriate to the courtiers of a noble lord who might expect a *guerdon* or *grace* rather than *hyre*.[2] It would appear that, underlying the identification of the God of Love, is an insulting, socially-derogatory implication. His tyranny is not that of a great lord; more that of a small employer, a village tyrant.

Well may Chaucer exhibit nervousness of the wrath of the God of Love, for despite his own reputation as a poet of love and philosophy, he was to become a seasoned despoiler of the reputation of that jealous god. In the *Knight's Tale* he returned rather less deviously to a similar assessment of him. Theseus, whose white banner bears the red figure of Mars as symbolic assurance of the balance he maintains between compassion and harshness, compared with the excesses of the red banner of Arcite and the white of Palamon,[3] Theseus, the ideal ruler who balances pity and rational justice in his dealings, reflects upon the nature of love after he discovers the fruitless single combat between Palamon and Arcite:

> *Se how they blede! be they noght wel arrayed?*
> *Thus hath hir lord, the god of love, ypayed*
> *Hir wages and hir fees for hir servyse!*
> (*CT*. I, 1801–3)

30

To Theseus, their conduct is irrational and the emotion (or god) which impels them is to that extent worthy of condemnation; but such behaviour is common experience, and as such merits his compassion and forgiveness.

The problems of the essential irrationality of love, the amoral way in which it is bestowed regardless of obvious merit, its inaccessibility to rational analysis, its disregard for established order and even statutory law, are problems which exercised both Chaucer and Gower, and indeed form a major theme of the *Parliament of Fowls*.[4] The image of the God of Love as a tyrant, coupled with a certain rationalistic distaste of the passion, expressed by means of a social slur, is a brilliant and inventive opening for a poem which proceeds to relate a vision of civil and cosmological order as a precursor to a revelation of the unadaptability of love to the ordered procedures of law.

Inevitably, Chaucer's depradations upon the character of the God of Love eventually lead to retribution: he is called to account in the prologue of the *Legend of Good Women*. Whether or not the actual circumstances of the composition of the *Legend* were, as Lydgate claimed, an instruction from Queen Anne to redress the unfavourable balance of his earlier writings, we shall never know. It is at least plausible that some courtiers, followers perhaps of the amorous orders of the Flower or the Leaf, found his morality too narrow and his treatment of Criseyde exceptionable.[5] These, at least, are the accusations made against him by the God of Love, who confronts him in a springtime dream. Chaucer is alleged to be the opponent of Love, a slanderer and abuser of this powerful lord, who now prepares himself to deliver justice:

> *Thow art my mortal fo and me werreyest,*
> *And of myne olde servauntes thow mysseyest,*
> *And hynderest hem with thy translacyoun,*
> *And lettest folk to han devocyoun*
> *To serven me, and holdest it folye*
> *To truste on me. Thow mayst it nat denye.*
> (*LGW*. G-text, 248–53)

The accusation is extended over many lines in the G-text, and the god becomes more and more threatening, until at last Alcestis intercedes on behalf of the speechless Chaucer. The situation is clearly a judicial one, and Alcestis, who is an example of constancy in love, here fills the rôle of counsellor to the offended prince, a rôle strikingly similar to that of Prudence in the *Tale of Melibee*:

> *'God, ryght of youre curteysye,*
> *Ye moten herkenen if he can replye*
> *Ageyns these poynts that ye han to hym meved.*

31

A god ne sholde nat thus been agreved,
But of his deite he shal be stable,
And therto ryghtful, and ek mercyable
He shal nat ryghtfully his yre wreke,
Or he have herd the tother partye speke.
                                    (*LGW*. G-text, 318–25)

Alcestis acts as the philosophical restraint to a potential tyrant. She offers a lesson in natural justice, using some of the technical language of legal procedure (*poynts . . . to him meved*), but also clearly echoing the theme of judicial tyranny in the phrase *yre wreke*, and in the insistence on the rational balance of justice and clemency (*ryghtful, and ek mercyable*). The whole passage takes on the characteristic moral psychological flavour that we have found informing passages of advice to princes in the last chapter. 'This,' says Alcestis, 'shulde a ryghtwys lord han in his thought:'

And not ben lyk tyraunts of Lumbardye,
That usen wilfulhed and tyrannye.
For he that kyng or lord is naturel,
Hym oughte nat be tyrant and crewel,
As is a fermour, to don the harm he can.
He moste thynke it is his lige man,
And that hym oweth, of verray duetee,
Shewen his peple pleyn benygnete.
                                    (*LGW*. G-text, 354–61)

The argument is one of sentiment. A lord should not be unswervingly just and severe, but he should be ready to show compassion upon that man who has been born into his service – as all men are to the service of Love. Unswerving harshness may be expected from a landlord, but the personal ties of the feudal system should predispose a natural lord to clemency. As in Theseus's reaction to Palamon and Arcite, contrition is to be taken as a further argument for mercy, even in the case where guilt is not in doubt:

And if so be he may hym nat excuse,
But axeth mercy with a sorweful herte,
And profereth hym, ryght in his bare sherte,
To ben ryght at youre owene jugement,
Than ought a god, by short avisement,
Considere his owene honour and his trespas.
For syth no cause of deth lyth in this cas,
Yow oughte to ben the lyghter merciable;
Leteth youre yre, and beth somwhat tretable.
                                    (*LGW*. G-text, 389–97)

Chaucer's attempts to justify himself are, however, cut short 'for Love ne wol nat counterpletyd be/In ryght ne wrong', and he is allotted the penance of writing the biographies of various ladies whose faith in love

32

has become exemplary. The penalty is relatively light because of the intercession of Alcestis whose compassion helps to moderate the severity which Love's ire demanded. Thus, once again, even as his *persona* is compelled to make amends to Love, and if we believe Lydgate's story, as he himself is commencing his penance, Chaucer is repeating the charge that Love is irrational and arbitrary. His justice cannot brook argument and is not based upon reason: in those cases where it is harshly administered, it is tyranny; where it results in a happier outcome, the reason is pity rather than justifiable clemency. Love is arbitrary and depends upon favour rather than deserts; it has all the marks of tyranny.

The conception of the God of Love in his malevolent aspect as a tyrant, at least in the examples from the *Parliament of Fowls* and the *Knight's Tale*, derives ultimately of course from the relationship between two individuals, so that it is no surprise to find the accusation of tyranny levelled at one of a pair of lovers. Indeed in the works of Chaucer the situation in which a distant and superior beloved inflicts real or imagined suffering upon an aspiring lover furnishes more examples of the typical vocabulary of tyranny than any other situation in which the image is used. When put in these terms, the situation referred to is immediately recognisable as that of 'courtly love'. I have, however, avoided using this phrase because critical custom has come to regard it as referring to a relationship in which a man is persecuted by the *daunger* of a distant lady. The use of the tyrant *topos* in the love relationship is, however, appropriate to either sex, depending as it does upon discrepancy in power, interdependence, and arbitrary cruelty. In fact, Chaucer's commission to write the *Legend of Good Women*, with its stories of faithful and loving women and cruel and deceitful men, means that the accusation of tyranny in love is more frequently to be made against men than against women in Chaucer's poetry.

We may illustrate this by an example drawn from an early essay in the heroic style, but which contains much of the spirit of the later *Legend*. In *Anelida and Arcite*, Chaucer describes the betrayal of Anelida by her lover, Arcite. Alone and abandoned, the queen makes a formal complaint of her mistreatment; she accuses Arcite of being *routheles* (230) and showing her *cruelte* (271), and addresses him in other familiar terms:

> And to this plyte have ye me broght,
> Withoute gilt, – me nedeth no witnesse.
> And shal I preye, and weyve womanhede?
> Nay! rather deth then do so foul a dede!
> And axe merci, giltles, – what nede?
> (*AA*. 297–301)

The speech is typical of courtly rhetoric in the witty play on the specific senses of certain words, here reflecting chaotic shifts in the self-possession of the speaker. At first Anelida is proud and defiant: she makes a confident accusation of injustice; she will not compromise her dignity by begging for pity from a tyrant. The word *mercy* is then used in its technical sense as justifiable clemency extended to the guilty; a sense which carries with it associations of the need for contrition.[6] If she is innocent, how then can she ask for mercy? A few lines later, her self-sufficiency breaks down, and, with her idealism blinding her to the possibility of faults in her lover, she assumes that there *must* be some rational explanation for his cruelty. Her self-confidence becomes self-accusation as she seeks a reason for guilt; perhaps it can be found in her very complaint:

> *Now merci, swete, yf I misseye!*
> *Have I seyd oght amys, I preye?*
> *(AA.* 317–8)

This same agony, that of the mistreated lover, the victim of the arbitrariness of love, who yet cannot credit the concept of injustice inhering in their beloved, is repeated again and again, in both men and women, in Chaucer's poetry. Most memorably, perhaps, it is found in Troilus:

> *What wratthe of juste cause have ye to me?*
> *What gilt of me, what fel experience,*
> *Hath fro me raft, allas! thyn advertence?*
> *(TC.* V, 1256–8)

Troilus is here of one company with women like Anelida or Dido. All are idealizing lovers who fail to perceive one essential feature of human love: its arbitrariness, and its potential instability. Put in allegorical terms, they do not recognize the God of Love as a tyrant. Like Chaucer at the beginning of the *Legend of Good Women*, they all argue with Love, convinced that, within the relationship they have cherished, some seeds of order and justice can be found if the desire to discover it be strong enough.

The image of the tyrant is also used in the love situation in a rather different way: this is in those literary circumstances which we would immediately identify as the 'courtly love' situation:

> *Hir surname is eek Faire Rewthelees,*
> *The Wyse, yknit unto Good Aventure,*
> *That, for I love hir, she sleeth me giltelees.*
> *(Lady,* 27–9)

The lover is presented as the hapless victim of a capricious lady whose unconcern will slay him as surely as a dagger beneath the ribs. The only help for the suffering man is the lady's pity (*routhe, mercy, pitee, compassioun, grace*), which in actuality means her sexual compliance. The situation, and its language are highly conventional, but perhaps rarer in Middle English literature than we are accustomed to think, at least in an elaborated form, although allusions to it may be common enough. It is, in fact, something of a specialized development of the tyrant tradition as we have traced it. The lady may be regarded as capricious and arbitrary, but the emphasis is not here upon those aspects of the tyrant. Her behaviour might well be considered by the lover to be unreasonable, but she can hardly be wrathful, mad, or ravening for slaughter. Indeed, neither irrationality nor direct cruelty are truly appropriate to this situation. Yet, she is conventionally accused of the slaughter of the innocent, and consequently of cruelty. Such accusations, which are dependent upon an inappropriate parallel drawn between the love relation and the relationship existing between a tyrant and his vassal, are one of the reasons why this 'courtly love' situation often seems contrived and artificial to the modern reader. His reaction is a correct one. Indeed, it *does* depend upon a contrived image.

The justification for calling the distant lady a tyrant, and applying to her the vocabulary of tyranny is specious, and is twofold. Firstly, it depends on the peculiarly medieval conception of the tyrant as lacking pity, incapable of compassion, rather than his association with rage or irrationality. Secondly, it depends on a further literary convention: that unrequited love leads to actual sickness, which, if unremedied, may eventually cause death. As Professor Dronke has demonstrated, this idea, in which the lady figures as the only possible physician for the doomed man, is extremely ancient and widespread in literature. It also had a more limited career in reputable medical opinion.[7] Whatever the truth of the belief in sober scientific fact, its effect was to place the lover's life in his lady's hands: her capacity for compassion stood between him and inevitable death. Whilst there is clearly no strict parallel between the deliberate cruelty of the tyrant and the suffering involuntarily, and perhaps even unknowingly, caused by the courtly lady, nevertheless poets saw a connection in the failure of both to be impressed by suffering when it was revealed to them. The complaint 'Ye sle me giltelees for verray peyne' (*CT.* v, 1317) becomes commoner in literature in this love situation than its original judicial one.

The accusation of heartlessness at the distress of the innocent no doubt became a winning argument in the mouths of hopeful young men. Indeed the Lady of La Tour Landry finds it necessary to warn her daughters against those who would demand their notice on these grounds.[8] The tactician Pandarus uses it repeatedly to Criseyde in Book II:

> *If that ye don us bothe dyen,*
> *Thus gilteles, than have ye fisshed fayre!*
> (*TC.* II, 327–8)

35

The phrasing is that of arbitrary injustice, but the appeal is to pity. No grounds exist for an accusation of tyranny in the rational moralistic terms of Seneca: the implied crime is lack of compassion:

> *A womman, that were of his deth to wite,*
> *Withouten his gilt, but for hire lakked routhe,*
> *Were it wel doon?*
>
> (*TC.* II, 1279–81)

The only blame that attaches here is failure to show pity and to act accordingly. The reference to innocent suffering, like Pandarus's actual accusation of tyranny (II, 1240), is the dishonest use of persuasive rhetoric rather than a justifiable use of the tyrant analogy.

If the God of Love is a cruel master, arbitrary and unjust in his rewards, so too does Fame prove to be. In the *House of Fame* Chaucer is a privileged visitor to her hall, where he stands on one side watching the jostle of those eager to court her favour. Some petitioners, who genuinely deserve to have a good reputation, put this request to her, and are met with a blank refusal:

> *'Allas!' quod they, 'and welaway!*
> *Telle us what may your cause be.'*
> *'For me lyst hyt noght,' quod she.*
> (*HF.* 1562–4)

Their attempts to remonstrate would be pointless; Fame, like Love, takes no account of deserts and will not be reasoned with. Neither reason nor a concern for morality affects her decisions, but only the caprice of her will. Chaucer is at pains to make this clear, for when at length Fame actually does refuse a good reputation to a group who really do not deserve one, he heads off our possible feeling of satisfaction at seeing justice done by putting an explanatory speech in Fame's mouth. She is not acting, she says, from motives of justice, but simply for her own satisfaction:

> *Al be ther in me no justice,*
> *Me lyste not to doo hyt now.*
> (*HF.* 1820–21)

Fame exhibits in full the amorality, the pettishness, the irrational exploitation of despotic power, which in a king would make him *rex tyrannus*. It is inevitable that in such circumstances Chaucer will eventually have recourse to the typical vocabulary of tyranny and unjust oppression. As he looks on at the arbitrary mistreatment of people whom he knows to be worthy, he sadly thinks to himself:

> *'Allas . . . what aventures*
> *Han these sory creatures!*

> For they, amonges all the pres,
> Shal thus be shamed gilteles.'
> (HF. 1631–4)

If Fame is arbitrary, then Fortune is her sister. When Chaucer came to translate Boethius's lament against his unjust imprisonment, he found the evocative phrase *fortunae in nos saevientis asperitas* 'the harshness of fortune raging against us'. His rendering of this has a more personal and pointed form than the Latin, achieved by substituting a transitive verb for the verbal adjective of the original, and an alteration in the personal pronoun used: 'the scharpnesse of Fortune, that waxeth wood ayens me' (I. p. 4, 12). The cue offered by the Latin *saeviens*, familiar in the Latin tradition of the tyrant, and used by Gower of Richard II, is seized by Chaucer, whose translation intensifies the notion of the unjust persecution of an individual.

Yet, as the result of his more extensive reading in Boethius, Chaucer has rather an ambivalent attitude to Fortune. For, in Boethius's explanation of the causality of events, Fortune is eventually revealed to have rather less that absolute power. She is, as she herself explains in a short poem of Chaucer's, more properly to be seen as evidence of a divine order underlying creation. Indeed, there is a sense in which Fortune does not exist outside the minds of men. It is they who have made her in the image of the tyrant; an image to render familiar certain effects of a divine plan whose just motives they cannot perceive:

> Lo, th' execucion of the majestee
> That al purveyeth of his rightwysnesse,
> That same thing 'Fortune' clepen ye,
> Ye blinde bestes, ful of lewednesse!
> (Fortune, 65–8)

To regard Fortune as arbitrary and to rail at her as a tyrant is error. She is rather the *Executrice of wierdes* 'the agent of providence', and any true Christian should perceive this role, even though pagans might erroneously condemn the tyranny of Fortune.

In connection with this dualistic notion of Fortune, we should also briefly consider Chaucer's attitude to the pagan gods who repeatedly appear in his poetry. First of all we must be clear that, in fourteenth-century poetry, they are not considered to have any real personal existence. They occur in Chaucer's poetry in two main guises: firstly as a kind of historical recreation of the supposed pagan divinities of Troy or Athens in the pre-Christian era; and, secondly, as artistic devices of various kinds, mechanical, psychological, or rhetorical. A typical example of their psychological function would be their equation with planetary influences, in which they tend to become excuses for the actions of morally fragile characterizations such as the Wife of Bath, or explanations of the origins of dream visions such as that of the *Parliament of Fowls*.[9] But these functions do not concern us at present, and it is to their former role that we must turn our attention.

Chaucer deliberately sets certain of his poems in a pre-Christian age. Although he does not attempt a thorough-going antiquarian reconstruction, and is not scrupulous about excluding references to Christian doctrines and beliefs, nevertheless the philosophical conception of the world, man's place in it, and morality, is different, for the world he creates is lacking in the dimension of a loving and humane Christian God. Troilus, and the participants of the *Knight's Tale*, have read parts of Boethius, but they have not been granted the Christian resolution of the philosophical difficulties raised in the earlier parts of the work. Thus it is excusable, and to be expected, that characters in these poems complain long and bitterly about the gods, and about Fortune.

Although, in the *Knight's Tale*, Theseus has a conception of the divine providence of Jupiter, the god is distant, ill-defined, and impersonal, close to the Stoic *logos*. He does not appear in person in the tale, and the gods who play an active part – Mercury, Mars, Saturn, Venus, and Diana – are either simply disinterested, or indeed active persecutors of mankind. When Palamon exclaims 'O cruel goddes' at line 1303, there is the usual ambivalence about whether the Olympian pantheon is meant, since the language and ideas of the speech closely and inevitably echo those of Christian determinism, but the accusation of tyranny is unmistakable. The gods are rulers of a world in which:

> . . . slayn is man right as another beest,
> And dwelleth eek in prison and arreest,
> And hath siknesse and greet adversitee,
> And ofte tymes giltelees, pardee.
> What governance is in this prescience,
> That giltelees tormenteth innocence?
> (*CT*. I, 1309–14)

This is an ill-governed realm groaning under the sway of an unjust administration. The gods are tyrants who persecute and harass their human subjects. Even the queen of the gods, Juno, is 'jalous and eek wood'. And this assessment of the pagan pantheon is one which is widely spread throughout Chaucer's poetry. The epithets of tyranny – *cruel, wood* – are felt to be especially appropriate to Mars in other poems also.

The image of the pagan Gods as tyrannous rulers given especially in the *Knight's Tale* may usefully be compared with a speech on divine dispensation made by Dorigen in the *Franklin's Tale*. Although it is not perhaps very clear what the religious affiliations of the 'olde Britouns' were, Dorigen's speech is uncompromisingly medieval Christian. She is putting the problem of apparent evil and injustice in a reasonably ordered Christian creation in words that echo *Boethius*, I, metre 5:

> *Eterne God, that thurgh thy purveiaunce*
> *Ledest the world by certein governaunce,*
> *In ydel, as men seyn, ye no thyng make.*
> *But, Lord, thise grisly feendly rokkes blake,*
> *That semen rather a foul confusion*
> *Of werk than any fair creacion*
> *Of swich a parfit wys God and a stable,*
> *Why han ye wroght this werk unresonable?*
>
> (*CT*. V, 865–72)

Dorigen accepts the Christian doctrine of a just and loving God, but sees the dark rocks, which threaten shipping and, she fears, her husband's life, as a contradiction of such doctrine. The situation would have offered no problem to Palamon or Arcite, for they knew the tyrannous nature of their gods. But for Dorigen such an explanation is not possible. Mankind is esteemed as the noblest of God's creation:

> *Which mankynde is so fair part of thy werk*
> *That thou it madest lyk to thyn owene merk.*
> *Thanne semed it ye hadde a greet chiertee*
> *Toward mankynde; but how thanne may it bee*
> *That ye swiche meenes make it to destroyen?*
>
> (*CT*. V, 879–83)

Dorigen knows the orthodox answer to her question, that even the 'blakke rokkes' have a useful part to play in an all-enfolding divine plan, but, faced with the threat of the loss of her husband, she finds this answer hard to accept and emotionally unsatisfying. Indeed much orthodox Christian doctrine in medieval times, which depended upon faith in the existence of a divine plan working towards good at a level beyond human comprehension, must often have been scant comfort in those moments of need, which a more insecure world made commoner than in that of today. It is therefore not surprising that, even in a Christian context, there were many who were ready to identify Fortune as a tyrant, or were ready to blame the stars for the catastrophes which befell them, or were brought about by their own failings.

Two admirable reactions to disaster were open to Chaucer's contemporaries. The first was that which the pagans of the past had also cultivated, and that which Seneca had revered: the recognition of the arbitrariness of Fortune and the cultivation of Stoic fortitude, neither greeting good fortune with excessive joy, nor ill-fortune with lamenting. This self-sufficiency, which protects the wise man against any external evil, whether bad fortune or the persecution of tyrants, as Boethius explains (I, m. 4), would, however, be criticised by adherents of the second reaction for its exclusively secular nature. In the poem *Fortune*, Chaucer states clearly the Stoic ideal:

> But trewely, no force of thy reddour
> To him that over himself hath the maystrye!
> My suffisaunce shal be my socour;
> For fynally, Fortune, I thee defye!
> (*Fortune*, 13–6)

But in the same poem Chaucer goes on to point out the error of this attitude and to indicate the way to the second, which is patience in tribulation in the joyous knowledge that all suffering is part of some just purpose whose full workings no mind can conceive. Both Stoic and Christian ethics are apparent in Chaucer's works, but, whenever the two come into contact, there is no doubt which is to be considered superior.

Contempt for reversals in worldly affairs, whether from Christian or Stoic convictions, is a poise that few can maintain, and to Chaucer's contemporaries, unless they were most careful to remain philosophically alert, Fortune or planetary influences may seem as arbitrary and cruel masters as Chaucer supposes that they did to the pagan past. To the moral philosopher, however, conscious as he must be of Divine Providence and man's free will within it, such forces often concealed the true door at which blame should be laid.[10] Human foolishness, the subjection of the reason to tyrannical passions, were the real sources of the troubles which were projected upon the stars or Fortune. As a result of this awareness that the strength of these tyrants is merely the reflection of human weakness, a further ambiguity often enters into Chaucer's treatment of Fame, Fortune, and the gods. From the pagan point of view, and as a literary convention, they may appear to be all-powerful tyrants, but from the point of view of the moralist observing the back-sliding Christian, they are trivialised, they are simply *swich rascaille*. Certainly, Fortune herself, the most respectable of them all, is frequently regarded as an oppressive tyrant, wielding inexplicable injustice. But she is equally frequently viewed as a fickle and irresponsible woman, and it is quite arguable that Chaucer's conception of the moral psychology of his most enchanting creation, Criseyde, is to some extent bound up with this essentially feminine conception of Fortune. The famous phrase *slydynge of corage*, which is used to describe Criseyde, is unparalleled in Chaucer's work, but in his translation of Boethius, he renders the original's *lubrica fortuna* by the phrase 'slydynge Fortune'. The implication of the word, which itself is rare in Chaucer, seems to be that of slippery evasiveness and instability. The unaccountability of Fame, too, we may remember, means that she is presented as a wilful and capricious woman who will give no explanation of her actions, but that it pleases her to act thus. Similarly, the essential triviality of the pagan gods is repeatedly revealed by their childish squabbling, their vindictive natures, and their wilful and unaccommodating behaviour. There is, in the moralist's conception of Fortune, Fame and the gods, a sense of their pettiness which tends to prevent the elaborated application to them of the tyrant image. More often it is applied to them in the form of a passing epithet.

Now, if the pagan gods are frequently considered to be petty tyrants, the god of the Christians is the anti-type of the unjust master. We have already suggested that this distinction can be seen both in his conformity to reason and in his compassion, and both these ideals will be discussed in later chapters; but we may illustrate his antithesis with the tyrant from one of the diagnostic situations we discovered earlier. In the parable of the labourers in the vineyard, understood allegorically, God is seen as an employer, and indeed an employer who pays beyond justice. In *Pearl*, although the story is told for another purpose – to illustrate the doctrine of the plentitude of grace – when the Pearl-maiden achieves salvation, she speaks of it in terms of receiving prompt payment of her *hyre*. In *Piers Plowman*, Piers is a servant of Treuthe, and in his insistence upon his habit of paying promptly and in full, there is an unmistakable implicit contrast with those earthly lords whose kind Chaucer's Parson convicts of tyranny:

> *For þou3 I seye it myself I serue hym to paye;*
> *I haue myn hire [of hym] wel and ouþerwhiles moore.*
> *He is þe presteste paiere þat pouere men knoweþ;*
> *He wiþhalt noon hewe his hire þat he ne haþ it at euen.*
>   (*PP*. B-text, V, 549–52)

The concept of the tyrant and his opposite, the just king, are very poignant ones in fourteenth-century literature. And they are so not simply because of their long and authoritative descent from classical times, but because they had a special appropriateness to medieval society and patterns of thought. Both as symbols of psychological states and of qualities of hierarchical relationships their utility easily extended far beyond the political situation to which they properly belonged. In a world full of hierarchies, among men who delighted to argue by analogy, such symbols were bound to flourish. The relationships between God and Man, lord and vassal, courtly lady and her lover may analogically appear to be types of one another. They may, as C. S. Lewis pointed out more than forty years ago, employ much of the same vocabulary, and the proprieties of one relationship may migrate easily to another.[11] And, of these three hierarchical relationships, only that between Christian God and Man is free of the imputation of tyranny. Beyond these basic relationships are a whole series of other dyadic relationships of a similarly unequal kind: that between father and child:

> 'O litel child, allas! what is thy gilt,
> That nevere wroghtest synne as yet, pardee?
> Why wil thyn harde fader han thee spilt?'
> (CT. II, 855–7)

between a bird of prey and its victim:

> Ther was the tiraunt with his fetheres donne
> And grey, I mene the goshauk, that doth pyne
> To bryddes for his outrageous ravyne.
> (PF. 334–6)

or even between a husband and wife. The Wife of Bath recalls her treatment of her husband in terms that we have found significant:

> O Lord! the peyne I dide hem and the wo,
> Ful giltelees, by Goddes sweete pyne!
> (CT. III, 384–5)

That the Wife should be envisaged as a tyrant would perhaps be surprising if we knew no more of her history, for medieval orthodoxy regarded the husband as ruler over his wife. But in the characterization of the Wife of Bath, orthodox hierarchies are repeatedly overturned, and this one can be paralleled at lines 440–42 by her suggestion that her wilfulness should take precedence over his reason. This too is a scandalous reversal of proper order, and it is precisely the diagnosis of the disorder which creates the personality of a tyrant, for the tyrant had long been the image of a man whose reason is subject to unruly and wilful passions.

The moral symbol of the tyrant, which was transmitted to the middle ages from the moral and philosophical literature of Rome became, in the fourteenth-century, a literary commonplace applicable in a wide range of situations. It had a remarkable stability both in terms of concepts and vocabulary. This cohesion as a literary topos it certainly owed to its derivation from the Latin tradition which lay behind it: vernacular poets in England were only just bringing to their productions the conceptual subtlety which had previously been exercised in Latin and literary French. But, by the fifteenth century, poetry can be found in which the tyrant topos is used not rooted in the Latin tradition but as part of an overt imitation of Chaucer and Gower. Lydgate's *Complaynt of a Loveres Lyfe* is a blatant imitation of the *Book of the Duchess,* and contains lengthy echoes from the *Parliament of Fowls, Knight's Tale, Troilus and Criseyde,* and other Chaucerian works. The idea of the God of Love as a master who stints his servants' wages occurs immediately before a stanza which is unashamedly modelled upon the close of *Troilus and Criseyde:*

> *But Love, alas, quyt him so his wage*
> *With cruel daunger pleynly at the last,*
> *That with the dethe guerdonles he past.*
>
> *'Lo, her the fyne of loveres seruise.*
> *Lo, how that Love can his seruantis quyte.*
> (397–401)

A longer passage, too long to quote in full, tells us how the faithful lover has been undone by slanders and his place usurped:

> *O ryghtful God, that first trouthe fonde,*
> *How may thou suffre such oppressyon,*
> *That Falshed shuld have iurysdixion*
> *In Trouthes ryght, to sle him gilteles?*
>
> *Falsly accused and of his foon for-iuged.*
> *Without answer while he was absent*
> *He damned was, and may not ben excused:*
> *For Cruelte satte in iugement*
> *Of hastynes without avisement.*
> (269–78)

Here are the phrase *sle . . . giltelees*, the notion of judgement without right of reply, the cruelty of the judge, and perhaps most notably, the implication that the judgement is not that of reason, contained in the words 'hastynes without avisement'. The exercise of prudence in reaching decisions is an important theme in Chaucer's poetry, indeed it forms the main theme of his own tale on the road to Canterbury, and it has its own typical vocabulary. Prudence is lacking in the tyrant, and after *pitee*, is the supreme virtue of the ideal king, and it is prudence which forms the subject of the next chapter.

CHAPTER THREE

Practical Wisdom

WHEN, IN THE *Knight's Tale*, Theseus discovered Palamon and Arcite skirmishing in the woodlands outside Athens in complete disregard of his will and his laws, he was, we may remember, inflamed by anger. But, just as that anger undoubtedly was, it quickly died away when the ladies of Theseus's party made an appeal on behalf of the sworn brothers. Their king is no tyrant; *pitee* soon floods into his heart, and he pauses to consider events:

> *He hath considered shortly, in a clause,*
> *The trespas of hem bothe, and eek the cause,*
> *And although that his ire hir gilt accused,*
> *Yet in his resoun he hem bothe excused.*
> (*CT.* I, 1763–6)

Pitee and *resoun* are united in Theseus's *gentil herte*. As he analyzes the circumstances and the cause of their breach of the law, his deliberations are given in detail, thus emphasizing the rationality of his procedure. Although the outcome of these deliberations does little to answer the doubts which most readers of the poem entertain about metaphysical justice, they do clearly exhibit the processes by which order and good government are maintained in the environment of Athens.[1] This scene is an example of the good secular ruler at work. *Pitee* abounds in him, but no more so than the exercise of reason: in both respects, he is the antitype of the tyrant.

In the *Legend of Good Women*, too, where the potentially tyrannous God of Love is restrained by Alcestis, we find an emphasis upon the necessity for preconsideration. In the judicial function, a lord must act rashly on neither *ire* nor *pitee,* but must first pause to consider (G. 394). *Gentillesse* seems to consist as much in this consideration as in ready pity:

> *In noble corage oughte ben arest,*
> *And weyen every thing in equite,*
> *And evere han reward to his owen degre.*
> (*LGW.* G-text, 383–5)

In every aspect of his rule, a king must proceed with discretion, must strive to see the implications of his actions, and to act only with this knowledge. Such is the repeated teaching of *miroir de prince* literature. Modern politics has been called 'the art of the possible'; government to Chaucer was the art of the do-able, seen in terms of the acts of a ruler. Gower, indeed, places it within a special niche in practical philosophy:

> *Practique hath yit the thridde aprise*
> *Which techeth hou and in what wise*
> *Thurgh hih pourveied ordinaunce*
> *A king schal sette in governaunce*
> *His Realme, and that is Policie.*
> (*CA.* VII, 1679–83)

In the above scene, then, Theseus is acting naturally, as a wise man should, but at the same time is acting as the teachings of Policie dictate for a king. He is conforming to a stereotyped ideal and to a stereotype which Chaucer set out in greater detail in his own *Tale of Melibee,* and of which we have every reason to believe that he approved.

The *Tale of Melibee* is a lengthy prose narrative in allegorical mode which has attracted little popular attention. Indeed it has probably never been so popular as many of the verse tales, although manuscript evidence indicates that it found a somewhat specialist audience of rather austere tastes, for manuscripts exist in which it is bound up separately with both the Parson's and the Monk's tales, and it occurs in books where it is the sole Chaucerian work.[2] That Chaucer esteemed it too in this same sober spirit is suggested by his approach to it. He protests scrupulous observance of the proprieties for a serious literary work. This is a moral tale, to be treated with reverential care in the retelling. As its reteller, variation in words and phrasing will be allowed to him, but its valuable import will remain unaltered. Indeed, he has adapted new sentential devices to press the original meaning more fully. After the unhappy experience of his tale of Sir Thopas, he now, as the pilgrim narrator, begs to be allowed to reproduce this story in its entirety. As author, he avails himself of that freedom. There is no trace of ambiguity in Chaucer's attitude to the *Tale of Melibee.* In his *Retracciouns,* when literary masterpieces are falling all around, *Melibee* remains unscathed.

The *Tale of Melibee* is in the tradition of the *miroir de prince*. It is devoted to the counsels given to the ruler Melibee (the prosperous man) by his wife, Prudence. He has been the victim of an outrage by his enemies and is preparing his reaction to this. Instinct demands speedy vengeance upon the enemies who have injured him, and he calls all his friends together in the accepted manner to give him counsel. Their advice is conflicting. One wise old counsellor warns him that careful consideration is necessary before entering on such a risky course:

> Werre at his bigynnyng hath so greet an entryng and so large, that every wight may entre whan hym liketh, and lightly fynde werre;/ but certes what ende that shal therof bifalle, it is nat light to knowe.
>
> (*CT*. VII, 1039–40)

But this excellent advice is shouted down and a decision upon a war of revenge is reached. At this point Prudence enters, armed with a sheaf of *sententiae* – that proverbial wisdom with which Chaucer had promised to reinforce his meaning at the beginning. 'He hasteth wel that wisely kan abyde', she proclaims, and 'in wikked haste is no profit' (1054). In reaching a good decision, the heart must be empty of cupidity and ire, and the mind free of *hastifnesse*, since:

> ye ne may nat deeme for the beste by a sodeyn thought that falleth in youre herte, but ye moste avyse yow on it ful ofte.
>
> (*CT*. VII, 1134)

After giving advice on the choice of counsellors and the assessment of the worth of their counsel, Prudence goes on to analyse the errors that Melibee has made in coming to his decision to make war. She approves the wise adviser who said 'that yow oghte nat sodeynly ne hastily proceden in this nede,/ but that yow oghte purveyen and apparaillen yow in this caas with greet diligence and greet deliberacioun' (1342). She goes on to teach her husband how to analyse the crime and what his proper reaction to it should be, and her words echo the way in which Theseus considers the 'trespas' and the 'cause' in the *Knight's Tale*. The substance of Prudence's advice to Melibee is:

> Werke alle thy thynges by conseil, and thou shalt never repente.
>
> (*CT*. VII, 1003)

Good counsel, with well-chosen counsellors, must precede every decision by the wise ruler. Hasty action is to be decried and replaced by careful preconsideration; this is the essence of the teaching of Prudence.

Such a doctrine is familiar enough, but its practical value is not diminished by familiarity: the middle ages, on the whole, did not regard aphoristic wisdom with contempt. At the end of the tale, Harry Baily, that scourge of humbug, bursts out in comic vein before turning to the Monk for his contribution, but his humour is not at the expense of the *Tale of Melibee*. Indeed, it serves rather to extend its applicability, for the account he gives of his turbulent life with a ferocious and vengeful wife clearly points to the relevance to domestic life of that prudence which facilitated a happy settlement between Melibee and his enemies. The exercise of similar prudence and patience on the part of Goodelief might go far, Harry feels, to help him live more peaceably with his servants and neighbours. At present, her desires for vengeance at supposed affronts threaten to provoke him to murder:

> *This is my lif, but if that I wol fighte;*
> *And out at dore anon I moot me dighte,*
> *Or elles I am but lost, but if that I*
> *Be lik a wilde leoun, fool-hardy.*
> *I woot wel she wol do me slee som day*
> *Som neighebour, and thanne go my way.*
>
> (*CT*. VII, 1913–8)

Prudence, expressed in terms of self-restraint, of hesitating to consider an action, is applicable not only to rulers but in every station of life, and in a bewildering variety of circumstances. Its opposite, reckless, unpremeditated action, is in all circumstances to be avoided.

In his third book of the *Confessio Amantis*, which is extensively concerned with the concept, Gower discusses the kind of impetuosity which is antagonistic to prudent consideration. He discovers a name for it, *Folhaste*:

> *Noght only upon loves chance,*
> *Bot upon every governaunce*
> *Which falleth unto mannes dede,*
> *Folhaste is evere forto drede,*
> *And that a man good conseil take,*
> *Er he his pourpos undertake,*
> *For counseil put Folhaste aweie.*
>
> (*CA*. III, 1739–45)

The word *folhaste* is rare in Middle English usage: in *M.E.D.* all the citations, except two from contemporary moralistic works, are from Gower. Much more commonly, a similar concept is connoted by a group of other words, most notably: *hastif, sodeyn, reccheles, rakel,* and *unavised*. The examples of *folhaste*, expressed in words like these, are legion in the works of Chaucer and Gower. The latter tells how Tiresias's misfortunes arose from his failure to consider before making judgement. Called upon to arbitrate a dispute between Jupiter and Juno upon the sexuality of men and women, he gave his opinion hastily 'withoute avisemente' (III. 751), and was struck blind for his folly. The experience of Tiresias bears out the

47

precept of Melibee's wife: 'he that soone deemeth, soone repenteth' (1135).

Ill-considered speech is as much to be shunned as hasty action. In the *Manciple's Tale*, Phoebus regrets the reckless anger which has led him to murder his wife whom he fears may prove innocent:

> *O rakel hand, to doon so foule amys!*
> *O trouble wit, o ire recchelees,*
> *That unavysed smyteth gilteles!*
>
> *Smyt nat to soone, er that ye witen why,*
> *And beeth avysed wel and sobrely*
> *Er ye doon any execucion*
> *Upon youre ire for suspecion.*
>
> (*CT*. IX, 278–88)

The subject and the style of this passage might persuade us that it is an illustration of the irrational fury associated with the tyrant, and at the same time a warning against 'sodeyn Ire or hastif Ire, withouten avisement and consentynge of resoun' (*CT*. X, 541). It could be taken as an example of how the sin of homicide derives from ire. Whilst all these reactions are relevant to the passage, in Chaucer's tale it becomes, unexpectedly and perhaps rather trivially, a warning against officious and unconsidered tale-bearing, whether the information be true or false. For Phoebus takes vengeance upon the white crow who has shattered his happy ignorance by turning him perpetually black. The moral of the tale is that discretion may be the better part of honesty; one must think before speaking:

> *. . . God of his endelees goodnesse*
> *Walled a tonge with teeth and lippes eke,*
> *For man sholde hym avyse what he speeke.*
> *My sone, ful ofte, for to much speche*
> *Hath many a man been spilt, as clerkes teche;*
> *But for litel speche avysely*
> *Is no man shent.*
>
> (*CT*. IX, 322–7)

The wisdom offered here is more practical than elevated, but it merits the name of prudence, since preconsideration is being advised.[3] Gower tells as an example of *Folhaste*, the opposite of prudence, the story of Pyramus and Thisbe, where again too rapid an assessment of appearances leads to a hasty suicide when Pyramus 'sodeinly/ His swerd al nakid out he breide/ In his folhaste', and killed himself. Examples in which prudence is implicitly contrasted with *folhaste*, expressed by the vocabulary listed above, could be multiplied from the works of both Gower and Chaucer, but the detailed examination of one more instance should be sufficient.

In the *Merchant's Tale*, Januarie has made his decision to marry before he calls together his friends to ask their advice. Nevertheless he observes the formality, and at the meeting his opening words are intended by Chaucer to betray his importunate folly:

> *For I wol be, certeyn, a wedded man,*
> *And that anoon in al the haste I kan.*
> *Unto some mayde fair and tendre of age,*
> *I prey yow, shapeth for my mariage*
> *Al sodeynly, for I wol nat abyde;*
> *And I wol fond t'espien, on my syde,*
> *To whom I may be wedded hastily.*
> (*CT*. IV, 1405–11)

The repetition of the words *haste, hastily*, their collocation with *sodeynly*, and the refusal to *abyde* with reference to an undertaking like marriage, are sufficient to typify Januarie as an imprudent man. Moreover his insistence upon a young wife, when conventional wisdom encouraged the marriage of like with like, only serves to confirm this impression.[4] He closes his speech with an appeal to the assembly:

> *And syn that ye han herd al myn entente*
> *I prey yow to my wyl ye wole assente.*
> (*CT*. IV, 1467–8)

Now, it is obviously ridiculous to ask only for advice which is acquiescent to one's own declared intentions. But such a commonsense observation is not really adequate in assessing Januarie's behaviour, for he is not only acting unreasonably, but he is shown to be acting within a familiar literary situation of decision-making in a way directly contrary to the lines laid down by conventional wisdom for behaviour in that situation. Prudence's enumeration of the errors made by Melibee in calling together his assembly contains two which have specific relevance to Januarie's meeting:

> ye sholden oonly have cleped to youre conseil youre trewe frendes olde and wise, /ye han ycleped straunge folk, yonge folk, false flatereres . . . Ye han erred also, for ye han shewed to youre conseillours youre talent and youre affeccioun.
> (*CT*. VII, 1244–9)

The flatterer among Januarie's friends has the allegorical name Placebo. He is as aware as Januarie himself of the proprieties of a council such as Januarie is holding, and he takes his flattery from the ideal as it is portrayed in *Melibee*. Echoing a *sententia* used there, he praises Januarie for the 'heighe prudence' which decides him, following the words of Solomon, to 'Wirk alle thyng by conseil'. But the conditions under which Januarie holds his debate make nonsense of Solomon's wisdom. Placebo is opposed in debate by Justinus, apparently the voice of reason, despite his calumny of marriage. Justinus speaks the secure and familiar truths, recommending the exercise of prudence:

> Senek, amonges othere wordes wyse,
> Seith that a man oghte hym right wel ayvse
> To whom he yeveth his lond or his catel.
> And syn I oghte avyse me right wel
> To whom I yeve my good awey fro me,
> Wel muchel moore I oghte avysed be
> To whom I yeve my body for alwey.
> I warne yow wel, it is no childes play
> To take a wyf withouten avysement.
>
> (CT. IV, 1523–31)

Januarie remains unmoved by Justinus's repeated assertions of the need for *avisement* in such a serious undertaking. To him, Seneca and sentential wisdom are mere 'scole-termes' with which he has no patience. He has not gathered his friends to hear academic arguments. Wiser men, he claims, have accorded with his intention, and so, with that, they *rysen sodeynly* with the resolve that Januarie shall be married.

The means by which Januarie goes about the selection of his bride are purely irrational. This is made clear by Chaucer's imagery. He fills his heart with the images of various women in much the same way as a mirror set in a market-place may catch the likeness of every passer-by. This irrationality is emphasized by an implicit comparison with Walter's selection of a bride in the *Clerk's Tale*, where even the people, despite their notorious blindness in such matters, are impressed by Walter's wise perception:

> And for he saugh that under low degree
> Was ofte vertu hid, the peple hym heelde
> A prudent man, and that is seyn ful seelde.
>
> (CT. IV, 425–7)

When his selection has been made by these reprehensible means, Januarie again calls a meeting of his friends to endorse his judgement, and again he urges:

> That noon of hem none argumentes make
> Agayn the purpos which that he hath take,
> Which purpos was plesant to God, seyde he,
> And verray ground of his prosperitee.
>
> (CT. IV, 1619–22)

This final defiance hurled at reasoned argument will suffice to show the nature of Januarie's decision to marry. It follows the familiar outline of the decision-making process involving a lord and his council as it is recommended in the *Tale of Melibee*, but it overtly breaks the rules given there, both in letter and spirit. The wilful abandonment of the familiar dictates of prudence, the atmosphere of irrational haste effected by the repetition of a few words closely associated with the dichotomy between *prudence* and *folhaste*, lead to the identification of Januarie not simply as the foolish, amorous old man, the *senex amans*, but as the type of the imprudent man.

There is no further need to argue the literary vitality of the concept of *folhaste* in Chaucer's poetry, nor its antithesis with *prudence*. In terms of the need for preconsideration of actions, prudence, the Stoic virtue of Prudentia, was familiar to the Middle Ages as one of the cardinal virtues described by Cicero in *De Officiis*.[5] In terms of forethought, too, it had been a theme of English poetry from its beginnings, occurring in the gnomic utterances of the *Wanderer* and *Beowulf*.[6] In the fourteenth-century, although the theme is not marked by the use of the typical vocabulary clustered around Chaucer and Gower's exploitation of it, it is found too in alliterative poetry. When Gawain recklessly accepts the challenge of the Green Knight there is no mention of *folhaste*, but, with the advantage of reflection, the narrator advises Gawain to consider well what he has undertaken, and grimly remarks:

> For þaʒ men be mery in mynde quen þay han mayn drynk,
> A ʒere ʒernes ful ʒerne, and ʒeldeʒ neuer lyke,
> þe forme to þe fynisment foldeʒ ful selden.
>
> *(Sir Gawain, 497–9)*

The advice here is ironic, for it is too late to warn Gawain to behave as he should have done: the warning serves as a foreboding of disaster. Failure to consider the ends of one's actions, as Melibee's counsellor implied when advising against recklessly embarking on war, precipitates one into a threatening unknown.

Turning from the literary use of the concept of prudence to its definition by contemporary writers, we again find reference to the uncertain connection between an act and its consequences. According to Langland, whoever has the gift of prudence is able to surmount this uncertainty to some extent, since 'ymagenye he sholde,/ Er he dude eny dede . devyse wel þe ende' (C-text, XXII, 277–8). The *Book of Vices and Virtues* gives a wordier, and slightly different definition:

> For þat vertue al þat a man doþ or seiþ or þenkeþ, al he ordeyneþ and ledeþ and rewleþ to þe riʒt lyne of resoun, and in al his werkes he purueieþ hym þat þei gon bi ordenaunce and bi chois of God, and seeþ and iugeþ al þing.
>
> (p. 123, 5–10)

Here *prudence* is the virtue which ensures that a man's actions are rationally considered and are consonant with the will of God. In actuality, this definition does not diverge very greatly from that of Langland, since for Langland the highest end for every action is the eventual salvation of the soul, so that the noblest function of prudence is to assess courses of action with this end in view. Such a conception of *prudentia* is that of the major ethical thinkers of the Middle Ages. Authorities as disparate as Abelard and Aquinas agree in regarding *prudentia* as a power which discriminates good and evil in courses of action, serving as a guide to moral virtue.[7]

Seen in this light, prudence is far more than a desirable quality in a secular ruler; it is the essential ability possessed by all men to select the path which will lead to spiritual salvation. This is its highest function. But the way to Christian virtue may not be obvious for one reason or another, and here it was the business of the Church to act in the role of adviser instructing the well-intentioned person upon the requirements of God's law. Counsel may also be drawn by such a man from the voluminous literature which existed for his instruction; and indeed even literature which was not expressly didactic – narrative and historical literature – was often seen to fulfil this instructive function. In the Monk's words, the reader could 'be war by thise ensamples trewe and olde.' This injunction to *be war* by the misfortunes of fictional characters is as common in Chaucer as in more overtly didactic writing. The reader, made aware of the fragility of human happiness, could then take care to exercise prudence when similar circumstances befell him. Lack of foresight is all too common and indeed this is the only criticism which the Clerk can find to level at the otherwise exemplary Marquis Walter:

> he considered noght
> *In tyme comynge what mighte hym bityde*
> *But on his lust present was al his thoght.*
> (*CT*. IV, 78–80)

In the sparse, analytical manner of the Clerk, this is practically a definition of the function of prudence in the ordering of one's life. Such preoccupation with everyday affairs and present pleasures is reprehensible not only because of the threat it poses to ultimate salvation, but also because of the lack of resilience to worldly reverses that it brings with it. 'Accidie hath no purveaunce agayn temporeel necessitee,' remarks the Parson, and this lack of provision against disaster means that changes in fortune are always *sodeyn*, unexpected, and catastrophic: 'Fortune alwey wole assaille/With unwar strook' (*CT*. VII, 2763–4). And so it did when Death found the ale-drinker unprepared in the *Pardoner's Tale:*

> *And sodeynly he was yslayn to-nyght,*
> *Fordronke, as he sat on his bench upright.*
> (*CT*. VI, 673–4)

Prudence, then, is of supreme importance in the medieval theology of salvation. Lack of it leaves one exposed to Fortune and both in the secular world of *Policie* and the religious aspiration of individual salvation, it is central to the thought of any serious author in the Middle Ages. Yet, although we have stressed its importance to the moral psychology of actions, we have not yet given an adequate account of the breadth of its application to actions. We have still not fully answered the question 'what is prudence?' A little more than fifty years after Chaucer's death, Reginald Pecock, bishop of Chichester, wrote an answer to this question which he intended to be authoritative yet accessible to the layman.[8] His definition is complete and extensive, and although dating from after the time of Chaucer, closely reflects traditional scholastic thought as well as popular usage in Chaucer's time. It is, he says:

> a kunnyng or knowyng wherbi we knowen treuþis longyng to oure gouernaunce, þat is to seie, it is þe knowyng wherbi we knowen what is to be doon or to be left vndoon in oure governauncis, and in which maner, in which tyme, with what meenes, into what eend, and so forþ with whiche oþire circumstauncis it is to be do, or left to be vndo, and what is to be suffrid or not suffrid, and in which maner, tyme and place and meene it is to be suffrid or not suffrid; and so forþ of oþire circumstauncis.
>
> *(Folewer, p. 52)*

In effect, this is a fuller statement of what we have seen from other sources. Prudence is the faculty of assessing and understanding all the circumstances and consequences of any projected action, both deciding on its desirability and planning its execution. But Pecock goes on from this to see prudence at work in many more spheres than civil rule or individual salvation:

> Also as is kunnyng to knowe how we schule bere vs to plese oure maystris, oure lordis, oure fadris, how to chastise oure children and seruantis, how to lyue pesabli with oure neiʒboris, how to spende þat we falle not into pouerte, and so forþ of oþire lijk deedis and treuþis of hem perteynyng to oure gouernaunce.
>
> *(Folewer, p. 52)*

Here, in the punishment of servants and in the dealings with neighbours, we see the social function of prudence at the level of Harry Baily and his wife Goodelief. Pecock represents prudence at this level not so much as a virtue but as an accomplishment. Indeed to speak of prudence as a virtue in the modern sense of the word is misleading: it is rather to be conceived of as a kind of knowledge upon which actions are based. Pecock's formulation makes clear this conception of prudence as practical knowledge applied in sciences of the most diverse kinds, ranging from the moral function, through skill in eloquence – which Gower calls 'a gret prudence' (*CA*. IV, 2652) – to everyday thrift in domestic management.[9]

This broad conception of prudence can be clarified by examining the place Pecock allots to it in the whole range of human knowledge. He talks of the *kunnyngal virtues*, which are rational powers disposing a man to have some kind of knowledge. There are five of these, from which *intellect* must be subtracted since it is concerned only with self-evident truths without the need of external information. The four *kunnyngal virtues* which remain are concerned with knowledge which is the product of deduction from received information; these are: *opynyoun*, which is concerned with probabilities, *speculatijf science*, which deals with abstract knowledge, *craft*, which is concerned with the skills involved in the creation of a material product, and *prudence*, which is the science of actions. Pecock admits that this organization is in some ways eccentric, since the inclusion of *opynyoun* is unusual in such a schema of knowledge, but in most other ways the pattern is traditional enough. If we omit *opynyoun* as Pecock's innovation, we find that his schema of human knowledge divides itself neatly, first according to the need for deduction, into intellect and science, and then further into a division between practical and speculative sciences. A diagram of this simplified schema will illustrate its details more clearly:

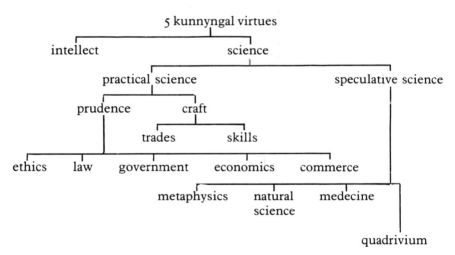

Let us compare the above diagram with one constructed from Gower's account of the education offered by Aristotle to King Alexander (*Confessio Amantis*, Bk. VII). Alexander evidently received a fourteenth-century

54

education in those arts deemed appropriate to a ruler. Naturally, therefore, craft skills are omitted, as in any case they often were from supposedly full accounts of *philosophye*:

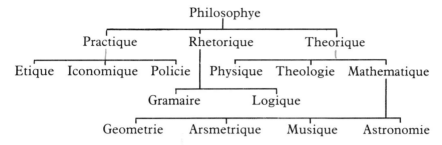

Gower elevates the linguistic arts to equality with practical and speculative sciences, rather than leaving them as part of practical science, but the general resemblance to Pecock's schema is obvious. Indeed, it is clear that Pecock's schema of human rational powers goes back to traditional scholastic categorizations of areas of organized study. These derive in turn, through Boethius and Isidore, from the Stoics and from Aristotle.[10]

Now, if we remove *Craft* from Pecock's schema in order to bring it into line with Gower and with established practice, we find that there is no longer any need for branching at the point marked *practical science*. We can therefore abolish the level *practical science* and equate it with *prudence*. In this new and further simplified scheme, shorn of variants and reduced to the basic, easily-memorable outline of humane studies, there is a simple dichotomy between practical science (*prudence*) and speculative science (*theorique*). Prudence, then, is often regarded as equivalent to practical knowledge and further sub-divided into the particular spheres of application of such knowledge. As a result, *prudence* becomes an inclusive term, just as the term mathematics includes arithmetic, algebra, and geometry. Prudence can therefore be substituted in appropriate contexts for a knowledge of economics and estate management, secular or canon law, government, or commerce. Each is a manifestation of prudence. Thus, Gower, forgetting his three-fold division, refers to eloquence as prudence, and includes *Iconomique* (the management of estates and households) within its range. Aquinas also lists this, and adds military skills, (*ST.* 2a2ae, 48,) whilst Pecock includes commerce and entrepreneurial activities on which he declines to comment further. Prudence seems often to signify what we today might call professional knowledge, and Pecock, perhaps somewhat grudgingly, admits merchant skills into this category. The irony in the apostrophe to merchant wealth in the prologue to the *Man of Law's Tale* is perhaps rather more subtle than it at first appears. The Man of Law may well be said to have a vested interest in merchant wealth, and his treatment of the aspirations of merchants is therefore more than generous:

> *O riche marchauntz, ful of wele been yee,*
> *O noble, o prudent folk, as in this cas!*
> *Youre bagges been nat fild with ambes as,*
> *But with sys cynk, that renneth for your chaunce;*
> *At Cristemasse myrie may ye daunce!*
> (*CT*. II, 122–6)

Poverty is to be decried, and the listener is warned to apply his practical knowledge to avoid it:

> *'Alle the dayes of povre men been wikke.'*
> *Be war, therefore, er thou come to that prikke!*
> (*CT*. II, 118–9)

Accepting these values, the *General Prologue* description of the Manciple whose 'wit shal pace/The wisdom of an heep of lerned men,' and the business of his masters who could act as stewards to any lord in England, keeping him within his income 'In honour dettelees (but if he were wood)', both are illustrative of such aspects of prudence as *yconomique*, *husbondrie* or *marchaundisyng*. The injunction of the *Man of Law's Tale* to avoid poverty echoes in advance Pecock's words on the prudence of 'how to spende þat we falle not into pouerte.'

But any such attempt to explain away apparent admiration of a rascally Manciple, or such whole-hearted enthusiasm for money, leaves us uneasy. This sense of unease, that by accepting all this at its face value of *bona fide* prudence we should be missing its irony, depends in part upon our expectations about the proper recipients of moral approval in the contemporary context: worldly wealth is usually held in contempt. But beyond this contextual knowledge, the very semantic structure of the concept of prudence and its related vocabulary (*avisement, forncast, purveyaunce, wise* and *war*) is our guide. We have recognized that prudence is directly opposed to *folhaste*, but in addition, our demonstration of the breadth of application of the term has shown what we might call higher and lower levels of prudence. To put this in other terms, we can say that the virtue of prudence is directly opposed to recklessness, but it is also gradationally opposed to less virtuous kinds of prudence. St. Thomas Aquinas observes this traditional distinction in discussing the virtue of *prudentia*, to which he opposes *praecipitatio* 'inconsiderate haste'. Gradationally opposed to it is *prudentia carnis* 'the prudence of the flesh'; what the Bible calls 'worldly wisdom.'[11] Now since the desirable and less-desirable kinds of prudence are equally called *prudentia* or *prudence* and function in the same way, differing only in their ends and intentions,

56

it is inevitable that when the lower kind of prudence is given praise due to the higher kind, connotations of that higher virtue may be ironically present in our minds. This will always be a potential when virtues are in gradational opposition to vices, and this fact of potential irony makes such semantic structures of inestimable value to the satirist.[12]

The wily Miller of the *Reeve's Tale*, Simkin, is sure of his superiority over the two Northern clerks who hope to catch him at his thieving. 'The gretteste clerkes been noght wisest men,' (*CT*. I, 4054) he assures his wife. His air of assurance echoes the prowess of the Manciple, and the proverb he is using was later to catch the attention of Pecock:

> Comonli suche marchauntis ben oftist wonyd forto holde in her witt and seie with her mouþ þat 'grettist clerkis ben not wijsist men', and þat for grettist clerkis kunnen not make bargens into greet wynnyng, neiþir be war of lossis, so wel as þei kunnen.
>
> (*Folewer*, p. 58)

Pecock acknowledges the truth of this opinion; but it is only true in a particular sense. Quoting Luke XVI, 8, he says of this claim by business-men against academics, that 'þe sones of þis world ben more prudent in her generacioun þan þe sones of liȝt' (p. 54). The contention is true, but true only in the wisdom of this world. He leaves us in no doubt that prudence in ethics, and in the law of God, is to be esteemed more highly than mere skill in 'marchaundisyng.' Such a distinction, however, is not one much honoured by the 'sones of þis world.'

The opening lines of the *Shipman's Tale* place us firmly in the world of merchant values:

> *A marchant whilom dwelled at Seint-Denys,*
> *That riche was, for which men helde hym wys.*
> (*CT*. VII, 1–2)

Few readers, however, would take these words at their face value. They are obviously ironic, representing as they do a limited conception of wisdom expressed in terms of a social judgement based upon skill in the accumulation of wealth. The opening lines set the tone for the rest of the tale, warning us to be alert for similar nuances later. Whilst there is no space for a full analysis of the *Shipman's Tale*, we may still see how fully the ironic potential of the vocabulary of prudence is exploited in it. The world of the tale is a world of payments, money transactions and practical merchant skills. When the central figure, the noble merchant (whom we may note is never individualized by a name) is visited by a monk rejoicing in the generic title of Dan John, we learn that this monk too is a skilful administrator: he is 'a man of heigh prudence' (64). For a monk, the appropriate sense must surely be one of the higher employments of prudence. But no, like the Manciple, his skill is in *yconomique*: 'To seen hir graunges and hire bernes wyde,' (66). Despite his calling Dan John is one of the 'sones of þis world,' as events will prove.

On the third day after the arrival of his sworn brother the merchant rose up and 'on his nedes sadly hym avyseth' (76). Whatever the associations of rising on the third day, the words *sadly . . . avyseth* imply matters of great gravity. But the merchant's concern is not with his soul's needs; he is bound for his counting-house to assess 'how that it with hym stood.' At length he emerges and, when he is reproached by his wife for his pre-occupation he replies with a dignified speech of self-justification, asserting the arcane complexities and uncertainties of the merchant's calling:

> *'Wyf,' quod this man, 'litel kanstow devyne*
> *The curious bisynesse that we have.*
> *For of us chapmen, also God me save,*
> *And by that lord that clepid is Seint Yve,*
> *Scarsly amonges twelve twey shul thryve*
> *Continuelly, lastyng unto oure age.*
> *We may wel make chiere and good visage,*
> *To dryve forth the world as it may be,*
> *And kepen oure estaat in pryvetee,*
> *Til we be deed, or elles that we pleye*
> *A pilgrymage, or goon out of the weye.*
> *And therfore have I greet necessitee*
> *Upon this queynte world t'avyse me;*
> *For everemoore we moote stonde in drede*
> *Of hap and fortune in oure chapmanhede.*
> (*CT.* VII, 224–38)

The curious dignity of the passage derives from the fact that it darkly echoes similar ones on the human condition, perhaps like that of Egeus in the *Knight's Tale* (I. 2846–9), where human life seems subject *unwar* to the sudden shocks of *hap and fortune*. The reference to pilgrimage recalls Egeus's conventional image of men blindly seeking a purpose in life; but this speaker knows precisely what men ask to have. The problem lies in keeping it. Pilgrimage is lightly set aside as an amusement unfitted to a man who:

> *neither pleyeth at the dees ne daunceth,*
> *But as a marchaunt, shortly for to telle,*
> *He let his lyf.*
> (*CT.* VII, 304–6)

Gravity, even ascetism, is as much the property of the merchant as of the clerk, and he goes about his business with a dedication equal to that of any clerk, concerning himself exclusively with 'this queynte world.' His prudence is in *chapmanhede* and he sees in pilgrimage no more than a diversion, a frivolous entertainment. The associations of higher philosophical speculations contained in the passage serve to illustrate the limits of his wisdom. Yet he is repeatedly called wise, and the epithets *war and wys*, applied to him in line 365, deserve more comment. This phrase is extremely common in popular romance; but it is rare in Chaucer, occurring only twice elsewhere: once in the early translation of the *Roman de la Rose*, and once in the description of the Sergeant at Law in the *General Prologue*. Now, as Donaldson has shown, Chaucer sometimes used the diction of popular poetry for ironic effect, so that it is probably not too much to regard this usage in the *Canterbury Tales* as ironic.[13] It may perhaps be more than coincidence that in these two occurrences, the phrase is applied to two professions, merchants and lawyers, whom Pecock later credited with frequent use of the adage about clerks not being the wisest of men.

Generally speaking, the representation of the merchant in the *Shipman's Tale* is not unsympathetic. Compared with the other protagonists he behaves with dignity. He accepts the circumstances which have befallen him with equanimity, and shows some practical wisdom; seeing that there is no redress 'for to chide it nere but folie' (*CT*. VII, 429). His hospitality and loyalty to his friend are exemplary, even if he is a little too eager not to give offence to any about him; yet, by the subtle evocation of the more elevated functions of prudence, and especially in the speech setting forth the life of *chapmanhede*, Chaucer manages to demonstrate the limitations of such a restricted view of human life and purpose.[14] The reference to money as the merchant's plough touches upon a more critical note, implicitly contrasting a useful productive life with income from capital, but such distinctively negative tones are rare.[15] This is a noble merchant, a man of affairs, who, although his financial dealings will not stand scrutiny against moral idealism, nevertheless appears nobler by the contrast with his immoral and avaricious wife and the venial and predatory monk. Yet no man, however skilled at *marchaundysyng*, if his skill is limited to that art, can appear truly wise to Chaucer. Wisdom in all its dignity resides in the higher functions of prudence.

Our investigation of the variousness of prudence has led us from its function as the restraint on hasty emotions, through the part it plays in assuring the soul's salvation, to its role in the practical wisdom of everyday life. It is time now to return to the beginning and consider its relationship to that love which springs up so readily in the *gentil herte*. What part does the vocabulary of prudence play in Chaucer's masterpiece about love, *Troilus and Criseyde*?

We may recall the epithet *sodeyn* applied to Diomede, the man of Martian character, who presses on with the advantage of Criseyde's insecurity, and it here seems to have pejorative associations. But the epithet is also applied to the love of Criseyde for Troilus. The narrator raises the

question in Book II of whether Criseyde's reaction to Troilus is foolish
and hasty love; he raises it only to deny it. Everything needs a beginning:

> *For I sey nought that she so sodeynly*
> *Yaf hym hire love, but that she gan enclyne*
> *To like hym first . . .*
>
> (II, 673–5)

But the fact that the narrator raises moralistic doubts inevitably damages
the quality of Criseyde's love in our eyes. A less ambiguously courtly poet
might easily have depicted love as sudden and overwhelming but never
have raised any moralistic criticism of haste, or at least avoided a flurry of
justification. Chaucer raises it as he also raised it when he spoke of Troilus
falling 'subgit unto love' in Book I, and he compounds the criticism by
clumsy attempts at a defence. Nevertheless, in justice, we must admit that
Criseyde does not plunge headlong into love as Troilus had done. The
growth of her feeling is traced in detail throughout the book. Her internal
debates are chronicled at length; the effect upon her of the songs of
Antigone and of the cedar-borne nightingale are recorded. The narrator
intrudes even beyond her waking life to tell of her dreams, and it is not
until more than half-way through the poem that she is at last united with
her lover.

Criseyde is well aware of the need for prudence in love, for the avoidance of precipitate action. On her own admission (Bk. III, 1210–11) she
had committed herself privately to Troilus long before she saw the circumstances as propitous for granting him her love. Prudence is a constant
theme of her speeches, overtly or otherwise. At the beginning, when she
hears of Troilus's love, she asks her uncles's advice and begs Pallas 'in this
dredful cas for me purveye' (II, 436). She struggles to see the consequences of Pandarus's request, and when the affair is commenced, it is
Criseyde who is the fount of practical common sense. The affair, by joint
consent, is conducted prudently:

> *And by hire bothe avys, as was the beste,*
> *Apoynteden full warly in this nede,*
> *So as they durste, how they wolde procede.*
>
> (III, 454–6)

In her practical abilities, Criseyde follows the talents of her uncle; for it is
Pandarus who is the consummate planner in the arts of love. Chaucer even
finds it appropriate to use of him an elaborate metaphor, originally used by
Geoffrey de Vinsauf of the art of literary composition in describing his
prudence in this field:

> *For everi wight that hath an hous to founde*
> *Ne renneth naught the werk for to bygynne*
> *With rakel hond, but he wol bide a stounde,*

60

And sende his hertes line out fro withinne
Aldirfirst his purpos for to wynne.
Al this Pandare in his herte thoughte,
And caste his werk ful wisely or he wroughte.[16]

(I, 1065–71)

Before the eventual meeting of Troilus with Criseyde, we hear that Pandarus:

with gret deliberacioun
Hadde every thyng that herte myght availle
Forncast and put in execucioun.

(III, 519–21)

And Troilus 'Al this purveiaunce/Knew at the fulle', (III, 533–4). With all this planning and preparation, all this care in its conduct and pausing on the brink, what is the sense of the imputation that the love of Criseyde for Troilus is 'sodeyn love?' One answer perhaps lies in Criseyde's lament as the affair disintegrates:

Prudence, allas, oon of thyne eyen thre
Me lakked alwey, er that I come here!
On tyme ypassed wel remembred me,
And present tyme ek koud ich wel ise,
But future tyme, er I was in the snare,
Koude I nat sen; that causeth now my care.

(V, 744–9)

Here Criseyde is referring specifically to her decision to allow herself to be exchanged for Antenor in the hope of later slipping back again into Troy. The prudence she is aware of lacking is that prudence in which her uncle excels, the ability to manage everyday matters; indeed both uncle and niece have demonstrated it thoroughly until Fortune has dealt them a blow which leaves them powerless. What she fails to see is that it is not a greater skill in this kind of prudence that she requires, for Fortune will at length find the means of outrunning the opportunist, but prudence of another and higher kind. This is the significance of the doubts about 'sodeyn love.' Criseyde's deliberations about her own safety, her arrangements made for immediate happiness, might have been replaced by considerations of a more distant end, which would have put in more serious question the advisability of entering upon the affair at all. One way of interpreting this is that, as she herself suggests (II, 117–9), her heart should have been set upon celestial love, but such an interpretation is unnecessarily restrictive. Equally applicable is an assumption that, in reference to *love, sodeyn* here has a connotation of recklessness, and that a more penetrating review of her circumstances would have rejected this affair in pursuit of more lasting secular happiness. The implied criticism of Criseyde's love is not exclusively Christian. Given its circumstances, the love of Troilus and Criseyde is as *brotel* as any love can be. Troilus's high-minded fatalism, the instability of the times, Criseyde and her uncle's opportunist attitude to the ebb and flow of Fortune make them all inevitable victims. The tragedy of Troilus and Criseyde is contained in the Senecan quotation given by Prudence in the *Tale of Melibee*: 'thynges that been folily doon, and that been in hope of Fortune, shullen nevere come to good ende' (VII, 1449). The charge of sudden love, then, is really a charge of ill-advised love whose dangers were always apparent to the moralist who looked over the shoulder of Chaucer the poet.

What helps to create this critical and moralistic perspective in *Troilus and Criseyde* and elsewhere is the lack of linguistic discrimination in representing the enormous breadth of the concept of prudence. The same set of words could be used to express a wide variety of situations and distinct levels of mental activity. When a fox contemplates a raid on a chicken run his exploit is 'By heigh ymaginacioun forncast' (*CT*. X, 448). Although there is a tendency to associate the word *forncast* with sub-rational formulations of events, it is collocated frequently with words like *avisen*, which undeniably implies rational premeditation, and the two uses are unlikely to have been kept semantically separate in usage. The confession of evil must be 'purveyed bifore and avysed; for wikked haste doth no profit' (*CT*. IV, 191). Finally, on the highest level, the divine plan for human history is called: 'the hyhe almihti pourveance,/In whos eterne remembrance/Fro ferst was every thing present' (*CA. Prol.*, 585-7). This huge breadth of the vocabulary of prudence, which reflects a gradational opposition between virtuous prudence and *prudentia carnis*, was a cause of distress to Langland, who saw popular usage as the perversion of a noble virtue brought about by the incurable worldliness of man's aspirations:

> 'For þe commune,' quaþ þis curatour. 'counten ful litel
> The consail of conscience . oþer cardinale uertues,
> Bote hit soune as by syght . som what to wynnynge;
> Of gile ne of gabbynge . gyueþ þei neuere tale.
> For spiritus prudencie . among þe peuple, is gyle,
> And tho faire vertues . as vices thei hem semeþ.'
> (*PP*., C-text, XXII, 453-8)

Chaucer, however, accepted popular usage and discovered the satirical power inherent in words whose area of reference includes the most noble knowledge and most venial folly, and, even more valuable, those graduated shades between. In the *Merchant's Tale* the studied absence of prudence forms part of a savage attack on folly and evil, but in the *Shipman's Tale* and *Troilus and Criseyde* the chiding is gentler. Both the merchant and the lovers have admirable qualities, but the stylistic manipulation of the vocabulary of prudence serves to indicate gently but forcibly their deficiencies: that common worldliness which in the eyes of the moralist amounts to folly.

CHAPTER FOUR

The Philosopher

ONE DAY, SOCRATES, in his old age, sat by his fire as his wife returned from the well carrying a heavy pitcher of water. Like the wives of many a lesser philosopher, she became irritated by his inactivity and berated him as a shiftless husband. He made no reply to the onslaught, so that her anger flared up, and with no more ado she emptied the water-pot over his head. The philosopher remained undisturbed; pulling his chair up closer to the fire, he mildly remarked that in the winter season, after a raging storm, one must expect a little rain.

This anecdote appears in Gower's *Confessio Amantis* (III, 639ff.) as an illustration of the virtue of *pacience*, of which Socrates is the epitome. Versions of the story were familiar to Antiquity and the Middle Ages.[1] Indeed the Wife of Bath's clerkly husband knows one (*CT*. III, 727–32) and uses it against her as part of his armoury against feminism. But the story is misused for this purpose since its essential significance is that which Gower finds in it: an illustration of the inner peace enjoyed by that wise man who has mastered such passions as anger, along with hope, fear and ambition, and is therefore undisturbed by the unexpected reverses which may befall him.

In order to understand the vocabulary and ideas associated with the moral ideal of *pacience* in the time of Chaucer and Gower, we must again look beyond Middle English to the Latin tradition which moulded their usage and shaped their conceptions. Contemporary belief, based upon scholastic Latin learning, preserved a view of the human constitution which descended from pagan classical times, but which had been modified to suit their purposes by generations of Christian authors. The efforts of these men had been directed towards preservation and redirection of the learning of the past rather than a revolution in thought, so that the broad outlines of human psychology, as perceived by the well-informed layman of Chaucer's time were closer to those assumed in Ancient Rome than to the theories of today.

Man was regarded as a unique creation compounded of a physical body and an immaterial soul. The precise nature of the soul may be a subject for debate, but it was widely believed, even in pre-Christian times, that that part of the soul which was concerned with rational processes transcended the physicality of the world and would in some form survive death, returning to its divine source.[2] As we have seen in the last chapter, by the exercise of prudence as a guide and a check on the desires of the will, the rational soul ensures the morality of actions; at the same time, by exercising control over the emotions, it gives the wise man that strength which enables him to overcome any suffering. In the well-constituted personality, then, the rational soul rules every aspect of the individual's behaviour, and that man can then be spoken of as 'living according to reason' or 'according to nature.' Virtue, like the order of nature, is felt to depend upon rational control. So much is commonplace, and, ignoring refinements, would be shared by the educated Roman and the fourteenth-century English gentleman. But there are aspects of fourteenth-century thought which enable us to draw more specific parallels between Chaucer and his contemporaries and the ancient philosophic tradition. Even today, in popular speech, the patient endurance of suffering is equated with stoicism, and indeed there are indications that fourteenth-century ideals of *pacience* used some of the same verbal and figurative currency as the more popularized stoic philosophy of earlier times. Gower, discussing the constitution of mankind, says:

> *For as a king in his Empire*
> *Above alle othre is lord and Sire,*
> *So is the herte principal,*
> *To whom reson in special*
> *Is yove as for the governance.*
> (*CA.* VII, 485–9)

The suggestion that the human organism should be ruled by reason is unremarkable, but the use of the word *principal,* together with the image of which it is a part, and also the fact that reason is situated in the heart, demand attention. There are striking parallels here to Stoic teachings; yet it is scarcely credible to argue from this and a few other uses of the word *principal* that Gower had any complete understanding of Stoic psychology. In its use as a technical term by the Stoics, the notion has been compared to St. Paul's conception of the spirit: it connotes all the higher activities of the human soul, the reason and the will.[3] It is that governing power upon which the rest of the personality depends. If corrupted, it represents the corruption of the individual. The concept of a *principale*, as Seneca calls it, is of a force not restricted to human beings, but is in fact the guiding and ruling principle of animals too, and indeed in the universe as a whole. Although there is no evidence that Gower was aware in detail of the technical import of the word he uses, he is nevertheless following Stoic traditions in two other matters. He situates reason as a ruling power in the heart, which is where the Stoics placed the *principale* in defiance of the Platonistic belief that reason inhabited the head. Furthermore, he adopts the same administrative metaphor which had originally given birth to the technical uses of *principale* in Stoic philosophy. The heart governs the rest of the body by reason, just as a king rules a kingdom. This analogy between the individual man and the state was a favourite one of Stoic writers. To them, all men, whilst in their own constitution reflecting the organization of a state, were themselves citizens of an idealized world-state by virtue of their rationality alone. Irrational men, together with animals, were excluded from this republic of the blessed. Real worldly kingdoms, which inevitably included such men, could therefore be only partial reflections of this ideal state whose administration and laws are those dictated by reason and the order of nature. Indeed, the image of the ideal state, Cosmopolis, as it was called, formed the Stoic archetype not only of the individual soul, but also of the order of the universe. Virtue in the individual was to be measured by the stability of his disposition, arbitrated by reason. Such stability and self-consistency were related to the order of the universe, and indeed were a reflection of it, for man was but a microcosm of the larger order. It is this pre-eminence of reason, this virtually synonymous esteem for order, which is implied by the medieval love of the image which relates man's soul to a kingdom:

> . . . *every man for his partie*
> *A kingdom hath to justefie,*
> *That is to sein his oghne dom.*
> *If he misreule that kingdom,*
> *He lest himself, and that is more*
> *Than if he loste Schip and Ore*
> *And al the worldes good withal:*
> *For what man that in special*
> *Hath noght himself, he hath noght elles.*[4]
> (*CA.* VIII, 2111–19)

In Gower's estimation, there is a direct parallel between the rational control which enables the individual to live in peace with himself, and his advice to the new king, Henry IV, to rule in justice and humanity, achieving peace and order in his realm. Reason assures the individual of philosophic calm, and ensures that the kingdom will achieve 'pees and reste unto the laste.' (*In Praise of Peace*, 35).

To Seneca and to Cicero – authors who although pagan were read and revered as moral authorities in the Middle Ages – self-control and its consequent calm and unconcern were the marks of a special kind of man; a wise and virtuous man whom they called *sapiens*, or sage. In *De Constantia*, xiii, 4, Seneca tells us that the moral good which is characteristic of the *sapiens* is unconcern: 'Securitas autem proprium bonum sapientis est.' This lack of anxiety and inner peace is equated with the perfect life:

> The calmness or tranquillity of mind which is the Chief Good of Democritus, *euthemia* as he calls it, has had to be excluded from this discussion, because this mental tranquillity is in itself the happiness in question.

> Democriti autem securitas, quae est animi tranquillitas, quam apellavit εὐθυμίαν, eo separanda fuit ab hac disputatione, quia ista animi tranquillitas ea est ipsa beata vita.
>
> (*De Fin.* V, viii, 23)

But Chaucer could have found this same concern for tranquillity and rational control in more familiar texts. Indeed he may have learned of the inner strength of the *sapiens* from his translation of Boethius. Misfortunes befall the wise man, but they are of no consequence, for his life is ordered by reason, and he knows that the only true good is the well-being of his soul, and this knowledge places him beyond the reach of what to others would be miseries. Chaucer translates from Boethius:

> yif it so be that thow art myghty over thyself (*that is to seyn by tranquillite of thi soule*), than hastow thyng in thi power that thow noldest nevere leesen, ne Fortune may nat bynymen it the.
>
> (*Bo.* II, p. 4, 134)

The dichotomy of human nature, in which the soul and body are often in contention, forms the source from which much medieval tragedy arises. Gower (*CA.* VII, 490ff) comments on how clerks tend to forget in their theorizing that soul and body are at once a part of the same organism, but are inevitably drawn in different directions. Whilst this is a cause of distress to the average man, it is paradoxically a source of strength in the *sapiens*, for, seen from the perspective of the rational and immortal soul, even the body in which it is housed becomes an external and perishable property. It is no more than one of those benefits bestowed temporarily upon a man by his fortune, and consequently it is accepted that it may be subject to sudden and unexpected recall. By contrast the soul is free, beyond external influence; it cannot be bound. A man may be unjustly put

67

to death for his beliefs, but he cannot be compelled to alter them or to fear his death, provided that he is strong enough to be master of his own emotions. Lady Philosophy exhibits these strengths in her follower in another anecdote from Boethius:

> Maystow evere have any commaundement over a free corage? Mays-tow remuwen fro the estat of his propre reste a thought that is clyvynge togidre in hymself by stedfast resoun? As whilom a tyraunt wende to confowde a freman of corage, and wende to constreyne hym by torment to maken hym discoveren and accusen folk that wisten of a conjuracioun (*which I clepe a confederacye*) that was cast ayens this tyraunt; but this freman boot of his owene tonge, and caste it in the visage of thilke wode tyraunt. So that the tormentz that this tyraunt wende to han maked matere of cruelte, this wise man maked it matere of vertu.
>
> (Bo. II, p. 6, 47–61)

Chaucer's translation itself needs some interpretation for us to appreciate properly the parallel between these two Boethian quotations. The first refers simply enough to the tranquillity of soul derived from rational self-control; the second expands this by referring to the invulnerability of that mind – *thought* (Chaucer); *pensee* (Jean de Meun); *mens* (Boethius) – which has as its proper possession a tranquillity deriving from a firm and self-consistent purpose, guaranteed by unflinching rational determination. In other words, the Boethian *freman*, although Boethius is far from being a Stoic, is as much an example of the *sapiens* as Socrates in our opening anecdote.

The essential properties of the Stoic *sapiens* are found in such exemplary figures quite outside true Stoic writings, but since this figure is most fully developed by the Stoics, it is convenient to discuss it within a predominantly Stoic context. In the midst of apparent suffering, Seneca tells us, he exhibits *tranquillitas animi* (*De Const.* IV, 3), since no injury can touch him, because, in a manner of speaking, he inhabits a different world from his tormentors and from all physical assaults upon him (*ibid.* IV, 1). Of course, the wise man feels pain just like any other man – he is not made of stone – but his self-mastery is such that he is neither angered nor terrified by it. The *tranquillitas* in which he remains is an unchanging, undisturbed state of mind (*stabilem animi sedem*) which derives from his recognition of the worthlessness of all temporal things, and from rational certainty of that knowledge. He is, in the fullest sense, self-sufficient, and from this derives his unconcern (*securitas*) for worldly possessions. Seneca, indeed, goes so far as to say that a reduction in worldly possessions, which will tend to make a man less susceptible to the reversals of fortune, contributes to peace of mind, since it places less strain upon self-control. Although poverty was not advocated as an essential condition of wisdom, the popular picture of the *sapiens* is often of a man lacking in worldly goods, and indeed Seneca rhetorically equates *securitas* with poverty in *De Tranquillitate Animi*, VII, 4. The poor man does not fear to lose property which he does not possess, nor should he hope to gain any, for hope as much as fear is considered a morally dangerous condition leading to instability (*instabilitas*) and inconstancy (*mobilitas*). By contrast, the untroubled state where all one's actions are rationally justifiable to oneself leads on to stability and self-consistency, to *constantia* and *firmitas*. Such, then, are the Stoic ideals towards which a man must strive in order to become a *sapiens*: strength of character, emotional control, and unswerving resolution are the means to virtue. *Patientia*, the Latin antecedent of Chaucer and Gower's *pacience*, is rarely mentioned, yet everywhere presupposed as that quality of being able to endure hardship without emotional disturbance or complaint. The purpose of these rules of conduct was the pursuit of happiness, and to the Stoics happiness was to be found within, in the peace of mind achieved by an ordered personality in tune with the order of the universe. 'What is the blessed life?' Seneca asks himself, and at once replies, 'Securitas et perpetua tranquillitas' (*Ep.*, 92, 3); and his words are the echo of those of Cicero.[5]

We may reasonably assume that Seneca's writings on Stoic philosophy were intended for consumption by a rather restricted and patrician audience. Yet, at the same time as he wrote, philosophical ideas of a similar kind were finding their way to a broader and more popular public. In part this more popular teaching is represented in the Cynico-Stoic diatribe, which we mentioned earlier in connection with the image of the tyrant, and there is also evidence that Stoicism was preached at the street-corner in Rome in the first century A.D.[6] The audience of these preachers, it seems, were much swayed by rhetorical argument, and although it is possible that they may have been willing to listen to intricate technical exposition, it is much more probable that pungent illustrative anecdote would carry more weight, in such conditions. The teaching of philosophical ideas probably reached its widest audience when embodied in exemplary stories. It was these stories too which most easily became detached from the system of ideas to which they properly belonged, and, subject to minor re-interpretations, moved out of philosophy proper into more general literary-philosophical discourse. Such was the case of the tale of Socrates and Xantippe, and such also is the case of the story of Diogenes and Alexander, which perhaps originally formed part of Cynic philosophical teaching.[7]

The scorn of Diogenes of worldly affairs and possessions was famous; it extended to the point where he chose to desert his home and live in a barrel, open at one end to admit the sunlight. Gower tells us how one day

King Alexander received news that Diogenes had insulted him. The philosopher had evidently referred to him not only as his inferior, but as the servant of his own servant. The king at once made his way to Diogenes and demanded justification of this claim. The philospher's reply was that throughout his life he had controlled the desires of his lower nature by the exercise of reason, with the result that:

> *Will is my man and my servant,*
> *And evere hath ben and evere schal.*
> *And thi will is thi principal,*
> *And hath the lordschipe of thi witt,*
> *So that thou cowthest nevere yit*
> *Take o dai reste of thi labour;*
> *Bot forto ben a conquerour*
> *Of worldes good, which mai noght laste,*
> *Thou hiest evere aliche faste,*
> *Wher thou no reson hast to winne.*
>
> (*CA*. III, 1280–89)

Thus Diogenes is justified. Alexander, who is the slave of his own will in his desire for glory and conquest, is indeed the servant of that force which the philosopher has subdued. Diogenes shows no fear of this conqueror, and he is equally careless of the favours he has to offer, for Alexander's offer of a generous reward for his teaching is answered by the simple request that he should stand aside to allow the sun to flood into the barrel. Diogenes requires nothing that the worldly conqueror can bestow upon him, being content with the few necessities of nature. Alexander is his antitype; he covets the world, and more, as Gower remarks:

> *al the world ne mai suffise*
> *To will which is noght resonable.*
> (*CA*. III, 2436–7)

The meeting of Alexander and Diogenes is the instructive confrontation of opposites. Diogenes, like Socrates, is the exemplar of the philosophical virtues of rational control, *pacience*, and *suffisaunce*, or content; Alexander is the embodiment of the restless cupidinous conqueror, the worldly man whose driving ambition leaves him lamenting the lack of further worlds to conquer. He 'al the world weelded in his demeyne/And yet hym thoughte it myghte nat suffise' (*CT*. VII, 2665–6). According to Gower, Alexander's tutor in youth, Aristotle himself, was supposed to have advised his charge that sufficiency lay in the needs of nature, for 'whan kinde is dueliche served,/It oghte of reson to suffise' (*CA*. VII, 4570–71). But the disordered personality represented by the moral symbol of the tyrant, or when the emphasis is upon unrestrained appetites, by the conqueror, can never achieve the tranquillity of the *sapiens* and can never find content.

The story of the meeting between Alexander and Diogenes is of particular interest to us because its evolution has been charted in some detail. The anecdote was known to Seneca, Cicero, and Valerius Maximus, and passed into the Middle Ages through their writings. But in the form in which they quote it, its significance was different from that of Gower's telling. Its moral purpose in these earlier authors was to illustrate the vainglory of a conqueror, accustomed to boast of his generosity, whose vanity is revealed by the philosopher who desires only that which it is beyond his power to give, yet which is freely available to all. Gower's version of the story represents a particular transformation of the original tale which is clearly associated with books of sermon *exempla,* and which is first found in the *Disciplina Clericalis* and the *Gesta Romanorum.*[8] It is a matter of some interest that in neither of these two works is Diogenes named, and in the former, neither is Alexander: the encounter in these retellings is, respectively, between an un-named king and Socrates, and between Socrates and Alexander. What are we to make of this, since in all other retellings of the 'servant of my servant' version of the story, the participants are those Gower uses? The answer lies in the obviously exemplary rather than historical nature of the anecdote. We have here a deliberate contrast between a philosopher and a conqueror expressed in the moral terms of which both are symbols. The structure of this moral opposition is what is important; the names of the participants are inconsequential, and either Socrates or Diogenes would be equally satisfactory in giving the story that piquancy which is derived from the pretence of an actual meeting. Alexander was of course the most famous conqueror of all, and had already become a moral symbol in Antiquity; the list of examples of *sapientes* was long – Heraclitus, Aeneas, Scipio Africanus minor and Cato had all been used as examples in various situations – but the legendary frugality of Diogenes made him perhaps the most effective contrast with Alexander.

In Chapter One we discussed the use of the tyrant as a moral symbol of the man dominated by his passions, acting irrationally and unjustly to those around him: it is now clear that the popular philosophical tradition of Late Antiquity matched this symbol with its opposite, that of the man of virtue, the philosopher, a symbol largely modelled upon the Stoic *sapiens.* It is the conceptual opposition of the tyrant and the philosopher which is largely responsible for the re-working of the Diogenes and Alexander story in terms of subjection to, or control of, the will, and the relative stability of this symbolic opposition means that the names of the participants can be varied with no more effect upon its essential significance than that of stylistic variation.[9]

71

If the image of the philosopher survives from Antiquity to Chaucer's time, it is also true to say that it retains a typical pattern of verbal usage in the same way as does the image of the tyrant. This associated vocabulary is partly of English origin, partly adoptions through French from the original Latin. It owes its stability perhaps to the custom, established in England for nearly two hundred and fifty years before Chaucer's birth, of teaching Latin through the intermediary of French. Only in the mid-fourteenth century was this method abandoned, but by this time a series of Anglo-French glosses of Latin terms was established in usage. Let us consider, as an example, the rendering in Chaucer's and Jean de Meun's translations of some of the key terms associated in Latin with the figure of the *sapiens*.

A few words are rendered by Chaucer with scarcely any change, the French version of the Latin being directly adopted: thus *sufficientia*, the self-sufficiency and content of the philospher, is rendered as *suffisance* by both Jean and Chaucer, and Chaucer's *attempraunce*, the moderation associated with philosophic virtue, represents similar forms in the other two languages, whilst *patientia* emerges nearly unchanged as Chaucer's *pacience*. That essential feature of the Stoic *sapiens*, his *tranquillitas*, is in fact only rarely mentioned by Boethius. Jean de Meun expands it into an explanatory phrase, *paix de ton courage*, which Chaucer renders *pees of thi thought* (II, p. 1, 35). This is in implied contrast with the technical phrase *perturbacion of my thought* which renders the Latin *mentis perturbatione* (I, p. 1, 87). In a gloss, Chaucer refers to the *tranquillitas animi* as *tranquillite of thi soule*, but this is exceptional. This conception is much more frequently rendered by the words *pees*, and, occasionally, *quiete* and *reste*. Most typically, some phrase linking two of these is used: *pesible reste, reste and quiete, reste and pees, quiete and reste*, and so on. The emotional composure of the philosopher, from which his strength is drawn, is represented in Boethius and elsewhere by the words *solidus, soliditas* and *conpositus*. These become in Jean de Meun's translation *ferme* and *forteresce*, but in Chaucer are replaced by a word of Old English derivation, *sad-sadnesse*. The word *ferme* does occur in Chaucer's *Boece*, but usually as the echo of Latin *firma*. It is a distinctly uncommon word in Chaucer's usage, frequently collocating with *stable* to form a phrase whose primary meaning is 'unchanging, secure', but it can also mean 'judicious and reasonable.' *Ferme* is a favourite word of Jean de Meun, as *firmitas* was of Cicero. The Latin term is a synonym of *constantia*, and sure enough we often find Jean representing the familiar Latin virtue by some form of the word *ferme*, or perhaps by the phrase *ferme establete*, which Chaucer renders *ferme stablenesse*. Partly through the influence of Jean, partly for his own inscrutable reasons, although *constantia* and the associated verb *consto* are common in Boethius, they are never adopted in

72

the obvious way by Chaucer. In his *Clerk's Tale* the prompting of the Latin is accepted, so that *constantia* is rendered as *constance,* but in *Boece* it always appears as *stedfastnesse, stablenesse,* or in some phrase employing the word *ferme.* In other words, the vocabulary representing the philosophical virtue of unchanging moral strength and certitude becomes partially obscured by a screen of unfamiliar substitutions and additions. A table will most clearly demonstrate the relationship of Chaucerian usage to that of his sources. The use of braces indicates that the enclosed words or phrases are relatively rarely rendered by the Chaucerian word or phrase against which they are listed.

Chaucer	*Jean de Meun*	*Boethius*
stable	estable	stabilis
stablenesse	establete	[incommutabilis
	fermete	constantia/consto
		quieta
		firma]
stedfast	ferme	firma
stedfastnesse	estable	stabilis
	[constance	constantia
	puissance	[fides
	force]	solidus]
ferme	ferme	firma
ferme stablenesse	[ferme establete]	[constantia]
fermely	fermement	firmiter
sad	ferme	solidus/soliditas
sadnesse	[forteresce]	[conpositus]

The substantial synonymy of *ferme, stable* and *stedfast* in Chaucer is obvious, as is the fact that they fulfil a place in his moral schema similar to that occupied in the philosophical ideal of Classical times by *stabilitas, firmitas* or *constantia.* Hence, it is evident that in the works of Chaucer and Gower we find the echo of a moral symbol of considerable antiquity and that this is still associated with a typical pattern of vocabulary. This pattern will be all the clearer if, in the above table, the low-frequency sets of relationships, enclosed in braces, are omitted, and our attention given only to correspondences of common occurrence. From the table and from earlier discussion, we can now assemble a short list of Chaucerian words associated with the figure of the philosopher: *tranquillite, pees, quiete, reste; constance, ferme, stable, stedfast, sad; pacience; suffisaunce.*[10]

Throughout the history of the symbol of the philosopher, as the anecdote of Socrates and Xantippe demonstrates, *ire* has been unthinkable in the philosopher. Together with ambition, its absence has always been considered one of the distinguishing features separating the Philosopher from the Tyrant. The latter is a man glorying in temporal power, so that the insult which arouses his anger is likely to be followed by swift vengeance; indeed Cicero defines *ira* as simply the 'desire for vengeance'.[11] This standard definition was echoed by St. Augustine in his *De Civitate Dei* XIV, 15, 2, so that it also became established in Christian discussion of the vice. In the thirteenth century, when pastors, charged by the Fourth Lateran Council with the duty of instruction in confession, turned to the analysis of emotions with renewed interest, this definition found its way into penitential manuals. Ire was one of the seven root sins, and its understanding and correction were necessary to any conscientious priest. By Chaucer's time, as the Summoner patronisingly remarks, 'every lewed viker or person/Kan seye, how ire engendreth homycide' (III, 2008–9). The penitential manuals had established a new set of stereotyped usages based upon, and added to, the old ones. Chaucer's Parson, patient as he was in adversity, is unlikely to have been much disturbed by the Summoner's scorn of the automatic skills of his kind, for he begins his discussion of Ire with the inherited cliché: 'Ire, after the discryvyng of Seint Augustyn, is wikked wil to been avenged by word or dede' (*CT*. X, 535). His organization of his treatment of the subject and its remedy echo the familiar opposition of the traditional vice of the tyrant, *ire,* and the *pacience* of the philosopher. The remedy of *ire,* we are told, is a 'vertu, that men callen Pacience or Suffraunce' (X, 645).

Chaucer's Parson is echoed by the usage of others writing on the same subject not only in explicitly penitential works but also in contemporary literature of a more entertaining kind. In the *Speculum Christiani* Ira appears as a dramatised figure and tells us his characteristics:

> *I chide and fyghte and manas faste*
> *Al my fomen I wyl doune caste.*
> *Mercy of hem wil I none have,*
> *But veniaunce stronge, so god me save.*
> (p. 64, 62)

Chiding and *manas* have themselves become semi-technical terms in this tradition, and we shall be considering a third, *grucching,* below. *Jacob's Well,* a mid-fifteenth-century guide to sermon material, defines ire in similar terms, employing its English synonym:

> wretthe is whanne þou art wroth and angry, felle,
> malycyous, desyringe wreche.
>
> (p. 90)

The familiarity of such associations was so great that its lexical reflection can be seen to occur in inevitable collocations, even when an author is not overtly concerned with these ideas. Attacking wasters who contribute nothing to the prosperity of the community, Piers Plowman remarks:

> *In lecherie and in losengerie ye lyuen, and in Sleuþe,*
> *And al is þoruȝ suffraunce þat vengeaunce yow ne takeþ.*
>
> (B-text, VI, 143–4)

The righteousness of God is affronted by the idleness of such men, and his anger, and therefore his vengeance, is restrained only by his long-suffering.[12]

Hidden in these words of Langland is an important implication of the difference between Christian and philosophical conceptions. To Seneca, the *sapiens* approached the more closely to an impersonal Stoic god exactly to the extent that he was impervious to emotions and controlled by pure reason. The implication of Langland's words, however, is of a god who is sufficiently human and perceptible to act as the direct example for human behaviour. In the C-text, I, 117 his anger is pictured as leading directly to vengeance, but elsewhere in the C-text is the suggestion that God is an example to man of patient restraint. God suffers: 'in ensaumple. þat we sholde alle suffren' (XIV, 201). The conception of a God who feels human passions is an important departure from the philosophical tradition, and we must discuss this in later chapters, but for the present it is sufficient to notice that the virtue of patience has been absorbed into the Christian tradition as an antidote to ire. Patience is, as we should expect, dependent upon reason, and it is the personification of reason who presents God as its exemplar in *Piers Plowman*. For the allegorically-named Prudence in the *Tale of Melibee* other Christian *exempla* of patience are to hand. When she advises patience to her husband in a long passage beginning at line 1490, she opposes vengeance and patience in the traditional way, and she quotes Seneca and Cato in support of her argument, but these authorities are joined by St. Gregory and by repeated reference to Scripture. The familiar injunction to mastery of the passions, with its implied opposition of the conqueror and the philosopher, is drawn from that epitome of wisdom, Solomon:

> 'It is moore worth to be pacient than for to be right strong;/ And he that may have the lordschipe of his owene herte is moore to preyse than he that by his force or strengthe taketh grete citees.'
>
> (VII, 1515–6)

The teaching of the old pagan philosophers is justified by Christian wisdom. For *exempla* of patience, Prudence uses not Socrates or Diogenes, the heroes of the philosophical tradition, but Job (999), the un-named saints and martyrs who have suffered tribulation without guilt (1505), and above all the deity in human form, Christ himself:

75

'Jhesu Crist . . . hath suffred for us and yeven ensample to every man to folwe and sewe hym; for he dide never synne, ne nevere cam ther a vileyns word out of his mouth./ Whan men cursed hym, he cursed hem noght; and whan they betten hym, he manaced hem noght.

(VII, 1502–4)

To the medieval Christian no better example of the philosophical virtue of patience could be found than that of the willing suffering of Christ. Possessing the power to overthrow all his adversaries, he chose rather to exhibit patience, humility and benignity through the most intense suffering. Now, although Stoic doctrine taught the would-be sage to welcome suffering as a school for virtue, and to endure without complaint, little value is placed upon humility in the ancient tradition. Indeed, in our discussion of the relationship between vengeance and patience, there has been a persistent assumption that they are in fact alternatives, that the possibility of vengeance indeed exists. The images of the tyrant and the philosopher tend to be images of men involved in great matters, wielding the power of action. They have never been far from the political analogy. Consequently the philosophical tradition placed greatest emphasis upon the control of the emotions and the unwavering resolution of the *sapiens*. In late Antiquity, however, the importance of *patientia*, the quality of the passive endurance of suffering, becomes emphasized, and this is the point of most of the Boethian examples of the confrontation of tyrant and philosopher. If *tranquillitas* and *firmitas* are the marks of the philosopher to Seneca and Cicero, to Boethius *patientia* is outstanding. The test of a self-professed philosopher is now 'yif that he wolde han suffrid lyghtly in pacience the wronges that weren doon unto hym' (*Bo*. II, p. 7, 130–32). Furthermore, he must do this without self-congratulation. Boethius's conception of the philosopher, then, stresses passivity and humility rather than determination and strength, and this is consistent with changes that came upon the tradition as it was adopted by Christian writers. From the beginning Christianity had been a popular movement and had espoused humility and ordinary everyday social values as its own. To the early Christian – martyr or less-blessed – the fact of vengeance might well be no more than a discreditable, but unfulfillable, desire. To him, the poverty which wealthy Stoics like Seneca extolled as a philosophical good, may be an uncomfortable actuality which he was compelled by necessity to bear. Patience was a capacity which enabled him to 'maken vertu of necessitee,' and the sweetness of disposition with which he contrived to bear persecution and suffering became more important in the Christian conception of that virtue as a whole. Indeed, it would be true to say that *patientia*, which was simply the description of a state of being in the Stoic wise man, became the name of a moral and religious virtue as the result of its adoption as a quality of the Christian saint and martyr.

The patient acceptance of poverty is an important theme of Christian writings. It is prominent in the Christian life as it is portrayed in the 'Life of Do-Wel' in *Piers Plowman*: for 'alle þe wise þat euere were. by oucht ich can aspie, / Preisede pouerte for beste . yf pacience hit folwe' (C-text, XIII, 140–41). Its praises are sung in the *Wife of Bath's Tale*, III, 1177–1206, where patient acceptance of poverty is seen as a road to wisdom. In the prologue to the *Man of Law's Tale*, a tale which exhibits the saintly patience of a lady named Constance, Chaucer takes mischievous delight in turning the tradition against itself by assembling a list of authorities on the moral damage that may result from poverty; it is a brilliant ironic *tour de force*. The point of this is that poverty is valueless unless patience follow, as Langland has said. The author of the alliterative poem, *Patience*, which commends the virtue by displaying its opposite, stresses the essential unity of patience and poverty, taken as virtues, and goes on to represent patience in the traditional way as control of the emotions in a novel version of the Beatitudes:

þay ar happen also þat can her hert stere.

(27)

The reluctance of Jonah in this poem to obey the word of God, and his grumbling against it, serve to illustrate a further transmutation of the opposition between patience and ire which takes place in penitential writings. The parish priest, searching the soul of his parishioners for traces of the vice of ire, must ask:

> *Hast þow be impacyent*
> *For any gref that god þe sent;*
> *Or elles I-gruched a-gaynes hyt,*
> *In herte or word oþer wyt?*
> *(Myrc's Instructions*, 1161–4)

In *Jacob's Well* impatience is equated with *grucchyng*:

> vnpacyence; þat is, whan þou grucchyst aȝens resounable chastys-ing of þi souereyn, and aȝens reprouyng of þi synnes, demyng þat all thynges are wrong þat arn don to þe aȝens þi wille.

(p. 90)

This equation between impatience and *grucchyng* is maintained also by Chaucer's Parson, the *Book of Vices and Virtues*, and by *Langland;* indeed it is clear that the word is a quasi-technical term of this area of moral discussion. Its relation to the seven root sins is variable, but it is usually taken as a manifestation of ire: that spirit of begrudging and grumbling with which men are apt to endure what they cannot avenge or rectify. It is specifically a creation of the penitential tradition, having no equivalent in earlier philosophical discussions of patience, and it contrasts with that essentially Christian conception of patience as willing and cheerful endurance. In colloquial Middle English, *to grucchen* stands in opposition to *to taken for the best*.

In discussing *grucchyng* and the vices and virtues tradition, we may seem to have been moving in territory far distant from the tyrant and his ire, and his opposite, the philosopher. In fact we are not so remote. Chaucer's Parson remarks that *grucchyng* is especially typical of servants who dare not stand openly against their master's orders (*CT*. X, 507). This view of it is also implicit in the quotation from *Jacob's Well* (above). *Grucchyng* is in fact *ire*, the vice of the tyrant, conditioned by powerlessness, just as *pacience* is a virtue of necessity. In the tyrant ire and cruelty are joined with might; in the servant they are not. *Grucchyng*, then, lacks the social cachet attached to power, and tends to connote ridicule rather than fear; it frequently seems to be associated with the social condition of the churl. Yet, from the point of view of the moralist, the *wode tyrant* and the *grucchyng cherle* are of a single kind: both lack compassion, and both are mastered by their own passions. Their social status may be different, the circumstances may differ, but the moral disorder is the same. The *grucchyng* of the churl and the *ire* of the tyrant differ only as the pirate does from Alexander, or a *lemman* from a *lady* in the *Manciple's Tale*.[13]

We should not assume, however, from the unanimous condemnation of *grucchyng*, and the encouragement of benign patience by penitential writers, that these authors envisaged a Christian church peopled by neo-Stoic *sapientes*, self-sufficient in their own *tranquillitas*. Although they were happy to use inherited conceptual schemata and verbal formulae, especially when they had been used already by the Fathers, they would have been shocked by any suggestion of this kind. In his two short poems, *Fortune* and *Truth*, Chaucer employs many of the philosophical commonplaces: that man who is governed by reason is proof against Fortune, for she has no power over the man 'that over himself hath the maystrye!/ My suffisaunce shal be my socour; / For fynally, Fortune, I thee defye!' (14–16). The *stidfast* Socrates is invoked as the example of such a man. In *Truth*, the audience is advised to desert ambition and seek *suffisance* in small things:

> *That thee is sent receyve in buxumnesse;*
> *The wrastling for this world axeth a fal.*
> (15–16)

But neither poem closes with these traditional counsels; simple self-sufficiency and *tranquillitas* are no longer the end. Fortune replies to the complainant against her. The fault for which he blames her lies in himself. Lacking insight, he has failed to perceive that Fortune is merely the

78

agent of a divine providence which had foreseen these events from the beginning of creation. In the poem *Truth*, the addressee, Vache, is directed to turn his thoughts away from the world to seek out the creator God. To the medieval Christian, the only true content, the only lasting tranquillity, was to be sought in divine salvation. Boethius had painstakingly argued the identity of *suffisaunce, pees* and true happiness in God, and this was the orthodox assumption.[14] The blessed life in this world was simply a prelude to the life of bliss in another and better one.

Although the aspirations of medieval Christians had a different ultimate end from that of earlier philosophers, they still found the example of the past relevant to their moral needs, and it was in fact a conventional manoeuvre of the preacher to cite the virtue of the past to the detriment of the present. Modern man, says Chaucer's Parson, should learn to be patient both from the example of Christ and from consideration of the final reward of salvation, because even without these incentives 'the olde payens that nevere were Cristene, commendeden and useden the vertu of pacience, (X, 669). In the *Knight's Tale*, Chaucer deliberately created a moral world lacking the hope of salvation, and asked questions about order, reason and justice in a pagan universe.[15] At the close of the poem Theseus is left to justify the events of the action. He gives a long and careful exposition of a pre-determined world in which man is afflicted by forces beyond his understanding and control. This world is presided over by the providence of a distant and impersonal 'Firste Moevere' who is unconcerned with the worth of men. The only virtue in this world is patience, and this is what Theseus recommends:

> *Thanne is it wysdom, as it thynketh me,*
> *To maken vertu of necessitee,*
> *And take it weel that we may nat eschue,*
> *And namely that to us alle is due.*
> *And whoso gruccheth ought, he dooth folye,*
> *And rebel is to hym that al may gye.*
> (*CT.* I, 3041–6)

Although we, the audience, have been shown earlier that Theseus's noble conception of the order of the world is misplaced, that it is in fact ruled by the casuistry of an arbitrary Olympian clique rather than by justice, this does not vitiate the value placed upon patience. What is inappropriate in Theseus's universe is the respect that he, and what Chaucer probably regarded as the noblest examples of the philosophic tradition, accorded to their conception of providence. For, in the absence of a benevolent God, Theseus is using the language and ideas of the medieval Christian, but ironically, they are grossly misapplied. *Grucchyng* is denounced because it shows a rebellious attitude to the plan laid down by divine authority. To oppose this plan is wilfulness and sin.

79

But we have been shown by Chaucer that in this world there is no coherent plan. The assumption that there is one is not of divine origin; it is the product of the thinker and administrator, the ideal philosopher-king, Theseus. The *wilfulnesse* (3057) which Theseus ascribes to the rebel against his supposed providence belongs not to his pagan world but to St. Augustine's definition of sin as self-will, a deviation from the will of the divine creator. In the Christian view, patient acceptance of trials imposed by the divine plan perfect the soul, and hope, rather than being a weakness, becomes a source of strength in suffering. The pattern of Theseus's thoughts, derivable from his usage, is essentially a Christian one, but it is tragically misplaced in a universe which is chaotically pagan. Instead of a loving God, there is a 'first mover'; instead of the hope of salvation, there is patience, followed by the narrator's evasion:

> *His spirit chaunged hous and went ther,*
> *As I cam nevere, I kan nat tellen wher.*
> (*CT*. I, 2809–10)

Survival consists in the hope of an enduring reputation. It is perhaps this discrepancy between the aspiration to virtue and idealism, and the lack of an appropriate reward which makes Theseus's speech ring so hollow to many readers of the *Knight's Tale*.

By contrast, Chaucer's Parson inhabited a relatively comfortable world of Christian certainties. Patience, for him, implied obedience to the will of God with equanimity and eagerness. The old philosophical formula of living according to reason or nature was reformulated as living according to the divine will. The old capacity for suffering, *patientia*, took on a marked teleological aspect. The saint suffers in order to achieve a divine end, for:

> the tribulaciouns of this world but litel while endure, and soone passed been and goon,/ and joye that a man seketh to have by pacience in tribulaciouns is perdurable.
> (*CT*. VII, 1508–9)

The network of associations of peace, patience and constancy, descending from the philosophical tradition becomes involved with humility and hope, and with the submission of the individual will to that of God. The true Christian must equate the old *constantia* or *firmitas* with a firm resolution to improve his life by constantly submitting his own desires to the will of God. When, in *Piers Plowman*, Activa-Vita asks what is perfect patience, he receives the reply:

> *Meeknesse and Mylde speche . and men of on-wil,*
> *þe whiche wil loue ledeþ. to oure lordes place.*
> (C-text, XVI, 277–8)

Resolution guided by charity towards a divine goal is the Christian ideal of patience. Stability of emotions, gravity, and steadfastness of purpose are the marks of a saint. The sinner should strive to exhibit these virtues to the extent that he can. When he goes to confession, he must do so with a truly contrite heart and be accompanied by a firm determination to reform:

> contricioun moste be continueel, and that man have stedefast purpos to shriven hym, and for to amenden hym of his lyf . . . as contricion availleth noght withouten sad purpos of shrifte.
>
> <div align="right">(<i>CT.</i> X, 305–10)</div>

Sad or stedefast purpos, and *pacience in tribulacioun* are the final development in the medieval saint of those virtues which distinguished the philosopher of earlier times. But they have been joined by others unfamiliar in the ancient tradition, by *mekeness,* by *benignitee* and by the hope of joy.

CHAPTER FIVE

Transformations of the Philosopher

AS WE SAW in the last chapter, the traditional philosophic virtues of patience, firmness of purpose and emotional stability underwent a marked change when they were absorbed into medieval Christianity. Their companions were now virtues which previously had either been ignored or regarded as positively undesirable: humility, meekness and hope. Indeed it is rare to find in Chaucer's own writings much trace of the old philosophical virtues existing apart from this community. More often, we find that the traditional virtues have been joined not only by humility and hope, but also by joy and pathos. Let us consider this mixture in a scene from the Second Nun's legend of St. Cecilia.

The story is set in Rome at the time of the persecution of the Christians. Cecilia, a noble Roman lady, and a Christian from birth, is married to a pagan Roman whom she quickly converts. In the midst of various miraculous revelations a number of other prominent Romans, including the officer sent to arrest them, are also converted. The conversions are so swift and automatic, so accompanied by joy and wonder, that it is incontestable that any man of good heart would be expected to follow suit. One by one, however, the converts are put to death by the Prefect, Almachius, who is thus branded as a man of more than usual evil. So it is that when Cecilia is finally dragged before him we are prepared for a confrontation between the Christian heroine and her implacable enemy. His agents have proved susceptible to Cecilia's wise counsel, but Almachius is the incarnation of the powers of darkness and will not be influenced. Cecilia is unafraid; her poise is established at once when she questions the rationality of the procedure in commencing her case. Her tranquillity astonishes the judge: 'Ne takestow noon heede of my power?'

he asks incredulously. But Cecile is unconcerned with worldly power; she simply points out the injustice of persecuting Christians. Cecilia's calm and reason is emphasized by the fury of Almachius as he threatens the captive with death. 'Why spekestow so proudly thanne to me?' he asks. But what seems pride to him is for Cecilia devotion to the truth. She is exhibiting the *constantia* of the saint: 'I speke noght but stedfastly' is her answer.[1] Here, in the tranquillity and rationality of the captive, contrasting with the fury of her captor, we can recognize in a transmuted religious form the confrontation between the tyrant and the philosopher. There is however a small irony. Almachius is no ordinary tyrant, for he claims for himself the philosophic virtue of patience. Like the Stoic *sapiens*, he can suffer insults to himself:

> *I recche nat what wrong that thou me profre,*
> *For I kan suffre it as a philosophre.*
> *(CT.* VIII, 489–90)

But his actions belie his words, and it is an outburst of fury which finally sends Cecilia to martyrdom. The pretensions of the pagan to objective justice based upon philosophical patience are demonstrated to be false and, as the Christian God is superior to his stone idols, so the saint's virtue makes nonsense of the philosophical aspirations of the judge.[2]

This story, like most of the others in the *Canterbury* collection, was borrowed by Chaucer rather than invented. Its precise source is unknown, although it may be that Chaucer used some version of the *Golden Legend* which no longer survives.[3] At any rate, Chaucer recognized his tale as a saint's legend, and it should therefore be read as reflecting the moral certainties of that genre. A modern reader might well be tempted, for example, to sympathize with Almachius, who in fact is unusually long-suffering for a tyrant-figure. It is possible to understand the dilemma of the administrator faced by an inflexible malefactor who is convinced of the moral right of her position, and whose repeated assertions of it become merely provocative. Yet such a reading would be misplaced sympathy. By definition, in a saint's legend, the saint is justified; her faith and constancy are her outstanding virtues. And here, although Almachius is an unusual tyrant, she is justified also from the point of view of the philosophic tradition, since it is she who remains calm whilst he explodes into fury.

The reaction of the audience to a story of this kind is not intended to be an intellectually-contrived understanding and sympathy with the pagan persecutor, but rather immediate inspiration and pathos at the unperturbed suffering of the saint. How dare Cecilia act this way in the face of death? How can a mere girl dispute so effectively with a judge, reducing him to incoherent fury? The answers to such questions lie in faith and grace which transfigure a young girl so that she is the superior of her judge in just those accomplishments at which he should be most adept: rational argument and emotional self-control. From the moment Cecilia speaks it is clear that she is no naturalistic characterization: her speech is reasoned and weighty far beyond what might be expected of a young woman. Chaucer loads it with polysyllabic words of Romance origin, and couches it in rhetorical phrasing:

> 'O juge, confus in thy nycetee,
> Woltow that I reneye innocence,
> To make me a wikked wight?' quod shee.
>   (CT. VIII, 463–5)

Cecilia is firstly a saint, and only incidentally a woman, hence the simplicity of expression expected of a philosopher gives place to high-sounding words whose vehemence seeks to inspire the audience by her example rather than represent any possible speech with verisimilitude.

The fact that this saint is a women is perhaps more significant than my previous sentence allowed, for it has been noticeable that all the examples of philosophical fortitude which were used in the ancient tradition were men. Christian saints and martyrs, on the other hand, are frequently women, and indeed in Chaucer's writings are invariably women or children. In some ways this may seem surprising since the irrationality and levity of women was a foregone conclusion in the medieval period, and it had been so since the very origin of the psychological theories by which it was to be explained. Chaucer's Parson warns husbands to treat their wives with consideration and respect since they 'kan nat paciently suffre' (X, 928) as a man can. In discussing the *constantia* of the sage, Seneca had discarded the taunts of women as a possible cause of pertur-bation. It was unthinkable that a philosopher should be injured by a woman's mockery, which must be meaningless, since women were known to be subject, like children, to unruly desires and lack of reason.[4] Although Chaucer's female saints seem to conflict with this estimate, there is also the Wife of Bath who not only fails to show patience, but whose views are in radical conflict with all established hierarchies. This iconoclast even demands that her husbands willingly submit to her tyranny, and her argument is casuistically based upon the alleged weak-ness of women. That same wilful rejection of reason that leads Januarie in the *Merchant's Tale* to scorn the counsel of Justinus, causes the Wife to demand obedience from her husband in contravention of every medieval assumption about the relationship of husband and wife:

> Oon of us two moste bowen, doutelees;
> And sith a man is moore resonable
> Than a womman is, ye moste been suffrable.

84

What eyleth yow to grucche thus and grone?
(III, 440–53)

Not only ardent feminists will applaud this adroit table-turning, but the claim that reason should become subservient to wilfulness – which is implied by the superiority of the wife – is directly contrary to the whole structure of medieval ethics, and, whilst applauding the Wife's audacity, the contemporary audience would have appreciated that she deserves moral condemnation. However persuasive of individuality certain aspects of her character and appearance are, the topsy-turvy moral framework of her characterization is clear throughout.[5] As much as she is a real woman, she is also a symbol, and this is the fate of many, perhaps most, of Chaucer's women characters. Cecilia is more a demonstration of saintly virtue than a woman; so also is Constance in the *Man of Law's Tale*. There is no possible argument over Philosophy in *Boece* or Prudence in *Melibee*, both of whom are mere personifications. In poems where religious as well as philosophical idealism is embodied in a female figure, and explicit allegory is not used, we may be slower to grasp the allegorical tendency. It is present nonetheless. Sometimes this function is suggested by the presence of language which we have learned to associate with moral idealism. Thus the description of the widow of the *Nun's Priest's Tale* marks her out as having symbolic force. There are those who, misled by the reference to *fruyt* and *chaf* at the end of the tale, have tried to find in it a multiple-levelled allegory, and consider this widow to represent Holy Church. But the implication of *fruyt* and *chaf* here is not that of exegesis, and there is nothing to associate the widow with Holy Church.[6] However, in the picture of one who leads a simple life *in pacience*, enjoying an *attempree diete* and *hertes suffisaunce*, there is much that identifies her with the contentment of the blessed life, and much to contrast her with the foolish vanity and worldliness of Chaunticleer.

That women should be chosen as symbols of moral-religious idealism is in the end not very surprising. In a prevailing literary climate of anti-feminism the virtues of prudence, resolution, emotional stability were as unexpected in woman as in children, and for much the same reason. Both were regarded as relatively irrational creatures. Youth and femininity were antithetical to reason, and a woman philosopher seemed as unlikely as a child-sage. Because of this very unnaturalness, both are common in hagiography.[7] What better way to demonstrate the power of the Holy Spirit in a human vessel than by picturing it in the weakest possible vessel, suspending the alleged laws of nature?

The choice of women and children to represent a moral-religious ideal also had a further advantage, and this is demonstrated by the reaction of the Canterbury pilgrims to the tales of the Prioresse and Physician. They become thoughtful, recognizing the exemplary function of the tales.

Harry Baily is deeply moved by the *Physician's Tale,* finding it a 'pitous tale.' It is here, in evoking *pitee,* that the choice of women and child heroes is justified. If it is heartrending to see the innocent in distress, it is doubly so to see the suffering of the weak and innocent. Women and children are free from any dissatisfaction an audience might feel at excessive passivity. They are physically weak and their suffering evokes pathos unchecked; but if they are spiritually strong their triumph, and the moral teaching to be gained from it, are the sweeter.

The greatest part of Chaucer's reference to these religio-philosophical themes is in passing, in setting the tone of a scene, or in sketching in the moral idealism of a minor character. Occasionally they may form associational resonances in creating a character where the primary interest is not hagiographic or blatantly moralistic. Some reference to these words and phrases is often inevitable. But in the tale which he gave to the philosophical Clerk, the theme of patience was given extended treatment. More than any other tale, the *Clerk's Tale* represents the tenets of Christianized philosophy which we have been discussing in these two chapters.

It would be easy to assume that Chaucer went to some trouble to match the story to its teller. His Clerk is a man of frugal life, an unworldly man, and a lover of philosophy and old learning. His manner of speech is brief and pithy, and his phrasing ordered and meaningful. His tale is written in the philosophical plain style, employing simple vocabulary, and exhibiting a marked sobriety in the use of rhetorical figures. It is, however, enlivened by discreet word-play and deepened by persistent allusiveness in phrasing. In addition, by comparison with its sources, which seem to be the use of Petrarch's Latin story of Grizelda and the Old French *Livre de Griseldis* in parallel, the philosophical theme and commonplaces are increased both in number and in the space allotted to them.[8] Yet, although Chaucer *does* make it a philosopher's story in these ways, he also blurs the clear outline of moral allegory which Petrarch had wrought from Boccaccio's *novella.* In particular, he develops the relationship between Walter and Griselda in more detail, showing greater insight into their motivations and reactions. As a result, Griselda, who is primarily a moral symbol in Petrarch, shows real affection for her husband and reflects nostalgically upon happier times from the depths of her suffering. The pathos is consequently greatly increased. The framework of the story, with its contrived contrast with such wives as Dame Alisoun of Bath or the turbulent Goodelief, complicates the situation even further, since it raises directly the problem of justification of the patience of Griselda in the context of more realistically-conceived fourteenth-century marriages. Much of what is gained by the use of a symbolic woman to win acceptance of total passivity, is at least potentially lost by her exposure to these larger-than-life representatives of an alternative mode of behaviour.[9]

The basic outline of the story, told as an example of the patience that man owes to God, falls simply within the thematic area which we have been exploring. Furthermore, Chaucer's decision to expand certain passages in an analytic way, and often his choice of language for purposes of amplification, make this even more obvious. Both Petrarch and the *Livre de Grisildis* give us some details of Griselda's character early in their telling of the story. The *Livre* says that she had a 'mature and old' mind (*courage meur et ancien*); Petrarch that her mind was 'old and manly' (*virilis senilisque animus*). Chaucer renders this by 'rype and sad corage'(220), a phrase which is a literal translation of neither source. Some lines later in the poem he refers to Griselda's 'wise and rype wordes,' and here his *rype* renders the Latin *maturitas*. Elsewhere, in the *Tale of Melibee* (1199), he translated a French allegation that the counsel of young people is to be avoided because it is not *rype* (*meur*). Clearly, the fact that Petrarch plants a manly and old mind in a young maiden is referable to the kind of clerkly prejudice we have been discussing; in its equation of philosophical virtues with age and masculinity, it goes back to Seneca and beyond. Together, the *Livre de Grisildis* and the French book of Prudence provide Chaucer with his translation of Latin *maturitas* in the word *meure*, which he then renders into English as *rype*; but the use of the word *sad* is quite unmotivated by the sources, and must derive from Chaucer's own familiarity with vocabulary appropriate to the tradition. In his translation of the *Roman de la Rose* the usual incompatibility of youth and wise composure is found. Youth, we are informed, is concerned with nothing but leading folk into foolish amusements and unruliness 'So is she froward from sadnesse' (*RR*. 4940). This precise sentiment does not appear in the French poem. In the *Clerk's Tale*, perceiving the implications of his sources, Chaucer has paraphrased them, asserting the unexpected maturity and self-restraint of his young heroine.

These qualities of Griselda are tested when the servant of Walter arrives to take away her first child. Chaucer follows his sources in telling how the pathos of this scene would have moved a nurse, but how Griselda blessed the child 'with ful sad face' (552), showing no emotion. He then adds an explanatory couplet to his sources:

> But nathelees so sad stidefast was she
> That she endured al adversitee.
> (*CT*. IV, 564–5)

The Marquis can find no change in her behaviour despite the suffering he has inflicted; she remains: 'evere in oon ylike sad and kynde' (602). This explanatory line, with its familiar philosophical vocabulary, is again Chaucer's addition. But the nature of his treatment of his material does not become clear until the final test is placed upon poor Griselda. She is to be divorced, cast out, and replaced by a younger woman. Chaucer leaves us in no doubt that he understands precisely the psychological mechanisms of patient endurance, and, writing free of his sources, he composes a passage in which the familiar philosophical terminology re-appears:

> *But whan thise tidynges came to Grisildis,*
> *I deeme that hire herte was ful wo.*
> *But she, ylike sad for everemo,*
> *Disposed was, this humble creature,*
> *The adversitee of Fortune al t'endure,*
>
> *Abidynge evere his lust and his plesance,*
> *To whom that she was yeven herte and al,*
> *As to hire verray worldly suffisance.*
> (IV, 752–9)

Griselda is constant; unchanged by the changing of Fortune, she seeks no more than to obey the will of her husband. She is the 'flour of wyfly pacience' (919), the epitome of 'wyfly stedfastnesse' (1050). Chaucer tells us again and again that she is 'ferme and stable' (663), 'stidefast' (789), 'meke and stable' (931), and all these are Chaucerian additions to his sources. The epithets *pacient, stable, ferme, stedefast, constant*, and *sad* echo through the tale. Often they are suggested by the wording of the sources, but equally as often the theme suggests to Chaucer a constellation of appropriate words for its expression. Whilst there is no doubt that Petrarch intended the tale to be an *exemplum* of patience, it is also undoubtedly the case that Chaucer perceived this theme and amplified it, using the full range of vocabulary which usage had made appropriate to its expression.

In emphasizing the outstanding constancy of Griselda by comparison with the broad mass of ordinary people, Chaucer has further recourse to the philosophical tradition, building upon no more than a hint in his sources. From the Cynico-Stoic diatribe onwards, would-be philosophers were adjured to distrust popular opinion. The philosopher finds his strength from within and distrusts the foolishness of the people, who represent the fickleness from which he is a fugitive. Griselda finds that the favour of the citizens fluctuates wildly, turning from ecstatic acclaim to rejection in her darkest hour. Chaucer, taking his cue from Boethius (III, p. 6) exclaims: 'O stormy peple! unsad and evere untrewe!' (995). Popular esteem is as fleeting as fortune, so that the wise set no store by it.

Chaucer's handling of Petrarch's moral tale, then, is a curious one, although perhaps typically Chaucerian.[11] As we have seen, he is able to draw upon the vernacular representation of an ancient philosophical tradition to amplify the ideal of patience with which man should accept the inevitable. He develops this by stressing the moral strength of

Griselda, so that a figure who might be thought of as a saint becomes less theological and corresponds better with the older stereotype of the philosopher. Yet, at the same time, he develops human relationships, pathos, and consequently moral questioning, based on an assumption of the literalness of the events described. The result is an artistic and philosophical problem. Perhaps Chaucer was aware of this, for in his translation of Petrarch's explanation of the significance of the story, he makes his own Clerk alter the sense subtly. Neither Petrarch nor the *Livre Griseldis* utterly deny the possibility of a realistic interpretation of Griselda's behaviour, although they regard it as unlikely. In both cases the possibility remains that, should such an ideal wife be found, she would be regarded as an admirable creature. Chaucer's Clerk, by contrast, apparently feels that not only is the story unlikely to be echoed in actuality, but also that it is intolerable that it should be:

> *This storie is seyd, nat for that wyves sholde*
> *Folwen Grisilde as in humylitee,*
> *For it were inportable, though they wolde;*
> *But for that every wight, in his degree,*
> *Sholde be constant in adversitee*
> *As was Grisilde.*

(IV, 1142–7)

This strong warning is limited to Chaucer's version. Before exceeding the bounds of reason in ironic mockery of the Wife of Bath, the Clerk presents a serious explanation of the *moralitee* of his story. The philosopher's story is appropriately a celebration of the philosophical and religious virtue of constancy, the theme we have seen amplified throughout; too literal an understanding is highly undesirable, since it will lead to awkward moral questioning. And this is exactly what the placing of the tale in the *Canterbury Tales* framework, together with Chaucer's amplification of human relationships within it, does achieve.

It is not only in the religious sphere, as saints, that we find women in Chaucer being described in the vocabulary of moral-philosophical discourse, and indeed representing its ideals. The borders between philosophical, religious, and courtly works are rarely very well marked in fourteenth-century writing, and linguistic terminology easily moves from one sphere to another. In his early translation of the *Roman de la Rose*, Chaucer encountered a major source of what one author has called 'courtly scholasticism.'[12] Apart from the formal devices proper to scholasticism, such as moralisations, glosses, and disputations (*moralizatio, glossatio, disputatio*), he found there a whole range of vocabulary transformed into French from scholastic Latin. A very small proportion of this is of interest to us in discussing feminine *exempla* of moral value, and we shall in fact consider only one word beyond those already discussed.

In the *Roman de la Rose*, whilst the adverb *simplement* is used technically (Paré, p. 49), the adjective *simple* is used very commonly without obvious technical significance in descriptions of the feminine personifications of courtly virtues, such as Beauty or Franchise (magnanimity). The word seems to represent an important virtue among that group which is desirable in a courtly lady. It connotes ideas of honesty and straightforwardness. Since C. S. Lewis has clearly explained the development of its senses in English,[13] and especially in view of the fact that its sense is often very similar to that of modern English, further discussion would be unnecessary but for the peculiar fact that it is an uncommon word in Chaucer. In fact, the majority of Chaucerian uses are in his translations of the *Roman de la Rose* and Boethius, and it is fairly certain that, although its contextual sense is often similar to that of modern English, its connotational value is distinctly different. Boethius uses the Latin word to refer to the *simplex* nature of God; that is to say, to a nature which is at once unchanging through the course of time, and also indivisible in itself. In earlier Latin writers, such as Cicero and Ovid, its moral senses 'uncomplicated,' 'undissimulating', 'sincere and open' were common, whilst Peter Abelard used it in the moral sense to refer to 'pure and unmixed' intentions.[14] Given the attractive alliteration to be found in Middle English with words like *sad, stedefast,* and *stable,* it is therefore a matter of no surprise that *simple* should become associated with these words connoting stability and moral soundness in describing a courtly lady. Unfailing sincerity becomes a prized virtue of the heroine of secular courtly poetry, and she then attracts the epithet *simple.*

In composing the *Book of the Duchess*, Chaucer was working in close harmony with the preconceptions and artistic procedures of *The Roman de la Rose* and its successors in the French tradition. In particular, as he paints the relationship between Blanche and the bereaved Man in Black he seems to have been heavily influenced by the *Remède de Fortune* of Guillaume de Machaut. At the beginning of his poem, Machaut represents himself as young and therefore unstable in heart, and undiscriminating in his mind, but ready to learn virtue from the noble example of his mistress. This is echoed in the situation of the Man in Black as he recalls it for his eager listener. Like Machaut, when he met Blanche he was young, innocent, lacking in discrimination and emotional stability:

> *For hyt was in my firste youthe,*
> *And thoo ful lytel good y couthe,*
> *For al my werkes were flyttynge*
> *That tyme, and al my thoght varyinge.*
> *Al were to me ylyche good*
> *That I knew thoo.*
>
> (*BD*, 799–804)

Sadnesse and youth, as we have seen, were traditionally incompatible, yet Blanche combines them. She is an example of philosophic virtue to her lover: at his first glimpse, he notices that 'She had so stedfast countenance' (833). *Stedfast countenance* here means 'modest demeanour' or 'composure', and to this he adds that her eyes, the mirrors of her soul, are 'debonaire, goode, glade and sadde, /Symple, of good mochel, noght to wyde' (860–61). Her face too is *sad, symple* and *benygne*. Her spiritual virtues are matched by the equability of her physical proportions. Her *mesure* is stressed, and her eloquence, which is based firmly upon reason (922), and has that weighty significance which we have learned to expect from the morally ideal. The purport of her speech persuades men towards good. Her glances seem compassionate, since this is her nature, but they remain well-controlled:

> *Hyr lokynge was nat foly sprad,*
> *Ne wildely, thogh that she pleyde.*
> (874–5)

The point of this is that in the courtly literary tradition meaningful looks play a most important role, being often the only communication possible between lovers, and frequently the means of initiating love affairs. In *William of Palerne*, for example, a romance translated from the French at the order of the Duke of Hereford in about 1350, we find the lines:

> *alysaundrine a-non . attlede all here þouȝtes,*
> *sche knewe wel bi kuntenaunce . of kastyng of lokes.*
> (941–2)

Since looks were so important a means of communication between lovers and so potent an initiator of affairs, they attracted the attention of religious moralists, and we find frequent disapproving reference to *fol lokynge*. Foolish looking is one of the follies ascribed to Eve in the fourteenth-century *Livre du Chevalier de la Tour Landry*, which preceded the commission of the first sin, but in relation to love it occurs in Chaucer's *Parson's Tale* as the first of five steps which lead to lechery. Behind Chaucer's stress on the control which Blanche exercised over her glances is a whole spectrum of moral associations.[15] Like Walter in the *Clerk's Tale*, she is above reproach, and does not cast her glances around 'with wantown lookyng of folye.' (*CT*. IV, 236).

The overall picture of Blanche and the Man in Black which is drawn in the *Book of the Duchess* does not correspond very well with historical reality. In fact, when the historical John of Gaunt met Blanche of Lancaster, he was nineteen years old and she only twelve. Blanche, as she appears in Chaucer's poem, is, to say the least, a highly idealized portrait of any young woman who actually existed. Indeed it is perhaps wisest to regard Chaucer's creation as the representative of a group of courtly ideals for a woman. To what extent the historical Blanche actually fulfilled them cannot be guessed; we can only assume that the discrepancy between actuality and the poetic portrait was not such as to make the latter ridiculous. Whether Blanche really did correspond to the woman in *Complaint to his Lady* and represent paradoxical 'sadnesse in youthe' is imponderable; what is striking, however, is that even in describing an actually existing person, well-known to all, the power of the literary-philosophical tradition guided Chaucer towards idealization.

The complete conception of the ideal courtly lady is of course a very complex one, and the portrait of Blanche includes many elements beyond those of moral stability with which we have just been concerned. Yet there is no doubt that, in Northern Europe at least where the ideals of courtesy were to a large extent formulated by clerks, the religio-philosophical ideals which we have found exemplified by philosophers and saints played an important part in their formation. It is not difficult to find correspondences between such idealizations as Blanche and the consecrated virgins of the St. Cecilia type. Vincent of Beauvais wrote a book on the education of the sons of gentlemen, towards the end of which he spoke too of their daughters. He borrows his ideal of the young noblewoman from St. Ambrose's treatise on Christian virgins. Young women, he says, must be humble in heart, weighty in words, prudent in spirit, very expert in speech, and studious in reading.[16] Lowered eyes are a sign of modesty (xlvi) as also is brevity in expression (xlix, 31ff) and sobriety of demeanour (xlvi). Such recommendations of behaviour do not contrast with those of the philosopher in the ancient tradition, but more significantly, they closely match the behaviour required of Christian wives by the evangelists in Scripture. These are women:

> Whose adorning let it not be that outward adorning of plaiting the hair, and wearing of gold, or of putting on of apparel; but let it be the hidden man of the heart, in that which is not corruptible, even in the ornament of a meek and quiet spirit, which is in the sight of God of great price
>
> (I *Peter* III, 3–4)

Moralistic writers seized upon the wearing of golden hair ornaments and extravagant fashions in dress as indicative of a boldness and worldliness which Vincent of Beauvais feared that excessive familiarity with court manners and *mores* might encourage in a young girl. The author of the thirteenth-century lyric, *Ubi sunt que ante nos fuerunt,* represents exactly this kind of adornment as typical of worldly vanity.

Chaucer's notion of the ideal courtly lady, then, subscribes to a view which is essentially moralistic, and which draws both on philosophical and more religious conceptions of morality. The characterization of Blanche is a full and complex description of such a lady, and is in fact a moral idealization. From the points of view of emotional stability and self-restraint, which are the aspects of moral behaviour which concern us here, it is a striking fact that there is a marked contrast between Blanche and the Man in Black. When he is discovered by the narrator, he is in the depths of despair, to such an extent that it is necessary to present him with a conventional list of *exempla* as a warning against suicide. He considers himself overwhelmed by ill-fortune, and bitterly complains of Fortune's instability and his own loss of *suffisance* (703). The narrator conventionally invokes the example of Socrates as a champion against Fortune, but the Man in Black is no philosopher, and the reference has no effect on him. In point of fact, his moral constitution seems hardly to have changed from his account of his youthful instability at his first meeting with his mistress. What are we to make of this contrast? Blanche is an ideal courtly lady, resplendent in regular and proportioned beauty, accomplished in all the appropriate arts, and with the moral and emotional poise of a philosopher or a saint; the Man in Black is a creature of passions who is overwhelmed by the loss of the sole object of his desires. The schematic contrast is heightened by the chosen names, Black and White. If we hold to the traditional view that the poem is an elegy for the death of the historical Duchess of Lancaster, and that the Man in Black is indeed John of Gaunt, we must assume that, somewhat mysteriously, the familiar discrepancy in worth between the lady and her lover has been recast in moral-philosophical terms to the disadvantage of John of Gaunt. Alternatively, it may be argued that the poem is a more tactful exercise in consolation by which it is suggested that excessive grief is a betrayal of his love for Blanche. Indeed, if as it is tacitly implied, the love of Blanche was a maturing influence on the young John of Gaunt, it is little compliment to that love that its influence should vanish so soon with her death. A third possibility remains; that the poem has less to do with John of Gaunt than it has to the case of all lovers deserted by their ideal ladies. Lovers may speak of *stidefastnesse* (*AA.* 143), of remaining *sad and trewe* (*Complaint*, 9) but from the philosophical point of view, as to the religious commentator, such usages are improper, since they may only be justifiably applied to transcendental things, to the human soul and to God. To expect steadfastness in externals, and to put all one's hope of *suffisance* in a worldly object is to make no fortification against the blows of Fortune. To this extent, the psychological history of the Man in Black is that also of Troilus and of other medieval lovers, whom Reason considers, in best Stoic tradition, to be suffering from a sickness (*RR.* 4810).

Troilus's mistress, however, does not die; she deserts him. In other words her steadfastness is limited not only by the universal limit of death, but by an essential failing in her own character; she falls far short of the ideal exemplified by Blanche. In the final Book of the poem comes a famous description of Criseyde, placed symbolically between her two lovers. Her physical beauty is stressed. She is of moderate stature, and all her features are proportionate. Her hair hangs behind her back and is caught up with a golden thread. There may be nothing sinister in this, but this part of the description echoes that of the sensual Venus of *Parliament of Fowls*, 267–8, which in turn may recall the moralists' censure of golden hair ornaments. In any case, it is immediately followed by the telling detail that Criseyde's eyebrow's are joined, in sharp contrast to those of Beauty in the *Romaunt of the Rose*, 1018.[17] A moral description in proper rhetorical style follows:

> *She sobre was, ek symple, and wys withal,*
> *The best ynorisshed ek that myghte be,*
> *And goodly of hire speche in general,*
> *Charitable, estatlich, lusty, and fre;*
> *Ne nevere mo ne lakked hir pite;*
> *Tendre-herted, slydynge of corage.*
>
> (V, 820–25)

We may place this beside a description of her in Book One, where she is described as:

> *Simple of atir and debonaire of chere,*
> *With ful assured lokyng and manere.*
>
> (I, 181–2)

The language is reminiscent of that used of Blanche. Criseyde is *sobre, symple, wys;* she is fully composed and controlled in her behaviour and glances. But there is no mention of her moral stability: she is never called *sad, stedefast,* or *stable.* Instead, her emotionality is stressed; she is tender-hearted, easily affected, and *slydynge of corage.* This last phrase is important. *Slydynge* means 'slippery', 'impossible to grasp or pin down', and is strongly associated with ideas of changeability. The word is used very sparingly by Chaucer: it is applied in another form to the joy of love which is easily lost (*PF.* 3), and to hope or ambition which is deceptive or impossible to realize (*Bo*, IV, m. 2, 14; *CT*. VIII, 682). Twice in *Boece*, it renders the Latin *lubrica*, which Jean de Meun translated as *escoulouri-able*, 'slippery'; and in its application to hope, Jean indicates its poor foundation by adding the word *decevable* to his translation: an addition which Chaucer also adopted.[18] It may not be without significance that Chaucer followed the reference to her *slydynge corage* with the description of a physical imperfection, her joined eyebrows, which as well as being antithetical to established canons of beauty, were considered by

94

medieval commentators to indicate an unstable character. These associations of deceit and instability are also essential in another of Chaucer's rare uses of the word *slydynge,* for he chose it as the translation of *lubrica,* applied to Fortune in *Boece* I, m. 5, 34; Fortune, of course, is the epitome of fickleness. In the Latin tradition, too, the word *lubrica* had had a moral significance, since in Cicero's usage it implied changeability, and was particularly associated with hastiness and the imprudence of youth; whilst in medieval Latin, Alan of Lille used it in opposition to the concept of stability.[19] It is evident from this that in describing Criseyde Chaucer chooses the word *slydynge* with some care and awareness of its associational potency. She is in many more superficial ways a courtly idealization, but at the same time she is a negation of the ideals of moral philosophy: an example of instability.

Awareness of the ideals of moral philosophy was not confined to men like Chaucer's Clerk; it was flattering to anyone to be regarded as wise and stable. The Wife of Bath herself points out that it is dear to women to be so considered:

> *And somme seyn that greet delit han we*
> *For to been holden stable, and eek secree,*
> *And in o purpos stedefastly to dwelle.*
> (*CT.* III, 945–7)

This is true of Criseyde: she constantly seeks for good repute, professing the desire to adopt the religious life or praising the worth of prudence. In Book V, after bewailing the limits of her prudence, she resolves to return to Troilus: 'This purpos wol ich holde, and this is best,' she says; but, as the narrator concludes:

> *er fully monthes two,*
> *She was ful fer fro that entencioun!*
> *For bothe Troilus and Troie town*
> *Shal knotteles thorughout hire herte slide;*
> *For she wol take a purpos for t'abyde.*
> (*TC.* V, 766–9)

Criseyde's *slydynge* heart cannot hold to any one intention, one *purpos* follows another as the changes of Fortune demand. This does not prevent her from adopting the esteemed pose of *philosophre*: in making her resolution, she says, she cares nothing for the opinions of idle bystanders; ignoring them, she will place herself above the fickleness of popular opinion and seek true happiness in self-sufficiency:

> *And as for me, for al swich variaunce,*
> *Felicite clepe I my suffisaunce.*
> (V, 762–3)

95

But Criseyde is no Socrates. For her and her like, these words have lost their proper meaning. Unlike the narrator of the poem *Fortune*, whose *suffisaunce* is the strength of his rational control, what Criseyde means by *suffisaunce*, and where she hopes to find the blessed life, is really in a kind of dependence. In common with the Man in Black (*BD.* 1037) and other lovers, *suffisaunce* has become for her one of the endearments spoken between lovers. She refers to Troilus as her 'owene hertes sothfast suffisaunce' (IV, 1640) and welcomes him to her arms with language which, in another context, might have had philosophical significance: 'Welcome, my knyght, my pees, my suffisance' (III, 1309). For Troilus and Criseyde, each is the other's *suffisaunce*, and as they lie in each other's arms 'in lust and in quiete', they seem to have found the greatest happiness. But as the philosophical tradition, whose words and concepts they are abusing, teaches, and as experience will make clear, such tranquillity and felicity are illusions which vanish with the mutability of Fortune. The only lasting good in their pagan world lies in individual virtue, and if, as in Criseyde, the stability essential for this is missing, there can be no lasting happiness even within the limited span of life in this world.

The courtly love ideal of constancy in commitment between lovers is stated in the *Romaunt of the Rose* in a passage which fully exploits the literary topos of the confrontation of the tyrant and the philosopher:

> A, Bialacoil, myn owne deer!
> Though thou be now a prisoner,
> Kep atte leste thyn herte to me,
> And suffre not that it daunted be;
> Ne lat not Jelousie, in his rage,
> Putten thin herte in no servage.
> Although he chastice thee withoute,
> And make thy body unto hym loute,
> Have herte as hard as dyamaunt,
> Stedefast, and nought pliaunt.
> In prisoun though thi body be,
> At large kep thyn herte free;
> A trewe herte wole not plie
> For no manace that it may drye.
>   (4377–90)

Such invariability in good or evil fortune is the mark of true love and friendship alike (*RR*, 5225ff.). Like prudence, of which according to the author of *Patience* they are the product, constancy and patience are virtues which can be valued at various levels and in situations far beyond their proper lodging in the philosopher or saint. In any sphere, patience may be seen as a desirable alternative to haste and rashness. It is the key to tranquillity, and Gower expresses this in sentential form:

Suffraunce hath euere be the beste
To wissen him that secheth reste;
(CA. III, 1639–40)

For suffrance is the welle of Pes
(III, 1672)

This is a lesson which the Wife of Bath finds applicable to marriage when she recalls the story of Socrates and Xantippe, a lesson which is more respectably adopted by the Franklin. For him, the opposition between the tyrant and philosopher is forgotten, and his recipe for happiness in marriage is mutual tolerance. In recommending it, however, he slips easily into the familiar patterns of language:

Pacience is an heigh vertu, certeyn,
For it venquysseth, as thise clerkes seyn,
Thynges that rigour sholde nevere atteyne.[20]
(CT. V, 773–5)

There are also echoes of the ideas found expressed at the beginning of the alliterative poem, *Patience,* when willing suffering is advised as an ideal preferable to *grucchyng:*

Lerneth to suffre, or elles, so moot I goon,
Ye shul it lerne, wher so ye wole or noon.
(CT. V, 777–8)

A wise man who knows about self-restraint will moderate his behaviour on some occasions rather than seek redress (784–6). And so, Arveragus, 'To lyve in ese, suffrance hire bihight' (788). Whatever the subsequent vicissitudes, patient sufferance on both sides is the basis of a marriage from which peace and tranquillity may grow, and out of which the *Franklin's Tale* is made to reach its improbably happy end.

We may now close this discussion of patience and constancy by re-iterating the comparison with which it began. The self-control and sense of order which leads to tranquillity in the soul of the wise man is also the basis of peace in his reflection, the state. If every citizen exhibited the philosophic virtues, the state itself would necessarily approach the ideal of Cosmopolis, and the Christian world would become the City of God. Accordingly, Chaucer exhorted Richard II to 'wed thy folk agein to sted-fastnesse' (*Stedfastnesse*, 28), and since the well-being of a kingdom depends upon its *principale,* Gower recommended his successor, Henry IV, to rule in justice and humanity and to exercise wisdom in achieving peace and order in his realm. Borrowing the traditional opposition, he says that Alexander achieved fame by conquest in the ancient world, but the Christian world requires other virtues. The course of Solomon is now to be followed, and by the exercise of wisdom and tolerance the Christian ruler will find 'pees and reste unto the laste' (*In Praise of Peace*, 35).

Chaucer describes an ideal king at the beginning of the *Squire's Tale:*

> *Hym lakked noght that longeth to a kyng.*
> *As of the secte of which that he was born*
> *He kepte his lay, to which that he was sworn;*
> *And therto he was hardy, wys, and riche,*
> *And pitous and just, alwey yliche;*
> *Sooth of his word, benigne, and honurable;*
> *Of his corage as any centre stable;*
> *Yong, fressh, and strong, in armes desirous*
> *As any bacheler of al his hous.*
>
> (V, 16–24)

There remains something of the balance between wisdom and chivalry, but the heroic aspects which the Knight gave to Theseus are suppressed. The younger generation apparently valued moral virtues more greatly than prowess. *Trouthe* (faith and integrity), the stability of the heart, without traces of *slydynge*, are what Gower chooses to emphasize when he analyses the symbolic significance of the royal crown. The hardness of the jewels, he tells us, employing the same image as that used by Jean de Meun of the constancy of the lover, signifies:

> *Constance,*
> *So that ther schal no variaunce*
> *Be founde in his condicion.*
>
> (*CA*. VII, 1757–9)

A king must above all be of firm and stable moral fibre; he must be of impeccable integrity and resolute. For Gower and Chaucer alike the age of heroic rulers was over; what they both admired was neither the conqueror nor the tyrant, but the philosopher-king. The fourteenth-century ideal of a monarch was no longer Alexander, but Solomon.

CHAPTER SIX

The State of the Heart

IN THE PHILOSOPHICAL tradition the tyrant had been distinguished by his arbitrary exercise of power, by his persecution of the innocent, and by his own subjection to overwhelming and uncontrolled passions, and especially to ire. He was a symbol of irrationality and disorder which was capable of endless reinterpretation, and, directly opposed to him in these aspects, was the symbol of the philosopher, marked by his rational control, calmness, and self-restraint. But, for the fourteenth century, important as this opposition on rational grounds was, a further characteristic of the tyrant was equally important to his definition, and this was not traditionally in opposition to any quality possessed by the philosopher. This was the idea that the tyrant was typically hard-hearted, and furthermore that this hardness of heart was in itself reprehensible. No doubt tyrants in actuality had always been hard-hearted – a tender-hearted oppressor is hard to imagine – but in the ancient philosophical tradition no emphasis had been placed upon this aspect since the central concern had been with rationality and the curbing of destructive emotion. The medieval tyrant was, however, hard-hearted, and this could be seen in his lack of pity for his victims, his refusal to grant clemency, or exhibit any humane feeling. The exemplary tyrant, Nero, gazed unmoved upon the body of his own mother, murdered upon his orders:

> he lookede on every halve uppon hir colde deede body, ne no teer ne wette his face, but he was so hardherted that he myghte ben domesman or juge of hir dede beaute.
>
> (*Bo.* II, m. 6, 8–12)

A picture of the tyrant whose heart is affected neither by filial piety nor

99

humane pity is found in the Latin text, but it is to the medieval translators' tendency to gloss their original that we owe the explicit diagnosis of hardness of heart. A hint is given in Jean de Meun's version (*fu si dur*), and is expanded by Chaucer to the familiar compound *hardherted*.

In medieval Latin, too, condemnation by this phrase is found. Gower, we may remember, stigmatized Richard with the words 'rex induratum cor semper habet'. This hardness of heart prevented him from extending compassion or mercy to the victims of his atrocities: 'Nil pietas munit, quem tunc manus invida punit'.[1] How marked is the contrast made with 'pius Henricus.' In *his* hour of triumph Henry is mild and benign. He seeks no vengeance on his enemies; indeed Gower says that his enemies found no hostility in him. Rather than savagely condemn to death 'the *pietosus* king raised up and graciously prolonged the life' of the unfortunate Bagot. Unlike the 'most cruel' Richard, who even denies a defeated enemy an honest burial, 'probus Henricus', ever the friend of *pietas*, delivers over Richard's own body to proper Christian interment (III, 452–3). Like Theseus in Chaucer's *Knight Tale*, for whom *pitee* is the precursor of mercy, Henry's heart is accessible to pity, and indeed, in the contrast maintained between him and Richard, it might legitimately be considered his distinguishing characteristic. If Richard is *rex tyrannus*, *crudelissimus rex*, whose heart is *induratum*, then Henry is *mitis, probus*, and, above all, *rex pietosus*. The distinction between the tyrant and his opposite is re-defined in terms of affectivity rather than reason, and the validity of this re-definition would immediately have been recognized by Chaucer's Parson. Selecting his quotation from Seneca's *De Clementia*, and inadvertently altering its sense, the Parson states:

> Ther is no thing moore convenable to a man of heigh estaat than debonairetee and pitee.[2]
>
> (*CT*. X, 467)

Henry, then, is the ideal king from whom humanity, pity and mercy flow; Richard is the hard-hearted tyrant.

In Chaucer's English usage, and that of the courtly tradition as a whole, we find the reflection of this opposition. Hardness of heart is associated with the failure to feel compassion on the sufferings of others, whatever their cause, and whether any previous relationship existed or not. This is well illustrated in Chaucer's translation of the immensely influential *Roman de la Rose*, where the allegorical portrait of Sorrow acts as a stimulus to a pity which, it is alleged, would affect even the hardest heart:

> *In world nys wight so hard of herte*
> *That hadde sen her sorowes smerte,*
> *That nolde have had of her pyte.*
> (*RR*. 333–5)

This passage finds an echo in *Troilus and Criseyde* to emphasize the grief of the lovers at their imminent separation. Their sorrow is such:

> *That in this world ther nys so hard an herte,*
> *That nolde han rewed on hire peynes smerte.*
> (*TC*. IV, 1140–1)

Nevertheless, the man whose heart is of such a temper that it is inaccessible to pity is common enough in Chaucer's poetry. He, and often she, occurs in all those situations of life into which we have found the image of the tyrant transformed in our discussion of him as a symbol of injustice and irrationality. The Wife of Bath is so inhumane as to laugh heartily at the sufferings of her husbands, and her laughter is echoed by tyrannical Fortune. Like the Wife, she is 'so hard that sche laugheth and scorneth the wepynges of hem, the whiche sche hath maked wepe with hir free wille' (*Bo*. II, m. 1, 12–14). Tyrannical fathers, too, who mercilessly persecute their children, may be called *harde* (*CT*. II, 857; *TC*. IV, 95); but above all, in the courtly tradition, hardness of heart, like other aspects of tyranny, is found in the relations between lovers. The parallel is explicit in the *Merchant's Tale*, where it is placed in the ironic context of May's compliance:

> *Som tyrant is, as ther be many oon,*
> *That hath an herte as hard as any stoon,*
> *Which wolde han lat hym sterven in the place.*
> (*CT*. IV, 1989–91)

In the *Complaint to his Lady*, hardness is seen to displace womanly virtues:

> *But the more that I love yow, goodly free,*
> *The lasse fynde I that ye loven me;*
> *Allas! whan shal that harde wit amende?*
> *Wher is now al your wommanly pitee,*
> *Your gentilesse and your debonairetee?*
> (98–102)

Outside the courtly tradition, hardness is also encountered as a condition which inhibits emotional sensitivity. In the *General Prologue*, the Friar contemplates the case of the man who is of such obduracy that, although desirous to do penance for his sins, he cannot find it in himself to show remorse. Tears of contrition are beyond his emotional constitution. A man of such hard heart, claims the Friar, may show his repentance by a cash payment to the friars. More reputable clerical opinion held a different, if more puritanical, view of the matter. The exemplary Parson tends to regard that hardness of heart which denies visible signs of contrition as a species of *malitia*, obduracy in sin, and a sin against the

Holy Spirit (X, 486).³ From the point of view of the religious, equally as well as that of the courtly man, hardness of heart, a condition which precluded pity and remorse, was deplorable. Although no literary capital is made of the fact in the passages mentioned, it is evident that the vice of the unrepentant sinner is identical psychologically with that of the tyrant. In fourteenth-century writings, hardness of heart, and consequent lack of compassion are deficiencies which are decried as features in the tyrant *topos*, but they extend beyond it, and historically, they invaded it from outside.

I have felt justified in speaking of hardness of heart without further comment, since the phrase is widely current in modern English and its sense is readily understood, at least for the purposes of the discussion so far. However, to understand the fourteenth-century connotations of the phrase, and of the adjective *hard* in the senses we have been discussing, a lengthy digression will be necessary. We shall try to understand the implications of this usage by considering the verbal company it keeps, and also by the way it fits into the medieval psychology of cognition.

In the second Book of *Troilus and Criseyde*, Pandarus undertakes to persuade his niece to give her love to his friend Troilus. The situation is one borrowed from the world of romance. Pandarus, seated upon a stone of jasper on a gold-adorned cushion, receives a letter from Criseyde which contains the first indications of her growing feeling for Troilus. Pandarus turns to her and says:

> nece myn, Criseyde,
> That ye to hym of hard now ben ywonne
> Oughte he be glad, by God and yonder sonne;
> For-whi men seith, 'impressiounes lighte
> Ful lightly ben ay redy to the flighte.
>
> But ye han played the tirant neigh to longe,
> And hard was it youre herte for to grave.
> (*TC*. II, 1235–41)

Here Pandarus inhabits a world of figures and mixed metaphors, yoking together hardness of heart, tyranny, and words like *impressiounes* and *grave*. These latter words appear to take up the metaphor of hardness and relate it to the impressions made by a seal in wax, and an engraving upon some hard stone or metal. Criseyde's heart has been hard, resistant to the impression of Troilus's worth, and like a tyrant, she has been unmoved by his suffering; but, as Chaucer remarks in the *Franklin's Tale*:

> By proces, as ye knowen everichoon,
> Men may so longe graven in a stoon
> Til som figure therinne emprented be.
> (V, 830–2)

In Pandarus's estimation, Troilus has succeeded in making an impression upon Criseyde, and the implication of the imagery is that the difficulty, or the length of the process of creating this impression, bodes well. In the same way as figures laboriously cut in stone will outlast those impressed in soft wax, so will Troilus's effect upon Criseyde's heart outlast too easy an impression. Such imagery, in which the creation of a figure, an image or impression upon a material, hard or soft, represents the heart's receipt of emotion or sense data, could be multiplied from Chaucer's writings. In few of these occurrences does the image of the tyrant also figure; yet the conception of the tyrant as a man whose heart will not accept the impression of pity occasionally brings together two disparate streams of imagery. Whilst the tyrant image is descended from popular moral and political philosophy, the image of impressions upon the heart is derived from cognitive psychology and from medical science. These two streams meet in the synthesis of courtly literature.

All the major systems of cognitive psychology which descended from the ancient world to the men of the Middle Ages envisaged the process of perception as the gathering of sense data followed by its resolution into images which were, so to speak, projected on to some receptive faculty of the human organism, or less concretely, of the soul. This is seen as a mechanical process, and the operation of cognition and committal to memory is by an analogous mechanical process. The explanatory imagery used of the process is of very ancient lineage, for both Plato and Aristotle, when discussing memory, speak of the impression of images made by a signet ring in wax, and they are echoed by most of the classical instructors of the Middle Ages: Cicero, Quintilian, the author of the *Rhetorica ad Herennium*, Martianus Capella, and St. Augustine.[4] Boethius's account of Stoic opinions on the matter was translated by Chaucer together with some explanations added by the thirteenth century commentator, Nicholas Trevet. The Stoics, he says:

> wenden that ymages and sensibilities (*that is to seyn, sensible ymaginaciouns or ellis ymaginaciouns of sensible thingis*) weren enprientid into soules fro bodyes withouteforth (*as who seith that thilke Stoyciens wenden that sowle had ben nakid of itself, as a mirour or a clene parchemyn, so that alle figures most first comen fro thingis fro withoute into soules, and ben emprientid into soules*); ryght as we ben wont sometyme by a swift poyntel to fycchen lettres emprientid in the smothnesse or in the pleynesse of the table of wex or in the parchemyn that ne hath no figure ne note in it.
>
> (*Bo.* V, m. 4, 6–19)

Boethius uses the familiar image, but rejects the Stoic view of perception, preferring a neo-Platonic notion in which knowledge of the external world proceeds from a process of recognition by which the intelligence

'matches' its knowledge of the divine forms with their material represent-
atives perceived through the senses in the world of everyday. Nevertheless, his conception still requires the imagery of impressions, and it
would be misleading to try to relate this imagery to any particular philosophical system. It is found in all of them, playing a rather different role in
their overall theory of knowledge yet always referring to the process of
sense-perception. Popular imagination seized upon these images of the
perception process, so that they are found commonly in literature as well
as technical writings.

We have referred to the use of the word *impressioun* and the common
analogies associated with it as the use of imagery, yet such a literary
classification is misleading, for this is not in its technical use a metaphor
at all. When we today speak of another being hard-hearted, or of ourselves
having an impression, or being impressed, we may dimly perceive two
dead metaphors in our usage. To Chaucer, however, not only were these
apparently disparate phrases intimately connected, but they were to be
understood literally. True, they were somewhat removed from their
proper contexts, but these proper, literal, contexts were those of live and
vigorous scientific theory. The imagery of seals in wax, of stones being
engraved, were not metaphors so much as explanatory analogies of scientific belief. In John Trevisa's translation of a favourite medieval
encyclopaedia, Bartholomew Anglicus's *De Proprietatibus Rerum*, the
medieval physicians' view of perception is given. For them, the brain is
actually divided into three cells or cerebral ventricles.[5] The foremost of
these contains the power of the imagination which forms mental images
from data collected by the senses (p. 98). It is this to which Chaucer refers
when he discusses the suffering of Arcite tormented by the 'loveris
maladye of Hereos' and mania caused by melancholic humour in his 'celle
fantastik' (*CT*. I, 1376).[6] This foremost cell is actually considered to be
warm and soft (pp. 173–4) so as to receive more readily the impressions of
the senses. Indeed the rapidity with which the mind seizes upon impressions fed to it by the senses is explicitly considered to be dependent upon
the physical consistency of the material of the cells of the individual's
brain (p. 176). Hence, when discussing the courtly psychology of perception, we should not imagine that the language of poets is utterly divorced
from that of science; rather, it frequently echoes it at some remove.

Yet Chaucer, in common with other poets, does not cleave to any one
doctrine. He can quote the view of the physicians, but more commonly
follows the philosophers. He does not, however, subscribe to any particular philosophical system. His spirit is more akin to the Boethian metres
than the prose: he was no philosopher, but a 'philosophicall poete', and
preferred that philosophical teaching which had became thoroughly
poeticized and absorbed by literary tradition. It is, for example, normally

104

the case in poetic usage that the heart rather than the brain, or some abstract faculty of the soul, is the recipient of sense impressions. Stoic tradition associated the heart with the faculty of imagination, and scientific opinion held it to be the centre of feeling, but the specific image of the heart as physically resistant to impression seems for Chaucer to have belonged rather to literature than to the contemporary scientific writings.[7]

The discussion of perception in vernacular literature nevertheless employed certain widely disseminated scientific assumptions together with their technical vocabulary, and it will be necessary to recognize some of these before we can go on to discuss courtly psychology. Briefly, everyone in the Middle Ages agreed that Man was, according to the scholastic definition, 'a resonable two-foted beest' (Bo. V, p. 4, 199). To this, the Parson adds a more obviously Christian qualification, ascribing it to an untraceable 'philosophre': 'A man is a quyk thyng, by nature debonaire and tretable to goodnesse' (CT. X, 658). Taken together, these quotations form a complete, if brief, popular philosophical definition of Man. As part of the animal creation, he is an organism capable of growth, movement, sensation and reproduction, but as a man, he also possesses the faculties of reason and will. These are what essentially distinguish man from the beasts. Like animals, he is possessed of five bodily wittes (i.e. the five senses) whose object is the material world around him; he possesses also the power of ymaginacioun by which sense data is formed into images, as it were, reflections of the world around him, and which can re-create these images in the absence of the objects themselves. Unlike the animals, however, he also had a wille, an intellectual faculty which predisposes him to seek and desire whatever it perceives to be good, and a faculty of resoun which analyses universal features from the simple images created by the ymaginacioun, giving him the ability to learn by inductive and deductive reasoning. In its function of guiding the wille by distinguishing true from apparent good, the resoun is often called prudence. A more elevated level of the resoun is known as intellect, and this is that rational level which perceives theological truths and those things inconceivable from ordinary experience. It is therefore a faculty not much invoked by the literary tradition, which concerns itself more with senses, will and reason.

Within its sensible function, below the operations of reason, the soul has various capacities: the receipt of sense data (vertu of felinge); the envisaging of things which are not, or which may never appear before the eyes, such as green knights, golden hills, or unicorns (vertu ymaginatif); the simple discrimination of good from evil in a particular situation directed towards the preservation of the individual (vertu aestimativa). All these are possessed by animals, and indeed may guide most men,

105

unthinkingly, through everyday matters; but all are placed below the truest fulfilment of the unique capacity of Man, the operation of the reason, and its guidance of the will. Memory (*vertu of mynde*) proved difficult to classify in this schema, and is placed by some authors at the level of sub-rational 'thinking'. Albertus Magnus allowed it to remain at this level, but spoke, like Aristotle, of a power of 'reminiscence' operating as a rational use of memory.[8] Aquinas saw memory as essentially one of the sub-rational faculties, which at the same time partook of the rational since, for him, even abstract knowledge is derived by way of the senses. To a scholastic of Aquinas' persuasion, it is considered impossible for a man to know anything except by an image produced through the senses. The essential feature of the acquisition of all knowledge, of all communication between human beings, between the individual and the world around him, is seen to be the conversion of raw data produced by the senses into *phantasmata*, or images, in the *ymaginacioun*. The image is an essential first stage in perception, so it is therefore not surprising to see theoreticians exploiting the supposed mechanics of the mind to make their purpose more efficacious. St. Thomas, for example, recommends that abstract ideas should be committed to memory in the form of sensible images, whilst the theoreticians of preaching allege that ideas are more readily available to the minds of the congregation if presented in the form of images.[9]

Chaucer's words for these mental images vary. Frequently he refers to them simply as *ymages*, but also as *figures* and *formes*. They, together with whole complexes of images, like *lessouns* or *wordes*, are spoken of as being *impressed*, *emprented*, or even *graven* upon the *ymaginacioun*, or, as it is sometimes called, the *fantasie*. From here they are transferred to the *mynde*, *memorie*, or *remembrance*, which Pecock tells us is composed of a harder material to facilitate their retention.[10] Less technically and precisely, but much more frequently in literature, the *ymages* are impressed into the *herte*, *soule* or *thoght*.

Conventionally, in the literary treatment of love, perception of the beloved is essentially visual. The appearance of the lady strikes piercingly through the eye, leaving a visual image powerfully impressed in the soul and stimulating desire. Troilus, wandering through the temple of Palladion, and Palamon, glancing through his prison bars, are affected in much the same way:

> *He cast his eye upon Emelya,*
> *And therwithal he bleynte and cride, 'A!'*
> *As though he stongen were unto the herte.*
>
> (*CT*. I, 1077–9)

But the impression of the visual image is only an initial stage. The delectation of the beloved may be built up into a much more complex, composite image derived from other senses. The Man in Black sits lamenting his former lady, in effect carefully reconstituting her image from the storehouse of his *memorie*. His feat of recollection has won the praise of critics, who admire the refreshing blend of the traditional, rhetorical *effictio* (list of physical features) with the *notatio* (list of moral qualities).[11] It is however noticeable that the passage has a schematic organization of its own, but rather in the way in which cognitive processes were alleged to operate. That is to say that the physical features of the sensible image of Blanche preserved in the Man in Black's memory are each given an appropriate moral significance. If we were to relate this to that rhetorical doctrine which dealt with the memorizing of lengthy speeches, and which exploited the natural workings of the memory and perception to do so, we might say that each item of her physical appearance acts as a kind of index of an associated moral quality. The description descends as in the rhetorical *effictio* from her head downwards, replacing the expected reference to her mouth by an account of her manner of speech. Her eyes evoke a dissertation on her manner of looking. She guards the significance of her glances with the decorum that befits a lady. All in all, the reminiscences of the Man in Black, although they do not correspond precisely to the conventional format of *effictio*, are nevertheless schematized by contemporary beliefs about memory and perception.[12]

A briefer and less elaborate account of the lover's recreation of the image of his desired object, which may be compared with this, is that which appears preparatory to Tarquin's rape of Lucrece. The image is created exclusively from a series of sense impressions, and it comes to Tarquin's mind as he walks reflecting on his meeting with Lucrece:

> Th'ymage of hire recordynge alwey newe:
> 'Thus lay hire her, and thus fresh was hyre hewe;
> Thus sat, thus spak, thus span; this was hire chere;
> Thus fayr she was, and this was hire manere.'
> Al this conseit hys herte hath newe ytake.
>
> . . .   .
>
> Ryght so, thogh that hire forme were absent,
> The plesaunce of hire forme was present;
> But natheles, nat plesaunce but delit,
> Or an unrightful talent, with dispit –
>
> (*LGW*. 1760–71)

The recreated image provokes that wicked delight and desire which leads to a notorious rape.

The point where sense impressions are received and formed into the composite image of the beloved is rarely specified in amatory psychology by any other expression than the *herte*. In *Troilus and Criseyde* this image-forming role of the heart is acknowledged by referring to it as the 'brestes ye' (I, 453). Images of all kinds, simple and complex sense images, pieces of information, words, even emotions like joy and pity, are all indiscriminately spoken of as being impressed upon the heart. In the language of poetry, therefore, the heart does service for the *celle fantastik* of the physicians and the *ymaginacioun* of philosophical discourse.

The hard heart of the tyrant and the churl, the heart of the homicide in particular is conventionally considered to resist impression of all kinds, and this is evil. Yet, in love poetry, as we have seen, initial resistance may have good results, for images which are laboriously engraved are likely to be lasting, so that initial resistance is associated with eventual constancy and stability. Nevertheless, a sudden and unusually forceful impression, too, can be seen as having an enduring quality which springs rather from its force than the excessive tenderness of the individual heart. Troilus takes such a 'fixe and depe impressioun' (I, 298) at his first sight of Criseyde, and after the consummation of their love, he lies alone going over their first meeting, fixing every detail in his memory:

> *And in his thought gan up and doun to wynde*
> *Hire wordes alle, and every countenaunce,*
> *And fermely impressen in his mynde*
> *The leeste point that to him was plesaunce.*
>
> (III, 1541–4)

An image so forcefully impressed into the heart may lead to a disorder of the lover's power of perception. It is a measure of the sensitivity of the heart, the force of the impression, or of both, that the impression is so fixed and deep that it alters perception of the world outside. An excellent example of this is found in the mid-fourteenth century alliterative romance of *William of Palerne* where repeated contemplation of the image of the beloved causes his image to become so fixed in the heroine's heart that it cannot be erased (448); furthermore, it overwhelms new images of other men formed by data from the eyes.[13] Whenever Melior is confronted with another man, she sees instead the image of her lover, William:

> *him so propirli haue i peinted. & portreide in herte,*
> *þat me semes in my siȝt. he sittes euer meke.*
> *What man so ich mete wiþ. or mele wiþ speche,*
> *Me thinkes euerich þrowe. þat barn is þat oþer;*
> *& fele times haue ich fonded. to flitte it fro þouȝt,*
> *but witerly al in wast. þan worche ich euer.*
>
> (619–24)

The lover's total absorption with the image he creates of his beloved is classically exemplified by the story of Pygmalion, the sculptor who created an image without a corresponding living form, and fell hopelessly in love with his creation. Gower tells the story (*CA*. IV, 371ff.) in a rather individual way as an *exemplum* against pusillanimity, a sub-division of the vice of sloth, applied to love affairs. His rather contrived handling of the story is intended to encourage the lover to overcome imaginary fears and openly express his desires; for were not Pygmalion's prayers over-heard by Venus who graciously granted his wishes, turning his statue into a living woman? Despite this twist in the telling, the implications of Gower's tale are clear enough: Pygmalion's situation is in fact that of the typical lover, overwhelmed by an image produced in his own *ymaginacioun*, and unable to approach the real lady who is its origin.

If the lover's waking hours are spent in contemplation of his lady's image, in sleep dreams and visions may spring up from the impression he has received. Chaucer refers to the plight of lovers in the *House of Fame:*

> *Or that the cruel lyf unsofte*
> *Which these ilke lovers leden*
> *That hopen over-muche or dreden,*
> *That purely her impressions*
> *Causen hem to have visions.*
> (*HF*. 36–40)

The identification of the source of such dreams, dreams which trouble the deserted Troilus in Book Five of his story, or Chauntecleer in the *Nun's Priest's Tale,* or which form the subject matter of the *Parliament of Fowls,* is a repetitive theme of Chaucer's work. Are they divine warnings, indications of deeper truths, or of things to come? Or are they the result of the preoccupations of everyday life impressed upon the memory? Or, indeed, are they merely the consequences of an ill-considered diet? It is a typically Chaucerian stratagem to leave us in uncertainty.

In dreams, the *ymaginacioun* is not purely a passive, image-forming faculty. It can function creatively, building scenarios of varying credibility from everyday experience.[14] Both asleep and awake, these fabrications of the imagination may be of a terrifying nature. Chaucer's Miller is scornful of those who are scared by these idle fancies:

> *Lo, which a greet thyng is affeccioun!*
> *Men may dyen of ymaginacioun,*
> *So depe may impressioun be take.*
> (*CT*. I, 3611–3)

The Miller's scorn derives from the fact that he contrasts himself, a hard-headed and intelligent man, with those fools who are dominated by imagination; in Gower's terms, the victims of pusillanimity. The Miller, and those who like Pygmalion overcome imaginary fears, recognize that *ymaginacioun*, along with *memorie* and *vis aestimativa*, although they possess a kind of cogitative power, are yet merely irrational faculties.

There is a tendency, when watching a dog herding sheep or a fox shaking off pursuit, to assume that animals possess some rudimentary ability to 'think.' In the Middle Ages, it was accepted that animals, just as human beings, possessed and demonstrated an ability to organize their lives at the level of everyday practicality in a way which did not necessarily involve the use of an elevated reasoning power such as that of prudence. As we have seen, the memory was considered to belong more essentially to the sub-rational level, so that the recall of images into the imagination need not involve rational faculties at all. When the imagination exercised its creative role in this way, the *vis aestimativa* – which was also called the *racio sensibilis* or 'reasoning power with reference to sense data' – also fulfilled a quasi-rational role, deciding on the desirability or otherwise of the sense-images and scenarios formed by the imagination. According to Bartholomew Anglicus, this power of *racio sensibilis* (*vis aestimativa*) made an animal *war and wys*. An identical phrase is used also to indicate the function of the higher rational power of prudence, and in point of fact, popular usage often failed to distinguish between the lower levels of *prudence* and the operation of the *racio sensibilis*. This ability of animals to determine courses of action beforehand is most impressively demonstrated by Chaucer's account of the fox who threatens Chauntecleer:

> *A col-fox, ful of sly iniquitee,*
> *That in the grove hadde woned yeres three,*
> *By heigh ymaginacioun forncast*
> *The same nyght thurghout the hegges brast.*
> (*CT*. VII, 3215–8)

Here the use of the verb *forncast*, which we have also seen used in reference to the exercise of *prudence*, decisively proves the ability of the animal *ymaginacioun* to plan events in advance. *Ymaginacioun* is the faculty by which plots are laid, for this phrasing is repeated by the Parson to refer to premeditated sin:

> The especes that sourden of Pride, soothly whan they sourden of malice ymagined, avised, and forncast, or elles of usage, been deedly synnes.
>
> (X, 448)

A similar phrasing is used in the *Appeal of Thomas Usk* to imply malice aforethought.[15] It is evidently a legal phrasing:

> in thys wise, be fals compassement & ymaginacion to-forn cast, many of the worthiest of the town sholde haue be ther-by enpesched, and be execucion ydo so vpon hem, that they sholde noght haue bore no-more estat in the town.

The decoration of the Temple of Mars in the *Knight's Tale*, where pre-meditation precedes execution, serves to emphasize this point. The plotting is the work of the *ymaginacioun*:

> *Ther saugh I first the derke ymaginyng*
> *Of Felonye, and al the compassyng.*
>
> (I, 1995–6)

In the *Summoner's Tale*, a flatulent churl sets a difficult problem of *ars-metrike* as a trap for avaricious friars. His ruse is described by the lord of the manor as a work of the imagination, and he finds it scarcely credible that a churl should possess such imaginative resources. Now although popular usage, as represented in Chaucer's works, tends to confuse the borderline between rational planning and the functions of the imagination, the lord's incredulity does not represent a high regard for imagination so much as a low one for churls. Churls as a class are not expected to show such resource even in such a humble faculty as imagination. And indeed it is normally quite clear that *ymaginacioun* is regarded as a humble faculty whatever the vagaries of usage. *Ymaginacioun* and *vis aestimativa*, being irrational, were also amoral, since only rational consideration could guarantee the morality of actions. As such, for any author concerned with manners and morals, they were suspect. To the moralist, the excessive prominence of sub-rational faculties in relation to reason was to be condemned. Now, since every man is, from time to time, a moralist – especially when contemplating the deeds of others – it is inevitable that the allegation of thinking only at the imaginative level should imply criticism, and consequently that the use of the word *ymaginacioun*, and its synonym *fantasye*, should develop pejorative connotations. In Middle English, as if in preparation for Coleridge's later distinction, those unfavourable connotations are more commonly evoked by the use of the word *fantasye*, although it is important to realize that *ymaginacioun* too is frequently subject to the same pejoration.

The Miller's scorn for those who die from terror of idle fantasies unchallenged by rational criticism, is phrased at first in terms of *ymaginacioun*, as we have seen; later, however, as he warms to his theme, he alters his wording in giving details of the carpenter's fears:

> *he was wood,*
> *He was agast so of Nowelis flood*
> *Thurgh fantasie, that of his vanytee*
> *He hadde yboght hym knedyng tubbes thre.*
>
> (*CT*. I, 3833–6)

The gullible landlord has fallen for his tenant's trick; he has accepted without question the picture drawn by Nicholas of a world engulfed by water in which only three will be saved, floating above the waves in kneading tubs. His actions have been dictated by this awe-inspiring, cataclysmic, and ridiculous image, and he has thus been shown up as a fool, a man who doesn't use his head. His neighbours pour in to witness his downfall and 'gan laughen at his fantasye'. The carpenter has made himself patently ridiculous, and in quotations like this last the word *fantasye* is contextually synonymous with foolishness.

Other attitudes to *fantasye* may, however, be found: it is admitted to by one at least who is anything but a fool. When the Wife of Bath judges that she has sufficiently prepared her audience for the strong meat of her prologue – and she intends assertions which will come close to blasphemy, as well as injuring individual sensibilities – she asks for the company's indulgence. Her excuse is the familiar one that what she will speak must not be taken in earnest: it is a *game*, a jest, and entertainment for the road. She is certainly a good companion, but to the sober moralist a crafty villain too, for what she is suggesting to the pilgrims is what she once used as an argument for dominion over her husband. She suggests the subjection of the rational faculties to the lower levels of the soul. She begs the pilgrims not to apply rational condemnation to the fabrications of her *fantasye:*

> *I praye to al this compaignye,*
> *If that I speke after my fantasye,*
> *As taketh nat agrief of that I seye;*
> *For myn entente is nat but for to pleye.*
> (III, 189–92)

Under the colour of a jest, she can tell her immoral memoirs without challenge, and by representing them as products of *fantasye*, without moral responsibility too.

To those who are uninvolved in the fantasies of others, they may seem comic, ridiculous, or damnable; in any case, they are likely to be taken to illustrate the trivial-mindedness of their originator. But to the man experiencing these images, they may have rivetting force and may occupy his entire attention. The narrator of the *Book of the Duchess* tells us that, like Melior in *William of Palerne*, his *mynde* is fully occupied by *sorwful ymaginacioun*, so that he experiences neither feelings nor ordinary sense impressions:

> *Such fantasies ben in myn hede,*
> *So I not what is best to doo.*
> (BD. 28–9)

The lover 'refigures' his beloved in his heart (*TC.* V, 473) so that it reflects like a mirror, but unlike a mirror, its images are in the past or the future.

The reflection of images shared by both the heart of the lover and the mirror nevertheless makes the latter a potent image of the operation of the imagination. It is, however, a deeply ambiguous image, for although it is to be expected that a lover should eagerly contemplate the impression of his beloved, yet the action is one of essential irrationality and therefore amoral. Whether it develops the pejorative undertones associated with idle fancy depends upon a subtle interplay between the attitudes of the author and his audience. Deliberate emphasis of the irrationality of the process will carry with it a strong possibility of moral criticism. Troilus is overwhelmed by the sight of Criseyde at the feast of the Palladion and he retires to his chamber, where, we are told, he made 'a mirour of his mynde, / In which he saugh al holly hir figure' (TC. I, 365–6).[16] Perhaps there is a slight air of superiority in the narrator's choice of the verb *imaginynge* a few lines later, for the sense is clearly that of empty and uncritical fantasy, occurring as it does in the environment of repeated images of irrationality. Yet the narrator is not condemnatory, at least no more so than an adherent of a rationally-based ethic must be of any lover: the weight of condemnation is not brought to bear on Troilus, is not felt to be inherent in the use of the mirror image. Elsewhere, however, the mirror image clearly *does* imply condemnation, and this it does in two principal ways: firstly, in contexts where the contrast with rational procedure is explicitly invoked, and, secondly, where the mirror image is used as a symbol of instability.

In the world of the *Merchant's Tale*, Januarie is a wilful and determined scorner of the counsels of moral philosophy, which he lightly dismisses as mere 'scole-termes', inapplicable to his own actions. Like the Wife of Bath, he repeatedly requires his friends to suspend rational criticism of his actions. The image of the mirror is applied to his conduct in an extended metaphor of lack of discrimination:

> *Heigh fantasye and curious bisynesse*
> *Fro day to day gan in the soule impresse*
> *Of Januarie aboute his mariage.*
> *Many fair shap and many a fair visage*
> *Ther passeth thurgh his herte nyght by nyght,*
> *As whoso tooke a mirour, polisshed bryght,*
> *And sette it in a commune market-place,*
> *Thanne sholde he se ful many a figure pace*
> *By his mirour; and in the same wyse*
> *Gan Januarie inwith his thoght devyse*
> *Of maydens whiche that dwelten hym bisyde.*
> (CT. IV, 1577–87)

Throughout the early part of his story, Januarie is clearly represented as a wilful and improvident seeker after marriage. His mind is a mirror, and this suggests both his lack of consideration and his instability. Within the context of the *Canterbury Tales*, the point is best made by the contrast between the behaviour of Januarie in seeking a wife and that of Walter in the Clerk's exemplary tale:

> He noght with wanton lookyng of folye
> His eyen caste on hire, but in sad wyse
> Upon hir chiere he wolde hym ofte avyse.
>
> (CT. IV, 236–8)

Walter's preconsideration is rational, dependent upon the perception of virtue rather than a mere sensible image. There is no doubt that the use of the mirror image in the description of Januarie, occurring as it does among accusations of *fol-haste*, is condemnatory. The *ymaginacioun* has an essential function in arriving at decisions on actions, but if it usurps the role of *prudence*, no good can result. What the fortunes of life deliver up to the individual should be subjected to the scrutiny of reason rather than the reflections of the sub-rational faculties. The correct attitude to the tyrant Fortune is expressed by Chaucer in two lines from a short poem to which we have referred earlier:

> Yit is me left the light of my resoun,
> To knowen frend fro fo in thy mirour
>
> (Fortune, 9–10)

In this quotation, the self-sufficiency, the implied security offered by reason contrasts with the instability of Fortune, and the image of the mirror becomes an image of transience. Mirrors, like shadows, are momentary images which pass away as quickly as the real object which they echo. Strangely, the image of the shadow is not used by Chaucer of the fleeting impression of the lover's heart, but another short poem, of doubtful authorship, echoes in reverse the encouraging words of Pandarus to Troilus with which we opened this discussion:

> Right as a mirour nothing may enpresse,
> But, lightly as it cometh, so mot it pace,
> So fareth your love.
>
> (W. Unc., 8–10)

The mirror, with its momentary images, can become the epitome of the hard heart which nothing can impress.

In Chaucer's world, too hard a heart is reprehensible. Simply for the process of perception to operate, a certain tenderness is required in the heart, *ymaginacioun*, or *celle fantastik*. But beyond the physiological processes of perception, the degree of hardness or tenderness of the heart becomes problematic, subject to argument, and relative. Too hard a heart is associated with lack of pity and tyranny, and with that mocking *newefangelnesse* of a heart ever-ready to accept new images without deep impression. Yet a certain firmness is required to preserve impressions and

114

is a condition of constancy. A heart may be too soft, too easily affected, too deeply impressed. Such a one may be overwhelmed by the products of the *ymaginacioun* to unreasoning fear, the lover's malady, or to chronic inaction. Worse, the scenarios of an over-active *ymaginacioun* may supplant the dispensations of *prudence*, so that the man's actions lack moral significance, and he becomes no better than a beast. Soft-heartedness and the sub-rational faculties are indeed essential both to man's emotional and to his rational being, but the control of the sub-rational faculties and the appropriate state of the heart are a persistent problem in poetry which deals with love and philosophy.

CHAPTER SEVEN

Within Reason

IN ANTIQUITY, AS in the Middle Ages, the figure of the tyrant is a symbol of the disordered personality, distinguished by his irrationality and his furious emotions. He is opposed by the philosopher, whose life is ordered by reason and who lives in endless calm. The philosophical tradition held up examples of patience but not of human kindliness; the contrast between the two symbols of tyrant and philosopher was made largely in terms of reason. But, as we have seen, in passages representing ideal kings, Chaucer and Gower frequently build the contrast between the ideal monarch and the tyrant upon the contrast between the former's benignity and the latter's pitilessness; in other words, the contrast is markedly an emotional one. Herod rages in a way that the philosophical tradition would have taken to represent irrationality – and it could still be considered so – but his vengeful *ire* is now frequently considered to contrast with the *pitee* exercised by Theseus, for example, and the distinction tends to be seen in terms of malevolent and benevolent emotional attitudes. Such an assessment does not square very well with the values of the philosophical tradition, for pity and kindliness, irrational impulses as they are, were considered by the Stoics to be simply amoral, and, since they tend to disturb the tranquillity of the philosopher, they could be regarded as evil.

Let us recall the basis of Stoic morality. It was, in brief, fixity of behaviour in accordance with reason. Stability and constancy in a rationally-ordered life was the key to virtue: 'Virtue may be defined as a habit of mind in harmony with reason and the order of nature.'[1] This dominantly rational ethic persisted into the Middle Ages, but was modified by the

Christian conception of the need to reconcile the individual will with that of an all-powerful creator God. Fixity in purpose becomes allied to constancy in faith, and rational guidance is re-defined as the divine plan for creation, which it is the business of reason to perceive. God, reason, and nature are neatly reconciled by the scholastic formulation that the laws of reason are the voice of God written in nature. In other words, the order of the observable world is testimony to God's rational plan. Thus reason remains closely associated with virtue:

> Cum enim bonum hominis consistat in ratione sicut radice, tanto istud bonum perfectius quanto ad plura quae homini conveniunt derivari potest.
>
> (*ST.*, 1a2ae, 24, 3)

> For the root of all human goodness lies in the reason; human excellence will therefore be the greater, the greater the number of human elements under rational control.

Aquinas finds human goodness to depend upon reason. A rather less exclusively rational viewpoint, expressed in the *Book of Vices and Virtues* and ascribed to St. Bernard, really amounts to the same thing:

> Vertue is non oþer þing but assent bitwixe resoun and wille.
>
> (p. 152)

The will is by its nature compelled to seek good, but identification of true good is the function of reason, so that although the impulse to good may lie elsewhere, the realization of virtue still depends upon reason in medieval Christian belief.

Now, none of these Christian thinkers would have denied the value of emotions such as pity. Statements restricting good to the operation of reason would simply have been considered incomplete. Although the primacy of reason remained unchallenged, there was a readiness to accept that less elevated functions played a valuable rôle in human goodness. Indeed, even the Stoics of Roman times seem to have found the blanket condemnation of human emotion a questionable doctrine. Cicero, although not himself a Stoic, used many of their ideas on psychology and ethics, and was in the habit of considering emotion as a weakness; nevertheless, in *De Finibus*, 3.35 he deliberately avoids the traditional reference to emotions as a sickness (*aegritudo*) of the soul and prefers instead the more colourless term *perturbatio*. Indeed both he and Seneca present the later Stoics as accepting the concept of an emotion pervaded or controlled by reason. Opposed to the disorders (*perturbationes*) of the soul are the rational states of emotion (*constantiae*). Thus irrational desire, *libido*, is opposed to *voluntas* 'which is desire according to reason.' Similarly, *laetitia* (*hilaritas*) opposes rational *gaudium*, and *metus*

117

opposes *cautio*. Categorization according to the rationality of the emotional state becomes a common one, and indeed is used by Seneca to distinguish pity from mercy.[2]

This willingness to accept the existence of rational states of emotion which could legitimately be experienced by the wise man is of vital importance to medieval ideals of virtuous conduct. Certain desirable emotions could be seen to be sanctioned by reason, and so long as they remained under rational control many emotions could be considered beneficial. In themselves, emotions remained amoral. A man cannot be blamed for fearing or growing angry, but only according to whether such emotions are in harmony or in conflict with reason (*ST.*, 1a2ae, 24.1). The notion of the acceptability of emotions 'within reason' becomes the arbiter of morality, and we should not forget that this also implies 'within the law of God', even if this implication is often not expressed.

In adopting this modification of their opposition to emotions, the later Stoics had been admitting a proportion of Aristotlean psychology to their teaching, and indeed the *rapprochement* between the Stoics and the Peripatetics in Rome was considerable, if not always acknowledged. Equally as important as the acceptance of rational states of emotion was the adoption by Panaetius of the Peripatetic view that reason operated to select a mean between two vicious contraries, an excess and a deficit.[3] Virtue is conceived of as the middle way. This is the view adopted by Cicero in *De Officiis*, and this conception of virtue as a rationally-determined mean was endorsed by St. Thomas Aquinas and had become a commonplace doctrine of moral psychology by the time of Chaucer. Aquinas accepts the necessity, and therefore the desirability, of the sensitive part of the soul and its desires, but stresses that they must be moderated by reason. He denies that the Stoics recognized the existence of rationally governed passions, so that they therefore condemned all passions and sensual pleasures. The Peripatetics, on the other hand, he says, accepted as good and useful those passions and pleasures 'cum sunt a ratione moderatae.' However, he goes on, there was little real difference between the Stoics and Peripatetics other than in terminology, because the Stoics simply used a distinct term (*voluntas*) for rational appetites, reserving the word *passiones* for reprehensible motions of the soul *extra limites rationis*.[4] St. Thomas, then, saw the agreement between the two most influential schools of moral philosophy as consisting in the moderation of emotion by reason. Reason was to act as the rule or measure of the operation of the sensitive appetites and emotions. Virtue was conformity with measure, and vice consisted in falling short or exceeding the extent determined by reason.

Clearly the good of moral virtue consists in fitting the measure of reason. Clearly, too, between excess and deficiency the mean is

equality or conformity with reason. It is evident, then, that moral
virtue consists in a mean.

(ST., 1a2ae, 64, 1)

To say that virtue is a mean, however, is potentially misleading, for it
invites the conception of virtue as the mid-point of an imaginary line
whose ends are related vices. Such a geometrical conception, although
often popularly adopted, does not apply to the mean of virtue according to
Thomas, except in the case of justice, where the virtue does in fact strike a
balance of this kind. Rather, the mean is to be thought of as that measure
established by prudence as appropriate to the situation and circumstances
with which one is currently concerned. (2a2ae, 47, 7). For example, the
mean or due measure of expressions of joy or sorrow appropriate to a
certain individual in particular circumstances might well differ from that
appropriate to another man or woman in the same circumstances, and
indeed, different circumstances will require a different estimate of the
mean. The mean, then, is due measure of emotion or desire for the
circumstances. It is to be determined by the exercise of prudence, and this
prudential measure is virtue. This interpretation of the mean overcomes a
difficulty which seems to be implied by the single application of a blanket
mean; that is that the love of God may be excessive and therefore vicious.
For if the mean is what reason deems to be due measure, then it is
reasonable to believe that God cannot be loved to excess. Similarly, hope
can be seen as related to a particular situation, where it is a rationally
justifiable condition placed mid-way between irrational despair and
presumption; the former of which is a deficit, the latter an excess in
expecting greater things than is reasonable. The mean is not, then, a
simple mid-point in a structural opposition between abstract vices, but is
rationally and situationally determined. Nevertheless, the abstract conceptual structure had a powerful hold upon the imaginative organization
of ideas about vices and virtues, and in discussions conducted without
specific examples, this simplified notion often prevailed.

In courtly verse, the concept of the mid-point is frequent, and it frequently finds rhetorical expression as a catalogue of opposed epithets. In
Chaucer's translation of the *Roman de la Rose* we find the association
between reason and the mean made in this rhetorical form. The personification of Reason is described by pairs of gradable adjectives in order to
imply the moderation of reason:

> *But she was neither yong ne hoor,*
> *Ne high ne lowe, ne fat ne lene,*
> *But best, as it were in a mene.*
> (RR. 3196–8)

The mean here may have more relevance to aesthetics than to ethics, yet the evocation of a mean must have seemed to Guillaume de Lorris an appropriate garb for Reason, whom he says was fashioned in heaven in the image of God to be the primary faculty whose business it is to preserve men from folly. Ironically, a more typically Thomistic use of the word *mene* is that of Pandarus when he is trying to persuade Troilus to reveal to him the cause of his distress in Book One of *Troilus and Criseyde*. He argues that complete distrust of one's fellow man is a defect whose companion vice of excess is gullibility. The rational mean is a prudent decision to confide in one trustworthy companion:

> *And witteth wel that bothe two ben vices,*
> *Mistrusten alle, or elles alle leve.*
> *But wel I woot, the mene of it no vice is,*
> *For for to trusten som wight is a preve*
> *Of trouth . . .*
>
> *(TC.* I, 687–91)

Throughout *Troilus and Criseyde* Pandarus is capable of using the learning of the schools to argue his point of view. It is a feature of the urbane courtier that he can employ rhetoric or dialectic when needed, yet treat them with the same sceptical wit that he accords courtly literary pretensions when they are playing no useful purpose.[5] There is a touch of clerkish wit when Pandarus, referring again to the *mene*, uses the same word-form in three different significances, punning on the senses 'mean' and 'means':

> *That is to seye, for the am I bicomen,*
> *Bitwixen game and ernest, swich a meene*
> *As maken wommen unto men to comen;*
> *Al sey I nought, thow wost wel what I meene.*
>
> *(TC.* III, 253–6)

The same ironic way with clerkly concepts is noticeable in Jean de Meun's cynical account of faithless lovers who, unable to select the virtuous mean, choose the lesser evil as it seems to them:

> *But men this thenken evermore,*
> *That lasse harm is, so mote I the,*
> *Deceyve them than deceyved be;*
> *And namely, where they ne may*
> *Fynde non other mene way.*
>
> *(RR.* 4840–4)

Where virtue is impossible, Jean wryly suggests, self-preservation is to be seen as the lesser evil; to betray rather than be betrayed.

The concept of the mean of virtue and its close association with rational processes is familiar enough in vernacular poetry, yet the use of the word *mene* is rather rare in Chaucer's works. There, and indeed in much of the

French poetry by which he was influenced, the ideas were more frequently represented by three lexical items derived ultimately from Latin: *mesure, attemprance,* and *sobrenesse. Mesure* (Latin *Mensura*) refers to the due measure acceptable to reason: hence, the mean. *Sobrenesse* (Latin *sober*) seems in Latin to have developed a moral sense from a figurative extension of its earlier sense 'not drunk', and it implies quietness and moderation in demeanour. *Attemprance* is derived from the cardinal virtue *temperantia,* which according to Cicero is the quality which disposes a man to accept the rulings of reason. He carefully distinguishes it from *mediocritas,* which is his name for the mean of the Peripatetics.[6] In order to clarify this, we might say that *temperantia* predisposes the appetites to obey the rule of reason, which then selects the proper *mensura* for the situation, and the observable effect of this may be *sobrietas* in behaviour. In popular vernacular usage, however, causes and effects are confused, and a considerable degree of synonymy is found between the English derivatives. Indeed, for the purposes of understanding their effects in Middle English poetry, the fact of their collocation and the range of their connotations are of far greater importance than the minor distinctions in their senses. Let us first of all dispense with a number of senses which will not concern us. It is as well to note that *sobrenesse* has its ancient and modern sense of the antithesis to drunkenness in the fourteenth century too, and also that the word is found in colloquial utterances indicating earnestness or seriousness in speech or conduct. *Attemprance* has a wide range of senses in colloquial passages, implying order, balance, or mildness. It can signify training, schooling, or putting in order, and like *mesure,* can be applied to clement weather.

On the whole Chaucer's uses of the word *sobrenesse,* although associated with seriousness, often of a philosophical or religious kind, are not of a technical nature. The translator of the contemporary *Book of Vices and Virtues,* however, takes *sobrenesse* to be synonymous with the virtue of temperance, and uses it to denote that cardinal virtue: 'who-so haþ þis vertue,' he says, 'he haþ þe lordschip of his body, riȝt as men maistrieþ an hors bi þe bridele' (p. 276). He is employing two familiar images of the penitential tradition: the ethical one of the seigneury of reason, and a homiletic, but also originally philosophical one, of the impetuous irrationality of the flesh.[7] The virtue of *sobrenesse,* he tells us, keeps rational measure, not only in eating and drinking but in other virtues too. His reference to eating and drinking betrays the common associations of *sobrenesse,* and, as though to avoid possible ambiguity on this account, when he talks of it as this essential moderating quality, which puts 'ouer al mesure,' he collocates the word with the unambiguous *attemprance.*

Chaucer's Parson, in discussing remedies against gluttony, tries to specify some distinctions between these words:

The felawes of abstinence been attemperaunce, that holdeth the meene in all thynges . . . suffisance, that seketh no riche metes ne drynkes, ne dooth no fors of to outrageous apparailynge of mete;/ mesure also, that restreyneth by resoun the deslavee appetit of etynge; sobrenesse also, that restreyneth the outrage of drynke.

(*CT*. X, 833–4)

But these distinctions belong more to etymology than contemporary usage. Indeed the compiler of an early dictionary, the *Promptorium Parvulorum* glosses *mesure* indifferently by the Latin synonyms *temperantia, moderacio,* and also the technical term for the mean, *mediocritas*, which Cicero had taken such pains to distinguish (335). In the *Book of Vices and Virtues*, seven degrees of *sobrenesse* are mentioned, and these too correspond to everyday behaviour: *mesure* in speech, hearing, dress, behaviour, eating, and drinking are all recommended. The *Middle English Dictionary* furnishes an even longer list where *temperaunce* is defined: 'whanne a man passeþ not mesure in etinge ne in drinkinge, þenkinge ne spekinge, lokinge ne heringe, slepinge ne wakinge' (s.v. *mesure* 9c). Such exhortations to *mesure* in everyday things can be paralleled from the *Parson's Tale* and they find their way too into the more secular tales as part of the verisimilitude of their characterization. The Pardoner, a celebrated homilist, inveighs against gluttony:

> *O glotonye, on thee wel oghte us pleyne!*
> *O, wiste a man how manye maladyes*
> *Folwen of excesse and of glotonyes,*
> *He wolde been the moore mesurable*
> *Of his diete.*

(*CT*. VI, 512–16)

And a friar in the *Summoner's Tale,* in the course of an impromptu sermon, calls upon his spiritual charge:

> *'For Goddes love, drynk moore attemprely!*
> *Wyn maketh man to lesen wrecchedly*
> *His mynde and eek his lymes everichon.'*

(*CT*. III, 2053–5)

Although it is less markedly a feature of characterization, the Monk in his tale echoes the Parson's esteem of *largesse with mesure*.[8] In cases such as this, the subject matter of the tale or general suitability to character account for the use of the words *mesure* or *attemprance* in a way associated with homilies. In a few instances, however, the typical phrasing appears not as the language expected from the declared identity of the speaker, but rather as revelatory of his point of view or his moral stance. In the case of Justinus, the echo of the Parson's words in his premarital advice to Januarie (use . . . the lustes of youre wyf attemprely) serves, with other echoes of sermon style, to indicate his credentials as adviser.[9] In the wider context, they also help to explain his narrow-minded antifeminism and pessimism. His is not the practical wisdom of moderation so much as the doom-laden voice of religious asceticism. Indeed, much of the homiletic treatment of the idea of the mean of virtue tends in this direction. The *attempree diete* which sustains the health and vitality of the Nun's Priest's poor widow might seem to the modern reader to be distinctly on the worse side of moderation. As the author of the *Book of Vices and Virtues* points out – and in this he is, perhaps unwittingly, echoing St. Thomas –*mesure* is a relative concept:

> For among þes worldeliche goodes, þat þat is to moche to on is to litle to anoþer, and þat were outrage sum tyme for a pore man where litle ofte for a riche man.
>
> (p. 227)

The *Romaunt of the Rose* offers an answer to this problem:

> *For richesse and mendicitees*
> *Ben clepid two extremytees;*
> *The mene is cleped suffisaunce;*
> *Ther lyth of vertu the aboundaunce.*
> *(RR. 6525–8)*

In effect, this is to reconcile the Peripatetic mean with Stoic and Cynic ideas of sufficiency and the demands of nature: between poverty and wealth the virtuous mean is sufficiency; but who is to define that? Diogenes are few in reality, even if abundant in aspiration. So, in the absence of a fixed ideal, religious moralists tended to set *suffisaunce* and the mean at a somewhat ascetic level, close to that required by monastic vows. *Attemprance* is frequently collocated in moralistic passages with *abstinence*, and its sense tends to be affected by the association.[10]

Outside the context of the explicit exposition of vices and virtues, although never completely divorced from it, the vocabulary and ideas of rational moderation have an existence in secular social and behavioural theory. In twelfth-century Provence, *mezura* had been an essential component of courtliness, and the ideal of *mesure* is as important in the courtly verse of Northern France.[11] In Chaucer's work, it is rarely overtly discussed outside the 'courtly' poems of his early career in which he was most consciously imitating the French tradition. In these works, it is applied less to everyday appetites, as it is in homiletic and penitential writings, and more to general demeanour or emotional display. It is in fact closer to philosophical theorizing. Once again, it is contrasted with *outrage*, indicating excess, and often with a strong awareness of situational appropriateness. In courtly writings, too, *mesure* is distinctly less ascetic than in those infused with a religious morality. Thus, in describing the

123

virtue of the Duchess Blanche, the epithet *sobre* marks one pole of excess from which her virtue preserves her:

> *She nas to sobre ne to glad;*
> *In alle thynges more mesure*
> *Had never, I trowe, creature.*
> (*BD*. 880–82)

In this courtly world, although there is frequent stress upon moderation and the mean, it never implies asceticism or hardship of any kind. Even the settings of love-debates echo this more liberal interpretation of the mean. In the *Book of the Duchess*, as in most such poems, the setting is spring-like and the weather is *attempre*: 'For nother to cold nor hoot yt nas' (343).[12] *Mesure* is also evident in the physical appearance of the courtly participants, where it represents an aesthetic ideal. The arching brows of the courtly lady are 'smothe and slyke;/ And by mesure large' (*RR*. 542–3). Her lord's nose is also 'by mesure wrought ful right' (*RR*. 823). A similar ideal of beauty as measured proportion occurs, without any distinctive vocabulary, in *Sir Gawain and the Green Knight*, turning the court's awe at their visitor into admiration as they notice how well he fulfils their courtly canons of beauty:

> *Both his wombe and his wast were worthily smale,*
> *And alle his fetures folȝande, in forme þat he hade.*
> (144–5)

In social relations at this level, *mesure* is frequently invoked in French romances, and here it is especially useful to remember its opposition with the word *outrage*, where *outrage* can mean anything from an insult or injury through to lack of tact appropriate for the situation; indeed, sometimes no more than a minor breach of etiquette. In Chaucer's works, although the ideal of *mesure* is admirably demonstrated on numerous occasions, as in the initial exchange between the dreamer and the Man in Black in the *Book of the Duchess,* it is never expressed as such; Chaucer prefers to use such words as *debonairetee, curtesie,* or *benignitee*, which, for him, may have a more direct association with morals than manners. One example of Chaucerian usage, translated from the *Roman de la Rose,* is however worthy of consideration. Here Danger – a word which implies antagonism and haughtiness, and is personified as a churl – is mollified by the lover:

> *Daunger ne myght no more endure;*
> *He mekede hym unto mesure.*
> (*RR*. 3583–4)

The verb *meken* is rare in Chaucer, and apparently means 'to become gentle or conciliating.' It is used here as an antonym of *danger*, with the implication that the churl moved from his natural vicious extreme towards meekness until he reached the virtuous mean. Such reasonableness – and the familiar modern sense is suggestive here – is not considered to be the nature of the churl, and he is attacked for the aberration later in the poem. He is told he must be 'froward and outrageous;' it is not a churl's nature to be kindly and obliging: 'it sittith thee nought curteis to be' (4036). Churls are after all *vileyns*, and the personification Vilanye is 'proud and outragious' (*RR*. 174), whilst Curtesie is explicitly 'not nyce, ne outrageous' (1257). The God of Love denies *gentillesse* to all who are *outrageous* of demeanour (2191–2). The *Romaunt of the Rose* and those works in its tradition make a fairly clear division between the outrage of churls and the corresponding *mesure* of the courtier. However, since *mesure* is considered so integral a part of *curtesie*, it is frequently the case that the former concept is represented by the latter lexical item. The antithesis is expressed as existing between *curtesie* and *outrage*, and an extension of this opposition is amusingly demonstrated from outside the idealistic ambiance of the courtly tradition by Chaucer's Reeve. He tells of a cautious thief, a miller, who, on learning of the indisposition of the manciple whose corn he grinds, redoubles his thefts, throwing caution to the winds:

> *For therbiforn he stal but curteisly,*
> *But now he was a theef outrageously.*
> (*CT.* I, 3997–8)

Nothing could be more convincing of the set of synonymies and oppositions set up in usage between *curtesie* and *mesure, vileynye* and *outrage*, than this simple ironic remark.

Mesure is not a quality of the churl, but neither is it of that noble bird, the goshawk. Amid the gathering of birds, he is represented as a persecutor 'For his outrageous ravyne.' (*PF*. 336). There is implied tautology in this phrase, since no *ravyne* could really be considered to be within the bounds of reason. The force of *outrageous*, therefore, is pejorative and intensifying. If seeking a translation, 'merciless' might do quite well. Let us compare this with a passage from the *Tale of Melibee*. It is the familiar judicial situation in which Melibee is contemplating revenge justice on those who have harmed him: he intends to disinherit and exile them. Prudence protests in familiar terms against the sentence, which, she says, is cruel and against reason:

> And as touchynge that ye seyn ye wole exile youre adversaries,/ that thynketh me muchel agayn resoun and out of mesure,/ considered the power that they han yeve yow upon hemself.
> (*CT.* VII, 1847–9)

His antagonists have sought peace and placed themselves at his mercy; he must therefore judge more 'curteisly', and Prudence finishes her plea by reference to the judgement of God: 'Juggement withouten mercy shal be doon to hym that hath no mercy of another wight' (1869). The situation is one in which the ire of a lord – that is, his *outrageous* desire for vengeance – is moderated by the intervention of *prudence*, which, taking the circumstances into account, restrains him to *mesure*, whose direct result is *mercy* for the transgressors. If we deliberately blur the distinction between cause and effect, we shall see that in the judicial situation *mesure* and *mercy* often appear identical. The *outrageous* goshawk, then, is by the very fact of his irrational *outrage* a type of the tyrant, and is labelled as such by Chaucer.

Mercy and *mesure* are conceptual neighbours in fourteenth-century writings, and because of the chance alliteration they often keep close company on the written page also. The Parson puts Prudence's warning on divine judgement into other words, linking *mercy* and *mesure* almost as a formulaic phrase:

> wherfore I seye that thilke lordes that been lyk wolves, that devouren the possessiouns or the catel of povre folk wrongfully, withouten mercy or mesure,/ they shul receyven, by the same mesure that they han mesured to povre folk, the mercy of Jhesu Crist, but if it be amended.
>
> (*CT.* X, 775–6)

Similar phrasing is found when Criseyde envisages the opinion of her uncle Pandarus as a kind of judgement on her morals when she cries:

> *if that I, thorugh my disaventure,*
> *Hadde loved outher hym or Achilles,*
> *Ector, or any mannes creature,*
> *Ye nolde han had no mercy ne mesure*
> *On me, but alwey had me in repreve.*
>
> (*TC.* II, 415–9)

This apparent conceptual affinity between *mesure* and *mercy* leads us now to a consideration of the latter. Since it is apparently the equivalent of *mesure* in considering punishment, it is clearly a rationally-governed reaction, and indeed can be seen as a mean between emotional responses such as pity and savage cruelty. This in fact is how Gower does see it:

> *Forthi the lond mai wel be glad,*
> *Whos king with good conseil is lad,*
> *Which set him unto rihtwisnesse,*
> *So that his hihe worthinesse*
> *Betwen the reddour and Pite*
> *Doth mercy forth with equite.*[13]
>
> (*CA.* VII, 4167–72)

The judicial situation which we encountered in the judgement of Theseus in Chapter One furnishes a further instance of the importance of rational control of the emotions. Within that situation, the status of mercy has a fairly well-defined history, and one which leaves clear traces in fourteenth-century usage. Seneca in his treatise on clemency distinguished between *saevitia*, which signifies totally unjustified persecution (the vice of the tyrant), and *crudelitas*, which indicates harshness in justifiable punishment (but is often confused with *saevitia* when applied to tyrants). *Clementia* he considers to be opposed to *crudelitas*, since it implies rationally justifiable mildness in exacting retribution. *Misericordia*, however, since it is an irrational emotion and a sickness in the soul, is to be considered the true opposite of *saevitia*:

> Misericordia non causam, sed fortunam spectat; clementia rationi accedit.
>
> *(De Clem.* II, v, i)

> Pity considers the mischance, not the cause of it; mercy is in accordance with reason.

To the Stoic, either of the rational states, *crudelitas* or *clementia*, were preferable to the perturbation of pity, *misericordia*. However, when St. Thomas came to write on the subject he was less ready to dispense with beneficient emotions. Hence, he produces a rather more complex categorization. First of all, he follows Seneca in regarding *saevitia* as a bestial delight in persecution, and adds that it reveals a complete lack of humane feeling, an affective assessment which did not concern Stoic theory. *Crudelitas*, he says, is exhibited by those who have cause to exact punishment, but do so to excess (2a 2ae, 157.1). Although *misericordia* and *clementia* can be seen to be similar in effect, they are different in that the former implies an emotional identification with the person with whom sympathy is felt; the latter on the other hand, simply implies the rationally justified remission of a punishment. The rationally justified exaction of a punishment is now called *severitas*:

> Nam severitas inflexibilis est circa inflictionem poenarum quando hoc recta ratio requirit; clementia autem diminutiva est poenarum etiam secundum rationem rectam.
>
> (2a 2ae, 157, 2)

> For severity is unbending only when right reason demands it, and clemency also softens punishment only when and where this is fitting and reasonable.

Now, since *clementia* and *severitas* are both rationally justifiable, they cannot be truly in opposition. The opposition is therefore between *crudelitas* and *clementia* on the grounds that one is concerned with the excessive imposition of penalties, the other with moderating them according to reasonable measure. Alongside this opposition between a vice of excess and a virtue of moderation, there is a further opposition within the same sphere between the sub-human vice of *saevitia* and the superhuman gift of *pietas*.

Now although *pietas, misericordia, mansuetudo,* and *clementia* may be carefully distinguished in the *Summa*, as Thomas admits, their observable effects are similar (2a 2ae, 157, 4), and common Latin usage confuses *misericordia* and *clementia* very frequently. Indeed, from the earliest Christian Latin, there had also been a tendency to use *pietas* with the sense of *misericordia* and this is remarked upon by St. Augustine in *De Civitate Dei*.[14] If *pietas, misericordia* and *clementia* were confused in Latin, this tendency is even more clearly demonstrated by their represent-atives in the vernacular. Chaucer often uses *mercy* to render *misericordia* in his translations, but *pitee* is also a frequent translation for this word. When translating *pietas*, the obvious choice is *pitee*, but in fact *mercy* is also utilized. Hence it appears that *mercy* and *pitee* are interchangeable in his usage. It is therefore surprising, on closer analysis to find that this is not the case. There is sufficient evidence in the usage of both Chaucer and Gower to indicate that they recognized something of the ancient distinc-tion between rationally justifiable remission of a penalty upon a guilty person, and the irrational motion of sympathy towards a man irrespective of guilt.[15] Consider the example in *Anelida and Arcite* (301) where Anelida denies the need to ask *mercy* in a state of innocence.[16] Consider also the words of Alcestis to the God of Love in the *Legend of Good Women* (F. 404), where she stresses what Prudence has already told Melibee, that submission of the vassal demands *mercy* in a lord willing to bring reason to his judgement. Compare these with the words of the Parson:

> A man that hath trespased to a lord, and comth for to axe mercy and maken his accord, and set him doun anon by the lord, men wolde holden hym outrageous, and nat worthy so soone for to have remis-sioun or mercy.

> (*CT*. X, 992)

Mercy is seen to be rationally deserved by those who show true contrition and avoid presumptuous excess. The same idea is found in the poem *An ABC*, where the prerequisite of God's *mercy* is penance (120). Further evidence that Chaucer distinguished rationally deserved *mercy* from arbitrary, emotional *pitee* in a way echoing the distinction made by Latin writers between *clementia* and *misericordia* (or *pietas*) will be found in the next chapter; in the meantime, we may most conveniently demonstrate it from the work of Gower. In *Confessio Amantis* he plainly tells us that *mercy* is a derivative of *pitee*, created by the application of reason to an emotional impulse:

128

> *Bot Pite, hou so that it wende,*
> *Makth the god merciable,*
> *If ther be cause resonable*
> *Why that a king schal be pitous.*
> *Bot elles, if he be doubtous*
> *To slen in cause of rihtwisnesse,*
> *It mai be said no Pitousnesse,*
> *Bot it is Pusillamite,*
> *Which every Prince scholde flee.*
> *For if Pite mesure excede,*
> *Kinghode may noght wel procede*
> *To do justice upon the riht.*
> (*CA*. VII, 3520–31)

Although Gower's position is not precisely defined, he is certainly arguing in scholastic terms the importance of a rationally defined mean as the arbiter of virtue. *Pitee* is an emotion which leads on in suitable circumstances to *mercy*.[17] It seems to be considered a virtue, and is opposed to the vice of excess which is labelled *pusillamite,* and which inhibits the enforcement of true justice. Gower has something in common here with the *Book of Vices and Virtues,* for he classifies *pusillamite* as a subdivision of sloth. If we equate justice and reason in the following, the parallelism will be apparent:

> Iustice wiþ-oute mercye is cruelte . . . and mercie wiþ-oute iustice is lachesse, þat is slowþe.
>
> (p. 210)

It is evident that the judgement of Palamon and Arcite by Theseus, which we encountered in Chapter One corresponds precisely with the stereotype of the reasonable, merciful philosopher king, a role in which Gower was also eager to cast Henry IV.

At the opening of the *Parliament of Fowls* Chaucer summarizes the dream of Scipio. With its stress upon harmony, proportion and cosmological order, this summary represents a kind of disinterested love for the common good. The park into which he is then dragged in his own dream is an equally striking evocation of natural order, with its musical instruments 'in accord', its groves of everlasting trees, and its *attempre* air. This natural order is reflected later in the poem by the procedural order of Nature's parliament of birds, where the birds are met to fulfil Nature's plan of ensuring the immortality of the species through reproduction. The proceedings are highly formalized, but are disrupted by the inability of the female eagle to decide between three outstanding suitors. Her sensitivity, which forbids the commonsense remedies of the churlish ducks and geese, joins the sensuality of the Temple of Venus as elements destructive of natural, rational and ultimately divine order. Now, although the narrator emerges from the Temple of Venus with an almost audible sigh of relief, nothing in the narrative indicates that he disapproves of the behaviour of the eagles. To claim that Chaucer is satirizing courtly love is to take the side of the duck. This is not destructive satire, but rather the raising of serious questions in light-hearted form:

> *Ful hard were it to preve by resoun*
> *Who loveth best this gentil formel heere.*
>
> (534–5)

As the tercelet says, the extent of love is not accessible to rational enquiry:

> *But as for conseyl for to chese a make,*
> *If I were Resoun, certes, thanne wolde I*
> *Conseyle yow the royal tercel take,*
> *As seyde the tercelet ful skylfully,*
> *As for the gentilleste and most worthi.*
>
> (631–5)

Neither is the object to which love is directed always consonant with that which reason would select. In brief, human love, which passes beyond the rational modes of public good or procreation of the species – which latter is the purpose allotted to it by Reason in the *Roman de la Rose* – is extraordinarily difficult to reconcile with reason. In the ethics of Chaucer's day, it is therefore amoral and potentially tragic. Love may easily become the tyranny whose image opens the poem.

In treating this theme anew, Chaucer is precisely in the main stream of courtly literature on the topic of love. More than one book could be filled by the development of this theme, and in part of a chapter on the rational moderation of emotions no more than a few landmarks can be mentioned. For Jean de Meun, the reconciliation of reason with love is to be found in procreation. In the *Tristran* of Thomas, however, we find an author whom Frappier called a 'theologian of courtly love'.[18] Within a courtly milieu, he distinguishes a love which he calls *amour par reisun*. Love should be moderated by reason, he claims; it should not extend beyond the limits that reason perceives as justifiable. And, although reason is seen as a suitable cause for breaking off a liaison, it is also to be associated with faith and stability in love:

> *Mais trop aiment novelerie*
> *E home et femmes ensement*
> *Car trop par changent lor talent*
> *E lor desir et lor voleir*
> *Cuntre raisun, contre poeir.*
> (Sneyd Frag. I, 291–6; ed. Wind, p. 76)

(But both men and women are too fond of novelty, for too often they change their intentions, desires and wills, in contravention of reason and disregard of what is possible.)

Frappier remarks that this blend of love and reason lies at the heart of the ideal of *fine amour*. Whether or not this is true in all contexts, it is indeed true that a familiar verbal association with *fine amour* in France is that with *fol amour* or *amour par desmesure*. The implication of such phrases is of love passing beyond the rationally-defined limit. A common contrast, that with *fals amour*, might be applied not only to inconstant lovers but also to immoral, ill-intentioned suitors, such as those against whom the Knight of the Tower warns his daughters. But of course intentions in love are difficult to discern by rational enquiry, as the tercel said, and so Machaut in the *Dit dou Lyon* has to invent a test of true love (*l'Espreuve de fin amour*) to justify himself.[19] This test can only be passed by that lover who is well-intentioned and faithful (*li loial amant*).

As this rather heterogeneous assembly of French poetry shows, there is in the literature to which Chaucer and his contemporaries were so indebted a strong connection between *fine amour* and the idea of love moderated by rational virtue. This was greatly elaborated in the fourteenth century by Machaut. Although they rarely mention *fine amour* as such, fourteenth-century English writers wholeheartedly adopted the theme of love within reason. Gower's *Confessio Amantis* employs it as an orienting theme. In Book I Gower illustrates how the lover who puts aside reason rapidly comes to grief (*CA*. I, 1051) and at the end of the poem he exhorts lovers to rational love, which is the only kind he considers *honeste*:

> *Forthi, my Sone, I wolde rede*
> *To lete al other love aweie,*
> *Bot if it be thurgh such a weie*
> *As love and reson wolde acorde.*
> *For elles, if that thou descorde,*
> *And take lust as doth a beste,*
> *Thi love mai noght ben honeste;*
> *For be no skile that I finde*
> *Such lust is noght of loves kinde.*[20]
> (VIII, 2020–28)

But the accord of reason and sexual love is not easily achieved. Although Chaucer can suggest a reconciliation of reason and love in equable marriage, as in the *Franklin's Tale*, this is really no answer, for in marriage two essentials of Gower's love are absent: the constant desire for possession, and the lady's unconstrained bestowal of herself. Marriage entails possession and destroys desire, and legal right precludes the free gift.[21]

131

In most of his work, then, Chaucer follows the concern of the courtly tradition to maintain an uneasy balance between love and reason. His heroines constantly protest that reason rules their relationships. Criseyde claims to have fallen for Troilus's moral virtue, and in particular because 'youre resoun bridled youre delit' (IV, 1678). In Book III, as she prepares to surrender to Troilus, she hedges her commitment around with rational qualifications: he will have no more power over her 'than right in that cas is' (III, 172). She gives herself 'myn honour sauf' (III, 159). This last phrase finds an echo in the promises of one of the tercel eagles in the *Parliament of Fowls* (461), in the Man in Black's account of Blanche's commitment to him (*BD*. 1271) and in Anelida's words to Arcite (AA, 267). The circumstances are most clearly enunciated in the *Squire's Tale*, where a lady falcon recounts in her misery how she:

> *Graunted hym love, on this condicioun,*
> *That everemoore myn honour and renoun*
> *Were saved, bothe privee and apert;*
> *This is to seyn, that after his desert,*
> *I yaf hym al myn herte and al my thoght –*
> *God woot and he, that ootherwise noght –*
> *And took his herte in chaunge of myn for ay.*
> (*CT*. V, 529–35)

The exchange of hearts symbolizes the shared emotion and unity of will by which love is defined in scholastic writings. It is so defined also in the *Book of the Duchess*, where we are told that Blanche and the Man in Black's hearts suffered a single joy or sorrow (1289–95).[22] The falcon continues, explaining that:

> *my wyl was his willes instrument;*
> *This is to seyn, my wyl obeyed his wyl*
> *In alle thyng, as far as reson fil.*
> *Kepynge the boundes of my worshipe evere.*
> (*CT*. V, 568–71)

These last two lines contain the essential psychological circumstances of the courtly attempt to reconcile love and reason. Unity of will is moderated by reason, which establishes limits and ensures good morality according to the participants and situation. The falcon's behaviour has been exemplary; this is the conduct in love to which all other Chaucerian heroines aspire, or at least profess to in their speeches. But the decorum, the order and formality of the courtly relationship ruled by reason is doomed. In relation to love the rational mean only becomes absolute in the case of love of God. It is therefore a highly impractical guide for the conduct of a love affair, to which the lower functions of prudence may be more appropriate. Attempts to reconcile sexual love with reason tend

132

either to lead to the rigid formalism and inconclusive ending of the *Parliament of Fowls*, or else desire overcomes reason and the passion of love rules its blinded hosts. The rational ethic, the philosophical ideal, is then deserted, the lovers' fortune is either good or bad, ends in marriage or in tragedy. Indeed, love and reason are 'not of o governance.'

CHAPTER EIGHT

Beyond Reason

Illud satis est ad coarguendum furiosi hominis errorem, quod inter vitia et morbos misericordiam ponit. Adimit nobis affectum, quo ratio humanae vitae pene omnis continetur . . . accepit pro vitiis omnibus miserationis affectum, qui plane vocatur humanitas, qua nosmet invicem tueremur.

(Lactantius, *Divinarum Institutionum*,
III, xxiii. *PL*. 6, 423)

This is sufficient to prove the error of this madman, that he places pity among vices and diseases. He deprives us of an affection which involves almost the whole course of human life . . . the affection of pity, which is truly called humanity, by which we might mutually protect each other.[1]

If the sentiments of this passage sound modern, their polemic expression guarantees that this condemnation of Stoic theory belongs to an age when controversy was still live. The writer is a Father of the Church who was born in North Africa at the end of the third century. That is to say, little more than a hundred years after the reign of the Stoic Emperor, Marcus Aurelius, when Roman power and culture were still relatively untouched by the barbarian invasions. He is here attacking the founder of Stoic philosophy, Zeno, on the grounds that Stoic ethics are a doctrine of inhumanity, suppressing beneficent emotions along with less desirable ones. An identical accusation was later levelled at the Stoics by Augustine in *De Civitate Dei*.[2] To Lactantius, writing as a Christian apologetist, emotions might be morally valuable; indeed they were exhibited by Christ himself. Pity (*misericordia*), he argues, has been divinely placed in

134

Man for his own protection. God had created animals with robust bodies, teeth and claws; but mankind, in his weakness, needed from the beginning that mutual protection which grows from the consciousness of common humanity, and this is the function of pity. Properly understood, this consciousness is rather one of brotherhood, since all men are equally the children of God, and it is this sense of brotherhood which is the force unifying society. He attacks rival philosophical attempts to explain the origins of society and language in evolutionary terms according to which early men were forced to band together for protection, or from simple fellow feeling. For Lactantius, language and the basis of human society, *pietas* or *misericordia*, were created in man by God:

> He gave him, besides other things, this feeling of kindness; so that man should protect, love, and cherish man, and both receive and afford assistance against all dangers. Therefore kindness is the greatest bond of human society.

> dedit ei praeter caetera hunc pietatis affectum ut homo hominem, diligat, foveat, contraque omnia pericula et accipiat, et praestet auxilium. Summum igitur inter se hominum vinculum est humanitas.
>
> (VI. x)

Man is a social animal who values his own kind, and whoever wishes to deprive him of the affections necessary for such a role is denying his nature and depriving his soul of life:

> Therefore I can call them by no other name than mad, who deprive man, a mild and sociable animal of his name; who, having uprooted the affections, in which humanity altogether consists, wish to bring him to an immovable insensibility of mind, while they desire to free the soul from perturbations, and, as they themselves say, to render it calm and tranquil.

> Quare nihil aliud dixerim, quam insanos, qui hominem, mite ac sociale animal, orbant suo nomine; qui evulsis affectionibus, quibus constat humanitas, ad immobilem stuporem mentis perducere volunt; dum student animum perturbationibus liberare, et (ut ipsi dicunt) quietum tranquillumque reddere.
>
> (VI. xvii)

Now Lactantius's advocacy of the value of emotions is itself an emotional one. It was written against a background of the cruel persecution of Christians by their fellow men, many of whom, like the judge Almachius in the *Second Nun's Tale*, might have claimed some philosophical justification of their actions. Brotherly love was one striking difference between such persecutors and their Christian victims. Lactantius called Book Six of his work 'Concerning the False Wisdom of the Philosophers', and his intention in it seems to be to press home the point that reason alone is inadequate for the investigation of mankind, and especially of man's relation to God. The vigour of his attack on the philosophers and upon their rational ethic carries him to extremes, indeed to a condemnation of reason as a principle of action which itself would have provoked criticism from later medieval scholastics. As an example of this we may compare the Parson's injunctions to *resonable largesse*, which he contrasts with *fool-largesse* ('for thilke that passeth mesure is folie and synne.' X, 465; 811), with Lactantius's attack on similar views expressed by Cicero. The latter states that alms should only be given where reason considers them to be due.[3] Lactantius sees this as error; the measure of alms-giving is not to be the deserving nature of the case as assessed by reason, it is to be 'as much as possible.' In assessing this, one must consider the recipient as oneself: 'cum pietatis et humanitatis officia utilitate metitus es' (VI. ix. *PL*. 6, 675). The two attitudes are not perhaps mutually exclusive, but what occupies the attention of the Parson is rational measure, whilst Lactantius's concern is with sympathetic identification with the sufferer.

Lactantius was not alone among the early fathers in his opposition to pagan philosophy. Tertullian too accuses Socrates of failing to possess the truth in the closing chapters of his *Apologeticum* (*De Anima*, I, 2ff.), and as we have seen Augustine repeated these views. But all these men had been educated in the Roman system, and Lactantius and Augustine had held teaching positions within it, so that their modes of thinking and the language they used were greatly indebted to those authors whom they felt they must reject. Indeed, whilst Lactantius is denouncing the philosophers, his phrasing is often their own, and the story of how another father, Jerome, heard an angelic voice denouncing him as more a Ciceronian than a Christian is well known. Nevertheless, although their training was firmly rooted in the Roman schools so that they were the unintentional transmitters of much philosophical doctrine, a new approach to ethics, based upon Christian teaching, did emerge among the early Christian fathers. It was an ethic based upon the holiness of the heart's affections, upon the scriptural injunction to 'love thy neighbour as thyself'. Its basis was not rational self-sufficiency like that of the philosophers, but emotional inter-dependence: an ethic of relationships rather than individualism. The relationship involved was primarily that with God, but secondarily, and importantly, that existing between men. It fell to St. Augustine to develop a theocentric morality based upon love which existed alongside of, and often competed with, the rational ethic of the philosopher.

If Lactantius stressed the relationship of *humanitas* or *pietas* existing between men, Augustine clearly defined its relationship to God. In his *De Doctrina Christiana* (I, xxix, 30. *PL*. 34, 30) he alludes to the fellow-feeling, the sense of community, felt by the fans of an actor whom all admire; by analogy, he says, so is there mutual love between Christians whose prime love is for the same object, God. Employing a political metaphor, he identifies this Christian community with the membership of a city-state, which he calls the *civitas dei* 'the city of God.' In this conception, moral philosophy is united with a theory of history in which two great bodies of men exist: the citizens of the divine city, united by this sympathy which springs from their love of the same lord, and the citizens of the world, whose whole desire is fixed upon worldly things. This latter love Augustine calls *cupiditas*, whilst the love of God which unites the divine city is known as *caritas*.

Both *cupiditas* and *caritas* are species of *amor*, which is an all-embracing force comparable in some ways to the force of gravity in modern scientific theory. It is similarly difficult to isolate, adequately define, or set eyes upon. At its most abstract from human experience, it may represent the physical force by which natural objects seek out their appropriate place in creation, so that smoke rises whilst a stone falls, or water droplets run together into a hollow.[4] It also includes that sensuous appetite which makes one unthinkingly desire and pluck an apple from a tree. More important to us, however, is that intellectual love which is seated in the will and by which love can be defined as the consciousness of the desirability of a particular end or object.[5] This awareness of the desirability of the object is accompanied by a tendency to consider the object as related, or in some way relatable, to oneself. Scholastic writers refer to this as the perception of a *similitudo* between the lover and his object (see below).

Now, in monastic circles in the Middle Ages, and especially in the twelfth century, considerable attention was paid to a particular species of *amor* known as *amicitia* or 'friendship.' Treatises like that of Peter of Blois reveal this concept to have been institutionalized upon lines drawn ultimately from Cicero's *De Amicitia* and Aristotle's *Nichomachaean Ethics*, but it was considered to fulfil a valuable moral role within a Christian community.[6] What was envisaged was an enduring and mutually supportive relationship. The friends morally strengthened one another within a relationship based upon a concern for their mutual spiritual welfare and a total disregard of worldly goods. So it is that when St. Thomas came to discuss love in his *Summa*, he distinguished two essentially different kinds of love which he calls *amor amicitiae* and *amor concupiscientiae*. Before explaining what Thomas meant by these terms, it is necessary to stress that he was talking at a rather abstract level about basic qualities of love and not about easily recognizable everyday circumstances. His *amor amicitiae* is a conception based upon the ideal of *amicitia*, and we should not be too ready to equate it simply with actual friendship, extending it into an opposition with *amor concupiscientiae* as sexual love. That this kind of vulgarization took place is suggested by the use of the phrase *love of frendes* in *Troilus and Criseyde*, but it is not Thomas's meaning.[7] To the latter, an initial distinction is that *amor concupiscientiae* involves the desire of an object for our own good, whilst *amor amicitiae* is the desire of a good for our friend. Both kinds of love spring from a perception of some similarity between ourselves and the love object. This similarity can be of two kinds: firstly, an actual similarity of some quality, for example a shared interest in music; or secondly, a similarity of potential, for example that X may possess a skill at woodwork which Y lacks, but by association with him hopes to gain, thus realizing a potential in himself. In the first case, the resultant love is *amor amicitiae*, which is mutual and disinterested; in the second, it is *amor concupiscientiae,* which is self-interested, and perhaps one-sided. It is obvious that these two kinds of love do not simply correspond with friendship and sexual love; either could, for example, be called friendship in a suitable case, and on the other hand, either manifestation of love could be found within a sexual relationship. The disinterested and mutual love of *amicitia* is simply a different and more noble kind of love than the desire to possess which is the essence of *amor concupiscientiae.*

The essential feature of love of all kinds is considered to be an impulse towards union. In a trivial sense this merely means that lovers and friends seek one another's company. In a more basic sense it means that love involves union of affect, which is to say that the lover (understood in the widest sense) shares the sorrows of his beloved, and participates in his or her joys. In the case of *amor amicitiae*, indeed, each sees the other as a part of themselves, and total emotional sympathy is matched by identicality of will (*ST.* 1a 2ae, 28, 2). *Amor amicitiae* is, no doubt, in accord with reason, for the first stirrings of friendship were implanted in humans by God,[8] and the institution of friendship is directed to moral ends, but reason is less stressed in discussing it than the unity of will and emotional sympathy. It is as if the basic humane feeling of which Lactantius spoke, or the *caritas* existing amongst the citizens of Augustine's divine city, were being condensed and analyzed into that affection which unites two friends: *amor amicitiae* between individuals is echoed in amplified form by *caritas* in the Christian community.

The primacy of love, especially in terms of fellow-feeling, had been an essential feature of Christianity from the beginning. Love of one's fellow man is equated in the Gospels with love of God, and Augustine developed an ethical system based upon rightly-directed love. It is therefore not surprising to find that a whole range of words indicating love, forebearance, or beneficience became regarded as potential synonyms. Aquinas, as we have seen, remarked upon the similarity of effect of *pietas, misericordia, mansuetudo,* and *clementia,* and although he subtly distinguishes them, other writers in less analytic contexts, failed to do so. Thus the rational measure which in careful usage distinguishes *clementia* from *misericordia* is often forgotten. *Pietas,* which in classical Latin denoted those feelings of loyalty, love and respect which are due to one's family and national traditions had also adopted a sense synonymic with *misericordia* before Augustine's time. Thomas Aquinas, however, when he discusses *pietas,* re-imposes upon it the classical sense, but only at the expense of considerable argument to distinguish it from related virtues with which it was normally confused. In general, these distinctions are made in terms of the object towards which the special form of regard is directed: *pietas* towards family and country, *religio* towards God, *amicitia* towards fellow men, whilst *caritas* has a wider application altogether. Thomas acknowledges the frequent synonymy in usage of *pietas* and *misericordia* and regards it as indicative of the sanctity of works of mercy, whilst the tendency to confuse *pietas* with *religio* he suggests depends upon the habit of regarding God as a metaphorical father (2a 2ae, 101, 3).

Thomas's careful definition of his terms was necessary for any contemporary reader, since Christian Latin had always confused *pietas, misericordia* and *clementia,* tending to reduce all to the common denominator of emotional sympathy. Jerome's text of the Vulgate is itself guilty of this, and we have demonstrated Lactantius's indifferent use of *pietas, misericordia* and *humanitas.* Indeed Lactantius regards the classical definition of *pietas* as *falsa pietas,* and attacks the poets for misrepresenting its true nature, which is in its equivalence with *misericordia.* To him, true *pietas* is inconsistent with cruelty; it must be sought not among poetic accounts of the heroes of the past but among that small and unassertive band who know no battles, who preserve peace with all, who are friends to their enemies, and who have all men as brothers. The goal to which it is directed is mankind and not institutions, and it is associated too with *clementia.*

Since usage in Christian Latin is so confused, despite the efforts of authors like St. Thomas, it is not surprising to find that in fourteenth-century English bothe *pitee* and *mercy* are frequently used with the modern sense 'pity' (Latin: *misericordia*). Gower's usage testifies to the close relationship between these words:

> *Of Pite forto speke plein,*
> *Which is with mercy wel besein,*
> *Fulofte he wole himselve peine:*
> *For Charite the moder is*
> *Of Pite, which nothing amis*
> *Can soffre, if he it mai amende.*
> (*CA.* VII, 3163–9)

It would, indeed, be possible to assemble citations from Chaucer's works to illustrate the contextual synonymy of *pitee, mercy, routhe, compassioun, misericorde, grace*, and perhaps *charite*, and this synonymy would be dependent upon the confusion of affect and effect noted in Latin by St. Thomas.[9] The affect of all is associated with benevolence, their effect with beneficience; yet more than this, uniting the ideas of love and pity, and actions which imply love and pity, is the powerful concept of sympathy between the two human beings concerned in the relationship. In general use, the specific applicability of the vocabulary appropriate to this area is overlooked; what dominates their use is an immensely powerful connotation, that which Lactantius discerned, that of a feeling of shared *humanitas*, which is the basis of an ethic of love.[10]

The author of the *Book of Vices and Virtues* sees *charite* and *pite* as two sub-divisions of *Love*. The first is that by which Christians help and advise one another, the second is what we should probably call compassion, were not fellow-feeling a more descriptive term:

> as seynt Poule seiþ, we beþ alle membres of o body. After þis, alle þe membres felen and drawen to hem al þat a man doþ to eueriche, be it good oþer euele, be it joye, be it anguisse; whan a man smyt þe fot, þe mouþ bit, 'Let bee! þou dost me harme.' Bi þat we vnderstondeþ vertue of verrey pite þat we schulle haue in comune.
>
> (p. 146)

Paul is quoted again in discussing the virtue of mercy, whose sixth division is to have pity:

> seynt Poule seiþ, 'Who is seke, and I am not seke wiþ hym?' And seynt Gregori seiþ þat þe more parfiȝt þat a man is, þe more he feleþ oþeres sorwes.
>
> (p. 203)

Similar injuctions to shared emotion are repeated throughout the Pauline epistles, and as we have seen, found a ready response in Christian theology.[11] His instruction to 'be of the same mind one toward another' (*Romans* XII, 16), which Wiclif ambiguously rendered as 'Fele ȝe the same thing togidere', is repeated by Peter in an even more openly affective form: 'be ye all of one mind, bearing compassion one of another, love as brethren, be pitiful, be courteous' (I *Peter* III, 8).

Such an emphasis upon emotional unification, which is at the heart of both love and pity, and which had such a grip upon Christian belief that it brought about the extensive synonymy between *pietas, misericordia* and the other words we have mentioned, despite pedantic efforts to distinguish them, was inevitably opposed to the rational ethic of the philosophers. Indeed the relational concept of virtue itself would seem implicitly opposed to the self-sufficiency of that tradition. Whilst

Christian thinkers came to accept many of the analyses and classifications of the pagan philosophers, extensive modifications were often necessary. The mere equation of God's law with reason was insufficient, since this did not adequately explain the value of virtues which were essentially of an affective nature. In any case, the operation of God's law was often too mysterious to be explicable by earthbound reason. The answer was to supplement – though not dispense with – the rational moral virtues by virtues whose validity sprang not from human reason but direct from God. In the twelfth century the three theological virtues, faith, hope and charity, were explicitly added to the rational virtues of prudence, justice, fortitude and temperance. Furthermore, it was argued that in addition to virtue being developed by the creation of the habit of applying prudence to a series of individual acts, similar virtues could be infused into a man directly from God. These virtues, which sometimes have the same names as those formed by a disposition to do good, have a higher purpose than they. They operate in a divine rather than earthly context. In possessing and exercising them, men behave as citizens of the city of God rather than honest men of the world; they are, in other words, exclusively directed towards the divine end of salvation. St. Thomas gives an example of the distinction between the rational virtue of temperance and its infused counterpart: the former moderates desire for the sake of health and reason; the latter, by a divine rather than rational measure, requires abstinence to chastise the body, bringing it under the subjection of the spirit (1a 2ae, 63, 4). The question of *mesure* does not arise in this, and perhaps we can see here part of the reason for the tendency of moderation to slide into asceticism that we noticed earlier.

In addition to the divinely-inspired theological and infused virtues, there grew up, chiefly among Carolingian writers of the ninth century, a distinct tradition of seven 'gifts' of the Holy Spirit, based primarily upon a list which occurs in Isaiah. The editor of the relevant volume of the *Summa Theologiae* is at pains to argue that the gifts tradition is not based upon any one passage of Scripture, but that the idea of a free gift, as it were of moral powers, pervades the Bible.[12] The passage from Isaiah merely became a standard source for enumerations of them. Treatments of the gifts in early scholastic texts vary considerably. They are considered to precede the virtues, to be indistinguishable from them, or, like infused virtues, to be a kind of supernatural addition to them. Bonaventure, for example, claims that the gift of *pietas* exceeds the virtue of pity by looking at the sufferer not as a man but, in the Augustinian tradition, as the image of God. Aquinas distinguishes between the virtue of justice and the gift cf *pietas* by relating the former to the dictates of reason in doing right, the latter to righteousness out of reverence for God (1a 2ae, 68, 4). Whatever the detailed differences between scholastic treatments of the nature of the gifts, once again they turn out to be superadded qualities, promptings of the Holy Spirit with a transcendental end in view, and therefore surpassing the requirements of reason and purely rational morality. They spring from the theological virtues (68.4) which unite the soul with God. The function of the gift of *pietas* on earth is reverence for God and compassion and pity between Christians. In the future life, too, it will remain in essence a principle of shared emotion. Reverence for God will remain, but now the shared emotion will be mutual joy and honour, and also the saints' compassion for suffering man on earth. (*ST.* 1a 2ae, 68, 6; 2a 2ae, 121, 2).

The gifts which are bestowed upon man by God are of divine origin and therefore of the highest esteem; nevertheless they are bestowed upon all men, and indeed are necessary to perfect the virtues in order to achieve salvation. Whilst the philosopher may achieve virtue and tranquillity by the exercise of unaided reason, the saint requires the gifts for his salvation, for the gifts are a form of divine grace without which, according to Christian theology, one cannot be saved. Although the notion of gifts may not be a familiar one, that of grace is a common enough theological concept to be known to everyone. Yet, unless we have a more than ordinary interest in Christian theology, it is unlikely that we have considered it as more than some mysterious ingredient bestowed by God as a requirement of salvation. Etymologically, and in the usage of St. Augustine, the great formulator of the doctrine of grace, it means 'a free gift.' This sense was reflected in the Old English translation of the Latin *gratia* as *giefu* 'gift', but the transparency of the term was lost when *grace* was borrowed from the French after the Conquest. There are, in fact, a number of different kinds of grace, and it varies greatly in its manifestations, yet all are to be considered as free gifts bestowed by the Holy Spirit upon Christians. The words 'free gift' and 'Christian' are important in this definition, for according to St. Augustine's conception of grace, it is given freely and cannot be deserved. Moreover, it is given only to believers. The gifts of grace, then, are not a reward for virtue, but are the inevitable result of a commitment to faith and a determination to do good. If the gift of grace is accepted by the recipient and used to perform good works, then by this, he will achieve salvation. The theological and infused virtues, and the gifts of the Holy Spirit are all manifestations of divine grace which help to perfect the soul in search of its goal in religion. Loosely speaking, they may all be considered as special kinds of virtue, but they are bestowed upon man by God and are not the products of his own reason. The seven gifts, which were seen as virtues actually possessed by Christ, were considered to be bestowed upon the child by the Holy Spirit at the time of baptism.[13]

The gift of *pietas*, which is more perfect than the virtue of the same name, is considered also to perfect the nature of purely rational virtues like *justitia, severitas* or *clementia.* In this conception Christian ideals of justice temper the ancient rationalism with a concern for humanity. Indeed the very salvation of mankind, tainted by original sin as he is, depends upon the fact that God himself tempers strict justice by *pietas.* The theme that God's mercy extends beyond rational measure is a favourite one of homilists, and finds its way widely into fourteenth-century writings. Although Chaucer sees the Virgin as the intercessor who secures God's mercy for man, who in strict justice deserves condemnation (*ABC*, 23–4), his Parson speaks for many when he tells us that Christ's incarnation is to be seen as the supreme example of the *pitee* of God extending beyond justice:

> oure sweete Lord Jhesu Crist hath spared us so debonairly in oure folies, that if he ne hadde pitee of mannes soule, a sory song we myghten alle syngen.
>
> (*CT.* X, 315)

Gower echoes even more clearly this idea of the fellow feeling which united Man and God in the person of Christ:

> *It is the vertu of Pite,*
> *Thurgh which the hihe mageste*
> *Was stered, whan his Sone alyhte,*
> *And in pite the world to rihte*
> *Tok of the Maide fleissh and blod.*
> *Pite was the cause of thilke good,*
> *Wherof that we ben all save:*
> *Wel oghte a man Pite to have*
> *And the vertu to sette in pris,*
> *Whan he himself which is al wys*
> *Hath schewed why it schal be preised.*[14]
> (*CA.* VIII, 3107–17)

The idea is frequently found that the coming of Christ ushered in a new millenium ruled over by a different dispensation of justice. No longer is man to be judged by the severe and unrelenting standard of the Old Law of God and the prophets, but in a new spirit of forebearance introduced by Christ's law, the law of humanity, in the Parson's words, the 'law of pitee' (X, 889). Towards the end of *Piers Plowman,* in the gloom following the death of Christ on the cross, personified virtues gather, wondering at the sudden darkness and at the bright gleam visible over Hell. Mercy speculates that this might be the moment foretold by the prophets when Adam shall at last be released from Hell. Treuthe curtly denies this as a fanciful story; it is an idea also denied by Justice. Pees, however, corroborates Mercy's hopes. Despite all that could be rationally predicted, despite the principles of strict justice, mankind is to be saved, for it is revealed that 'crist haþ conuerted. þe kynde of ryghtwisnesse/ Into pees and pyte. of hus pure grace' (C-text, XXI, 190–1). The very nature of justice has been altered by the sacrifice of Christ, and a new era has dawned.

The perception of the actual union of God and Man in the person of Christ, and its relationship to the unity of love and compassion was made afresh in Western Europe around the year 1000. At about this time, as art historians have repeatedly pointed out, a change came over the figural representation of the Crucifixion. Christ, instead of the all-powerful hero conquering death for the benefit of mankind, began instead to be represented as undergoing real human suffering. Contemplation of the passion and compassion for the suffering of Christ became an important device for reinforcing devotion. The essential humanity of Christ is stressed by concentration upon a familiar human relationship, that between mother and son, and the suffering of Mary at the death of her son is the theme of a succession of vernacular religious lyrics, of which one of the briefest and yet most complete is the thirteenth-century *Pity for Mary*:

> *Nou goth sonne vnder wode;*
> *Me rewes, Marie, thi faire rode.*
> *Nou goth sonne vnder tre;*
> *Me rewes, Marie, thi sonne and the.*

Although this brief work employs few descriptive details, relying on word-play and connotational values to achieve its effect, detailed evocation of the scene becomes a common device of pietistic writings. The building of a composite image of suffering is achieved in the early prose *Wooing of Our Lord* by relating each detail of the crucifixion in the present tense, like a commentary, sprinkling it with exclamations 'lo!' and 'a!', and giving the whole an intensely personal tone:

> A, hwat schal I nu don? Nu min herte mai tobreke, min ehne flowen al o water. A nu is mi lefmon demd for to deien.

The intention is to create a personal and direct identification with Christ, to arouse pathos and to provoke charity. Weeping is the external sign of a heart moved to *pitee*, and indeed weeping in sympathy with Christ's suffering, and weeping in contrition for sins is encouraged. It often forms part of the work itself: a fourteenth-century Franciscan lyric concentrates its refrain upon the tear-drop falling from the eye of Christ, sacrificed for pity of mankind:

> *Luueli ter of loueli eyye, qui dostu me so wo?*
> *Sorful ter of sorful eyye, thou brekst myn herte ato.*

In literary *exempla*, the pathetic function of the crucifixion of Christ is echoed in a host of other descriptions of suffering in an affective religious setting. The righteous maiden martyred by a pagan tyrant can be treated either according to the philosophical tradition or in this pietistic way. The dutiful children, willing to sacrifice themselves or be put to death by their father for some justifiable cause, and then restored to life by a beneficient God, as in the romance *Amis and Amiloun;* the pious child martyred by the Jews and canonized by a miracle; to the pious, all are examples which recall the persecution of the innocent Christ, and all call forth awareness of the humanity which Christ shared with them, and those same feelings of *pitee* which caused God to send his Son for their redemption.

Pitee, then, was the cause of Christ's sacrifice and since St. Augustine greeted his conversion with a shower of tears, weeping had been esteemed as indicative of that tenderness of heart which enabled the Christian to feel sympathy with Man and God and regret his own misdeeds. In Chaucer's time the association between the gift of *pitee* and tears was so close that in his works the phrase *wepen for pitee* has virtually formulaic status.[15]

The association between *pietas* and *caritas* is a close one, since the latter is seen as the love which binds together the community of Christians, whilst the former implies compassionate regard for one's fellow man seen as the image of God. There is sufficient difference in this definition, however, for *pietas* occasionally to represent compassion extended to good men outside the ranks of the faithful. According to the strictest interpretation, the virtuous pagan, ruled by reason alone and ignorant of God, could not achieve salvation, since he lacked grace. It was argued, however, that Christ's sacrifice retrospectively bestowed grace upon those born under the Old Law, so that long-dead pagans could also be saved by divine *pitee* if they had been men of virtue. The favourite example of this is that of the Emperor Trajan, whose story is first told by a Whitby monk as early as the eighth century, and is also cited by Dante. Langland, too, uses his example when discussing what Chaucer terms the 'lawe of pitee', but alliterative convenience demands he call the 'lawe of love.' Trajan is a just pagan condemned to Hell as the result of his unbelief. In *Piers Plowman* he bursts on to the scene scorning written authority for the mercy of God and calling on his own experiences to witness how the love and compassion of Pope Gregory alone, without any ritual or observance, caused God to grant him salvation:

> *Gregore wiste þis wel. and wilnede to my soule*
> *Sauacion, for þe sothnes. þat he seih in myn werkes;*
> *And for he wilnede wepynge. þat ich were saued,*
> *God of hus goodnesse. seih hus grete wil;*
> *With-oute moo bedes byddyng. hus bone was vnderfonge,*
> *And ich ysaued, as ȝe may see. with-oute syngynge of masse.*

Loue with(oute) leel by-leue. and my lawe ryhtful
Sauede me Sarrasyn. soule and body boþe.

(C-text. XIII, 80–87)

Another fourteenth-century alliterative poem, *St. Erkenwald*, relates a very similar occurrence. The virtuous pagan remains incorruptible after death until he can receive the grace of God in a Christian baptism. This he does from a *pitous* tear falling from the eye of the Archbishop rather than in any formal baptismal ceremony. Human compassion is again revealed to be a greater force than the liturgical properties.

The willingness in these fourteenth-century vernacular poems to accept the virtues of the pagans of the past illustrates a markedly different attitude to philosophical virtue from that held by Lactantius. Now that they no longer posed a threat, the worth of the ancients could freely be admitted, and indeed they might be welcomed into the Christian world.[16] The emphasis placed upon humanity, and the attempt to apply the new humane standards of justice to pagan worthies, however, posed theological difficulties. Salvation was won by good deeds stemming from grace which was granted as a concomitant of faith, so that, clearly, dead pagans could not fit the proper procedure for entry into heaven. That the impulse of *pitee* for common and worthy humanity should so triumph over doctrine as to represent virtuous pagans as worthy of the *pitous* tears of Christians, and so achieve their salvation, came perilously close to the Pelagian heresy, and it is a measure of the strength of humanistic feeling that is found to be acceptable.

Gower, too, tells a story of the salvation of a virtuous pagan by compassion, but succeeds in avoiding doctrinal complications. Constantine is converted whilst still living, and he is saved not so much by his possession of rational virtues as by his own exercise of natural compassion and humanity. As Emperor of Rome he is informed that the only cure for his leprosy is that he should be bathed in the blood of young children. He gathers together the infants and their mothers, but is awakened from sleep by their lamenting. In a long speech, he reflects on the equality of man in terms of birth and innate capacities, how fortune places some in power over others through no special quality of either, and how that power confers the duty of responsibility. He is acutely aware of the common humanity he shares with the children and feels compassion for the distraught mothers. At length, *pitee* overcomes him and he sends the children away with gifts, preferring to suffer leprosy than to spill so much innocent blood.

In this account, Constantine is represented as a pagan philosopher behaving according to the highest principles of political reasoning and also gifted with natural compassion. His moral virtue, and because the story is about *pitee* and *charitee*, especially these two virtues at once

146

humane and divine, bring about his conversion and his cure. In a dream, Saints Peter and Paul appear to him and address him:

> O Constantin, for thou hast serued
> Pite, thou hast pite deserued:
> Forthi thou schalt such pite haue
> That god thurgh pite woll thee saue.
>
> (CA. II, 3339–42)

Constantine is duly baptized, and as his soul is saved, so too do the scales of leprosy fall from his body. *Pitee* and *charitee* shown to the innocent call forth the same from God, and although one cannot properly say that this grace is *deserved*, as Gower very nearly does, yet it is a commonplace that love is to be returned for love, and that *pitee* encourages *pitee*, both in relationships between men and also with God.

Those whose fortune places them in positions of power are repeatedly exhorted in medieval texts of all kinds to show mercy and be accessible to *pitee*, for by so doing they can expect that God will show equal sympathy to them in times to come. This idea, whose scriptural basis is sometimes cited as the Gospel of St. James, II. 13, is the advice given by Prudence to her lord Melibee:

> Wherfore I pray yow, lat mercy been in youre herte,/ to th'effect and entente that God Almighty have mercy on yow in his laste jugge-ment.
>
> (CT. VII, 1867–8)

It is implicit too in Piers' advice to the Knight in Passus Six, where he is sketching the political economy of a just society:

> 'Ye and yet a point,' quod Piers 'I preye [þee] of moore:
> Loke [þow] tene no tenaunt but truþe wole assente,
> And þouȝ [þow] mowe amercy hem lat mercy be taxour
> And mekenesse þi maister maugre Medes chekes.
>
> (B-text, VI, 37–40)

Mercy is to be greater than right in the Knight's dealings with those placed in his power; the Knight agrees, appropriately swearing by St. James.

There are then in the works of Chaucer and his contemporaries two possible systems upon which the morality of a poem may be based: the natural, earthbound, rationalistic ethic of self-sufficiency inherited from the popular philosophy of a pagan past, and the transcendental, affective, relational ethic implicit in the New Testament and further developed by the Church Fathers. It is the special glory of this latter ethic that although it is supernatural, it is not superhuman; it establishes the relationship between men, and their joint relationship to God as supreme, showing

147

readiness to forego strict rights and over-restrictive doctrine for the sake of it. The letter of the law is to be renounced for the sake of equity, and sacred texts are to be read in a way which corresponds with the impulse of charity, the letter giving place to the spirit;[17] even ritual observance must come second to compassion. No longer need one be a rationally-minded superman, a *sapiens*; it is enough to be a man and a Christian, for the eye of faith and the true intention of the will is as sure in seeking the path of virtue as the eye of prudence.[18] A simple man of good intentions is the equal of the philosopher or the prince. In his capacity to feel compassion, and in his will to act rightly he is the infinite superior of the powerful tyrant to whom, with his hardened heart, this path to virtue is as impassible as the rational way.

But there are real difficulties in an ethic based upon love. Dependence upon intention is its major weakness, for only God can read the motivations of the heart and know intentions. Peter Abelard, who developed a thorough-going intentional ethic, was willing to admit that it was really not well suited to practical worldly purposes.[19] Acts of beneficience, which may appear to spring from *pitee* or *charitee*, can easily be motivated by other concerns, which rob them of their virtue. *Cupiditas*, which is hidden within the heart, may be difficult to distinguish from *caritas* by its effects alone. Furthermore, an affective ethic is constantly in danger of being overwhelmed by emotion seen as an end in itself, so that overt weeping is more esteemed than inward piety. There is a danger that the affect may loom larger than the effect, and this is especially true in popular preaching, and in devotional works whose authors indulge in protracted orgies of pathos. Pious emotionalism can at any time become arrayed against reason, so that fanaticism and individual fantasy follow, scorning scholarship, logic and authority alike. Although these are abuses of the Christian theological ethic, and the balance between reason and emotion which we saw in the previous chapter is generally maintained, yet, in the fourteenth century, excesses of pietism are exceedingly common. The love of pathos in literature is widespread, and preachers like Chaucer's Pardoner must often have relied more on their skills in moving a congregation than upon rational argument. More respectably, the fourteenth century saw the emergence of numbers of individual mystical theologies which explicitly rejected the role of reason in seeking out the soul's pathway to God.[20] Gower, by no means a mystic, takes up again the cudgel laid down by Lactantius, but with a marked difference in tone. His phrasing is that of a man reciting the well-accepted facts of intellectual history, sure of the ground on which he stands, and of his audience's concurrence:

> *Les philosophres du viel temps*
> *Sur tout mettoiont cuer et sens*

> *Pour enquerir la verité,*
> *Les queux de tous les biens presens*
> *Sont de vertu plus excellentz:*
> *Les uns de grant felicité*
> *Delit du corps ont plus loée,*
> *Les uns richesce ont renommé,*
> *Les uns en firont argumentz*
> *Q'oneste vie en son degré*
> *Sur tous est le plus beneuré;*
> *Ensi dist chascun ses talentz.*
> *Mais Paul, l'apostre dieu loyal,*
> *Le grant doctour celestial,*
> *Q'estoit au tierce ciel raviz,*
> *Desprovoit leur judicial,*
> *Moustrant par argument final*
> *Qe sur tout bien doit porter pris*
> *La Charité par droit devis.*
> (*Mirour de L'Omme*, 13237–55)

(The philosophers of ancient times set their hearts and minds above all on seeking out the truth, which of all present goods are of the greatest worth: some praised bodily delight as the true happiness, others esteemed wealth, others argued that it was virtuous life in one's allotted station that was the most blessed. And so each said as he pleased. But Paul, the true apostle of God, the Heavenly Doctor, who was snatched up into the third heaven, disproved their opinions, showing by definitive argument, that by rights, Charity should be esteemed above all.)

There is, then, in the fourteenth century, a strong tendency to react against the dominant rationalism of the preceding century, which is found in all kinds of forms, even in attempts, like that of Gower, to place St. Paul's exhortation to charity within the rationalistic theorizing of the philosophical tradition.

Gower's attempt to place St. Paul as dominant within a secular philosophical tradition carries with it a danger which we have not so far mentioned. Concentration on affectivity as the basis of secular ethical theory may tend to separate it from its divine goal: liberal humanism of a kind traditionally attacked in pagan philosophers, *humanitas*, but of an emotional kind, may develop independently of the goal of salvation. And indeed, parallel to the Christian *amicitia* of the monastic communities these ideals of shared emotion, unified will, of forebearance beyond reason, were applied to ends other than the divine one;[21] to worldly ends, where, according to the very basis of the Christian ethic, they were totally inappropriate. Alongside the monastic communities united by *amor amicitiae* there are the secular courts, the expression of whose ideals, and whose terms of arguing them, often echo those used of *amor amicitiae,* but whose aims are worldly rather than transcendental. It is this courtly ethic that we must consider in our final chapter.

CHAPTER NINE

The Gentil Man

THE *Oxford English Dictionary* defines *churlish* as 'intentionally boorish or rude in behaviour', a definition which echoes in spirit the words of Chaucer: 'vilayns synful dedes make a cherl.' It is by deeds and by nature rather than by the accident of birth that churlishness is to be recognized. Churlishness resides in the heart, so that, if you act like a *vileyn* then at heart, that is what you are. What was still an argument in Chaucer's day, commonplace as it was, has since become accepted truth. We may still speak of villains and churls, but there is no longer any implication about their social status as there was in the fourteenth century; the words have a purely behavioural reference. Then, *vileyn* and *cherle* were words in opposition to two other lexical items which also connoted an uncertain mixture of moral evaluation and social description: *gentil* and *curteis*. Etymologically, *gentillesse* described the social fact of noble birth, *curteisie* a behavioural ideal connected with membership of the court. They had, not surprisingly, become more or less synonymous. In Chaucer's usage, a working, though not entirely accurate, distinction which may be made between them is that the former refers more regularly to morals, whilst the latter is concerned with the province of manners and accomplishments, but naturally, in describing attitudes in the interaction of individuals, there is considerable overlap in their use. In discussing what is essentially the same ideal designated by two terms, we should be aware that, what for the sake of simplicity I shall refer to as *gentillesse*, is not a monolithic concept. It varies considerably from author to author and from place to place, and even with different points of view within the work of the same author. As the discussion progresses, however, it will emerge that one or two ideals of *gentillesse* remain relatively stable in almost all treatments of it.

In what was *gentillesse* thought to consist in the estimation of Chaucer and his contemporaries? The question would ideally be answered by an extended reading of their works, but it is a question that was raised in this form by themselves, and relatively concise answers were offered. In the *Confessio Amantis*, Gower asks it of his instructor, the priest Genius, and receives a typical answer, the same answer indeed as Chaucer found in Boethius and gave to the Wife of Bath. Common usage, we learn, refers *gentillesse* to inherited wealth or to nobility of birth. Yet, since wealth is frequently lost, and since all men are descended from common parents, Adam and Eve, and pass through the same course of earthly life, both these claims appear vain. *Gentillesse* is a condition of virtue fixed in the heart:

> *For after the condicion*
> *Of resonable entencion,*
> *The which out of the Soule groweth*
> *And the vertu fro vice knoweth,*
> *Wherof a man the vice eschuieth,*
> *Withoute Slowthe and vertu suieth,*
> *That is a verrai gentil man,*
> *And nothing elles which he can,*
> *Ne which he hath, ne which he mai.*
> (IV, 2269–77)

Gower's use of the prefix *verrai* to his definition of *gentillesse* betrays his position as an advocate. His definition is in fact an argument against the view that *gentillesse* consists in birth, possession, skills, accomplishments or capacities; a view which he acknowledges to be widespread. Yet it is no more widespread than Gower's moral philosophical perspective of nobility as the habitual tendency to act well. In the *Tale of Melibee*, we are independently informed that the *gentil* man is to be judged by his moral virtues and by the care with which he strives to maintain his good reputation (*CT*. VII, 1601). Chaucer's Parson outlines the same Boethian argument as Gower, and gives a few specific indications of the virtues which, in his opinion, constitute *gentillesse*. They are, along with the general avoidance of sin, *curteisie, clennesse,* reasonable generosity, gratitude, the aspiration to a better life, and also kindliness towards all those in less fortunate estate. Seneca is quoted on the desirability of *debonairetee and pitee* in the sovereign (X, 467). The tendency, exemplified by Gower, to envisage *gentillesse* as a rational state equivalent to the philosophers' *virtus* is therefore complemented by the attempt of men like the Parson to capture *curteisie* and *gentillesse* for Christian idealism. Chaucer himself, exploits the implicit contrast between two kinds of heredity: the worldly one from Adam, and the spiritual from Christ. *Gentillesse* is explicitly distinguished from inherited wealth and is to be sought in the virtue of the individual, whose virtues are often Christian ones – *pitous, clene of his gost, besinesse* – and true *gentillesse* is associated with the example of Christ. Similarly, in *Pearl*, the Virgin is celebrated as the queen of true *curteisie*.[1] *Gentillesse* and *curteisie* are, already in the fourteenth century, treated as religious and philosophical ideals of a distinctly unworldly kind. Nevertheless, the latter very frequently connotes merely ceremonious behaviour or affability in demeanour, whilst the former can refer to the social niceties of courtly conduct: the clean nails, scrubbed teeth and polished boots prescribed for the lover by the God of Love in the *Romaunt of the Rose*. The breadth of application of these terms, then, is extremely wide.[2]

In attempting to reduce this variety of application to some underlying order, we may begin by the observation that *gentillesse* is particularly associated with *pitee*. On four separate occasions Chaucer uses a line which closely echoes thirteenth-century Italian sources: 'Pitee renneth soone in gentil herte.'[3] It is an essential feature of the *gentil* man that his heart is not hardened like that of the tyrant. When the God of Love begins his account of *gentillesse* in the *Romaunt of the Rose* he commences with a denunciation of the condition of the churl, speaking purely in moral terms:

> *Thise vilayns arn withouten pitee*
> *Frendshipe, love, and all bounte.*
> (*RR*. 2183–4)

The condemnation is entirely for lack of social virtues: *pietas, amicitia*, love and beneficience. Again and again we are assured that the *gentil herte* is 'fulfild of pitee' (*CT*. II, 660) whilst that of the *vileyn* lacks it entirely. *Frendshipe* is a quality describing an attitude of the courtly man to the world at large and does not describe any particular actual relationship; the courtly man is friendly-disposed to all his fellows. *Pitee*, too, is a quality of the *gentil* man; in fact that quality which we discussed as *pietas* in the last chapter. Sympathetic identification between members of the courtly community is as important a concept as it is between Christians. The capacity for feeling this compassion defines a particular kind of heart which Chaucer often refers to as a 'pitous herte', but alternatively, it may be called a 'gentil herte.' Our first presumption must be, therefore, that *gentillesse* is at least partly defined by the possession of a *gentil herte*, and that capacity for feeling is the acid test of this.

In the *Book of the Duchess*, the Man in Black phrases the description of his sorrow in a somewhat curious way. He is heartily lamenting a mysterious sorrow, and he presents his plight in the form of a test of feeling for any chance observer:

> But whooso wol assay hymselve
> Whether his hert kan have pitee
> Of any sorwe, lat hym see me.
> (BD. 574–6)

The idea of a test to see whether one's heart is capable of pity would seem bizarre were it not for the fact that it is established procedure in the literary tradition which Chaucer was following, and that matters of some moment hang upon it. In the *Romaunt of the Rose*, and also in *Troilus and Criseyde*, we find suggestions that failure to feel compassion indicates an undesirably hard heart, and such hard-heartedness is virtually inhuman:

> In world nys wight so hard of herte
> That hadde sen her sorwes smerte,
> That nolde have had of her pyte.
> (RR. 333–5)

The disapproval of hardness of heart implied in the effect of the allegorical portrait of Sorrow in the *Romaunt* is explicit in the *Book of the Duchess*:

> whoso wiste al, by my trouthe,
> My sorwe, but he hadde rowthe
> And pitee of my sorwes smerte,
> That man hath a feendly herte.
> (591–4)

No-one could relish the accusation of a 'feendly herte', and the test of a good heart is repeatedly the ability to feel pity on suffering. Pandarus employs this commonplace, echoing the idea of the courtly lady as the anti-type of the tyrant, when he supposes that

> in good herte it mot som routhe impresse,
> To here and see the giltlees in distresse.[4]
> (TC. II, 1371–2)

Pitee, then, is an ideal of *gentillesse*. The *gentil* heart is not hard and resistant, but soft and easily impressed by pity for the wretched. Curiously, in describing this ideal condition, Chaucer never uses the phrase 'soft-hearted'; for him the opposition with hardness of heart is expressed by a whole array of other phrases ranging from *gentil herte*, *tendre herte* and *pitous herte*, through to the simply evaluative *good herte*.

Now although there is considerable emphasis in Chaucer's work upon the capacity of the *gentil herte* to sympathize with the suffering of others, and a positive value is placed upon this, as in religious writings, this is not the complete story of the *gentil herte*. It is a mark of such a heart that it is also susceptible of other emotions, such as love and joy. It is strongly affected by the spirit of joy and vitality which animates the spring season. The Knight, with full confidence that his *gentil* audience will understand him, tells them that the 'sesoun priketh every gentil herte' (I, 1043), for had not Guillaume de Lorris declared, and Chaucer translated:

> *Hard is the hert that loveth nought*
> *In May, whan al this mirth is wrought,*
> *Whan he may on these braunches here*
> *The smale briddes syngen clere*
> *Her blisful swete song pitous.*
>
> (*RR*. 85–9)

The sympathy of the poet with the season is expressed by what at its earliest use must have seemed a daring image. The springtime clothing of the trees in green, known as the *reverdie,* is used directly of the poet's heart, which itself becomes green with the spring (*RR*. 720).[5] Many are the men and women in medieval literature whose hearts are similarly affected by the song of the birds in Spring, and whose thoughts turn from them to human loving. The second Book of *Troilus and Criseyde,* which Chaucer formed in the image of the twelfth-century French romance, illustrates well his own handling of these presuppositions. For there the exchange of hearts, which in Criseyde's dream symbolizes the union of affect which distinguishes lovers, is preceded first by the nightingale singing upon its 'cedir grene' and then by the Trojan song of Antigone. These conventions were already old in Chaucer's time, and indeed Criseyde might have been warned of the virulence of nightingales by a south-country owl of more than a century earlier. At the end of the twelfth century, the Anglo-Norman poet Hue de Rotelande also remarks in his knowing way that 'the song of birds and the sound of instruments is an aggravation of love.'[6]

Sensitivity, then, is a key notion in understanding *gentillesse,* and this is revealed by the ease with which the *gentil herte* is impressed by the moods of man and of nature external to it. But it is also revealed by the intensity with which it suffers emotion. Images from outside and emotions caused within are equally impressed with force upon the *gentil herte.* It is a function of the *gentillesse* of his heart that Troilus takes such a 'fixe and depe impressioun' of love of Criseyde, and the force of his emotions causes the same violent shifts in colour in other courtly heroes than Troilus, who changes colour some sixty times. The heroic suffering of the courtly man in love springs as much from his own sensitivity to passion as from external circumstances, although the latter, in terms of the inaccessibility of the lady, are more often emphasized in discussions of this narrative situation. It is often the case in literature that these powerful emotions come into conflict with some other ideal of courtly behaviour, and in these circumstances, the personality divided against itself may be threatened with self-destruction:

> *This is so gentil and so tendre of herte*
> *That with his deth he wol his sorwes wreke;*
> *For trusteth wel, how sore that hym smerte,*
> *He wol to yow no jalous wordes speke.*
>
> (TC. III, 904–7)

Suicide is conventionally threatened when matters reach this pass, and indeed the list of conventional *exempla* against suicide given in the *Book of the Duchess* (724–41) are intended to be suggestive of the intensity of the Man in Black's despair.

Yet, if emotional intensity is a feature of the *gentil herte*, it is its susceptibility to *pitee* which is its outstanding feature. In the courtly love situation, operating as it frequently does in the shadow of the tyrant image, *pitee* is very often the precursor of the fulfilment of love:

> *Anon hire herte hath pite of his wo,*
> *And with that pite love com in also;*
> *And thus, for pite and for gentillesse,*
> *Refreshed moste he been of his distresse.*
>
> (LGW. 1078–81)

This passage, with its schematic verbal organization (And . . . And . . . And . . .) and its use of the word 'Refreshed', has a distinctly ironic tone, but its irony consists in the wearied repetition of a series of conventional psychological stages, so that, despite its air of moral resignation at the way things happen in the world – perhaps even because of it – it is an excellent demonstration of the proprieties of the convention. We may supplement it by another passage from a poet following a convention equally closely, although with less consciousness of *déjà vu*; Lydgate in his *Temple of Glas*, explaining again the relationship between *pitee* and love:

> *That euenlich and with þe same fire*
> *She mai be het, as I nov brenne and melt,*
> *So þat hir hert be flaumed bi desire,*
> *That she mai knowe bi feruence hou I swelt.*
> *For of pite pleinli if she felt*
> *The selfe hete þat doþ myn hert enbrace*
> *I hope of rouþe she would do me grace.*
>
> (841–7)

Here the lover sees the function of *pitee* explicitly in terms of unity of affect by which the lady will participate in his own suffering, and so be led to grant him love. We may recall that in the last chapter it was stated that love, as much as *pitee*, implies union of affect; that is a sharing of identical feelings. *Gentillesse, pitee* and love are therefore interdependent and imply a union of feeling with one who is perceived to be our similitude.

This dauntingly abstract phrase, drawn from scholastic writings, can conveniently be exemplified from the *Squire's Tale*. Canacee has been given a ring which, when she wears it, enables her to understand the language of the birds. Out walking, she comes across an anthropomorphic falcon who shrieks in a 'pitous voys' and is rending herself with her beak. The Squire employs a variation of the 'no heart so hard' device:

> *ther nys tygre, ne noon so crueel beest,*
> *That dwelleth outher in wode or in forest,*
> *That nolde han wept, if that he wepe koude,*
> *For sorwe of hire.*
>
> (V, 419–22)

Canacee nearly dies 'for the routhe' and, looking 'pitously' on the unhappy bird, she asks the cause of its sorrow. The possible reasons she suggests sound a little precious, but they are those of the *Book of the Duchess* too:

> *Is this for sorwe of deeth or los of love?*
> *For, as I trowe, thise been causes two*
> *That causen moost a gentil herte wo.*
>
> (450–2)

Canacee expresses the compassion she feels; then the hawk swoons, revives, and at last replies:

> *That pitee renneth soone in gentil herte,*
> *Feelynge his similitude in peynes smerte,*
> *Is preved alday, as men may it see,*
> *As wel by werk as by auctoritee;*
> *For gentil herte kitheth gentillesse.*
> *I se wel that ye han of my distresse*
> *Compassion, my faire Canacee,*
> *Of verray wommanly benignytee*
> *That Nature in youre principles hath set.*
>
> (479–87)

The speech, awkward as it is, is a clear enough statement of the idea of *pitee* as the bond of common feeling uniting those who declare themselves to be *gentil*. The *gentil herte*, perceiving the suffering of its equivalent (*similitude*), is moved to *pitee* and to an identical feeling of sorrow. This sympathetic union alone is felt to be sufficient to indicate Canacee's *gentillesse*.

The courtly are united by their capacity to feel each others sorrows, and

157

further, courtly society, like the ideal Christian society envisaged by the early fathers, operates under the new dispensation of a kind of 'lawe of pitee.' Together with a readiness to sympathize comes a willingness to forego rights for another's sake. Verbal exchanges between courtly people are marked by the use of devices intended to avoid imposing the speaker's will upon the other. Elaborate efforts are made to ascertain the wishes of the interlocutor, and so achieve that mutuality of will which complements union of affect. On the Canterbury pilgrimage, Harry Baily has been granted the right at the outset to demand stories from any pilgrim he chooses, and sometimes he exercises it in a very peremptory way. But, when he comes to the Prioresse, he is the soul of courtesy:

> *My lady Prioresse, by youre leve,*
> *So that I wiste I sholde yow nat greve,*
> *I wolde demen that ye tellen sholde*
> *A tale next, if so were that ye wolde.*
> *Now wol ye vouche sauf, my lady deere?*
> (*CT.* VII, 446–51)

This speech, with its conditionals, its honorific titles, its respectful second-person plurals, Chaucer labels as *curteis.* Harry is dispensing with the authority which is his right, and courtesy calls forth courtesy in reply when the Prioresse gladly agrees to tell a tale. A somewhat different passage will illustrate further the point that *curteisie* involves the extension of human kindliness 'beyond right'. In the *Merchant's Tale,* Proserpin is quarrelling noisily with her husband, King Pluto, on the relative merits of men and women. An accusation, she implies, demands a right of reply, and she will not deny her tumultuous nature to waive that right:

> *I sette right noghte, of al the vileynye*
> *That ye of wommen write, a boterflye!*
> *I am a womman, nedes moot I speke,*
> *Or elles swelle til myn herte breke.*
> *For sithen he seyde that we been jangleresses,*
> *As evere hool I moote brouke my tresses,*
> *I shal nat spare, for no curteisye,*
> *To speke hym harm that wolde us vileyne.*
> (*CT.* IV, 2303–10)

Proserpin's refusal for courtesy's sake to curb a harsh reply is worth comparing with a few words in the description of personified Curtesye:

> *Of fair speche, and of fair answere;*
> *Was never wight mysseid of here;*
> *She bar no rancour to no wight.*
> (*RR.* 1259–61)

Curteisie, again like Christianity, demands that friendliness and under-standing be extended even to those who show hostility. Finally, we may recall a passage from the *Parliament of Fowls.* Towards the end of the poem, the formel eagle is unable to decide upon a mate. The three eagles who are her suitors all seem to resemble each other in nobility more than they resemble any of the other birds. Yet Nature states that if she were Reason she would advise the choice of the royal tiercel who is 'gentilleste and most worthi.' Now the point about the judgement of Reason is made without the necessity of distinguishing degrees of nobility discernable in the speeches of the three tiercels, and in any case the tiercels are ranked in order by the narrator, yet aesthetically it is desirable to find some dif-ferentiation within the speeches themselves. Nature sets the scene by stressing that the marriage must be made by mutual will.[7] Then the first tiercel speaks. His plea is one of total commitment. He places no obli-gation upon her and hopes only that his faith will lead to grace:

> *Thanne oughte she be myn thourgh hire mercy,*
> *For other bond can I non on hire knette.*
>
> (437–8)

The second tiercel's speech, by comparison, is one of self-justification, directed more towards competition with the first speaker than commit-ment to the lady; the brevity of the plea of the third, who claims commit-ment but is prosaically concerned with the delay caused to the other birds, disqualifies him from serious consideration despite the plausibility of his claim. The first tiercel, then, stands out as the most *gentil* largely on the grounds of his denial of this own merit and his complete trust in the humane qualities of the lady to extend *pitee* to him. His plea comes closest to the theological doctrine of grace where faith calls forth grace un-merited. *Gentillesse,* too, deals in beneficience rather than rights. The company of the *gentil* is defined by union of affect, mutuality of will, *pitee, grace, mercy* and love.

Yet, there is a qualification; for within the city of God *pietas* and *caritas* unite all Christians, but within the paradise gardens, where the union of affect signified by *pitee* connotes a delight and *myrthe* parallel to the joy which *pietas* extends among the saints in heaven, there are significant absences. The relationship of *similitudo* which defines the proper sphere of operation of courtly *pitee* becomes an exclusive device. Not all men have a *gentil herte,* and sympathy is by definition impossible with the hard-hearted, or those lacking in the requisite virtue. Among the vices to be excluded from the courtly paradise, and portrayed on the outside of its enclosing wall in the *Romaunt of the Rose,* are some which neither the Church nor philosophical tradition would find to be vicious: for example, Poverty and Old Age. In its narrower interpretation, then, *gentillesse* was

159

an exclusive doctrine: the *gentil* man was hardly likely to see his similitude in a churl, an old man, or a beggar. Christianity would see the image of God in all. By either standard, the Prioresse's *pitee* and *charitee*, extended to mice and little dogs, would appear ridiculous, since both *pitee* and *charitee* depend on the recognition of a similitude. It is fair to say, however, that such implications of courtly theory were not uniformly applied, so that respect for the aged is regarded as a part of courtesy in the *Pardoner's Tale* (VI, 739–47), where the attitude is influenced by scriptural authority, whilst there is no trace of satire in Gawain's regret for the death of his horse in battle. Indeed, the poet is at pains to tell us that Gawain is unconcerned at the loss of a valuable possession, or at the disadvantage in battle, he mourns only for 'þe dombe best þat þus shuld be dede.'[8] Whatever the allowable extent of sympathy, *gentillesse* had as its very root a concept which made it inevitably élitist; that which is implied by the urgency of the need to feel compassion. Some hearts were considered to be more sensitive than others, and it is upon this basis of the sensitivity of the soul that all else depends: the intensity of emotion, the capacity for love and compassion. *Gentillesse*, although sometimes interpreted in a way which confused the two, was not humanism, nor was it Christianity, since so many human beings and fellow Christians remained irretrievably locked outside the gates of its earthly paradise.

Beyond the emotional world of *gentillesse*, the sensitivity of the *gentil herte* had a further ramification which we have not yet mentioned, but which tended to increase the sense of élitism even further, and indeed to present the ideal *gentil* man as a superman in all respects. This arose from the scholastic theory of cognition, according to which the rational functions depended upon information from the outside world transmitted through the senses and the imagination. Clearly, if a man were of extraordinary sensitivity, in such a system he would be in a better position to think deeply, since the information at the service of his reason would be of finer quality. A mechanistic process of perception was already to be found in Plato (*Timaeus*, 76e) but is more elaborately treated by Aristotle. In his *De Anima*, Aristotle took the sense of touch to be paramount among the five senses, and stated that a refined sense of touch was causally related to a developed intellect.[9] In his commentary on this text, St. Thomas Aquinas greatly expanded this opinion, clearly relating the sense of touch to the whole sensitive nature:

> Unde ex hoc quod aliquis habet meliorem tactum, sequitur quod simpliciter habet meliorem sensitivam naturam, et per consequens, quod sit melioris intellectus. Nam bonitas sensus est dispositio ad bonitatem intellectus.

Therefore the finer one's sense of touch, the better, strictly speaking, is one's sensitive nature as a whole, and consequently the higher one's intellectual capacity. For a fine sensitivity is a disposition to a fine intelligence.

Further, subtlety of touch is a function of the harmonious *complexio* of the individual:

> Ad bonam autem complexionem corporis sequitur nobilitas animae: quia omnis forma est proportionata suae materiae. Unde sequitur, quod qui sunt boni tactus, sunt nobilioris animae, et perspicacioris mentis.

> Now nobility of soul follows upon a well-balanced physical constitution; because forms are proportionate to their matter. It follows that those whose touch is delicate are so much the nobler in nature and the more intelligent.[10]

Such thinking may well account for the assumed superiority of the *gentil* man; indeed it may be significant that the commonest Chaucerian rendering of the Latin *nobilitas* is as *gentillesse*.[11]

The intellectual capacities of the *gentil* man are revealed by the wit and subtlety of his eloquence, and by his accomplishment in a range of skills and activities. In England, he is described as *well-seiynge* and *wis;* in France, he is *bien parlers* and *enseigné*. One marked difference between Chaucer and his metropolitan contemporaries, and those popular romances which preceded them, is the former's familiarity with, and use of, a wide range of the popular scientific knowledge of their time. The themes discussed in this book, for example, belong essentially to the more sophisticated kind of secular poetry, and indeed might be taken to represent the reaction of the poet to the need among those who considered themselves aware of contemporary currents of thought for a poetry to express them in the vernacular: *Gentillesse,* from its beginnings, had been associated with the secularization and popularization of the theories of the clerks. The *gentil* man was by no means a clerk, but, just as today, the man of the world should be well-informed about the scientific speculations developed in more secluded circumstances.[12]

Poetry, too, was one of the accomplishments of a gentleman, and as it was frequently practised by those of ungentle birth, it tended to contribute to the conception of inherent superiority, for such men were apt to stress the élitism of the possession of a *gentil herte* and subtle mind over the advantages of birth. This is particularly noticeable in the poetry of Guillaume de Machaut, who repeatedly represents himself as a noble lover and a member of the charmed circle of the *gentil* by virtue of the nobility of his *fin coeur*. The poet must also be a lover and a *gentil* man, participating in the community of feeling of the *gentil*, recording it and interpreting it for them from the sympathetic beat of his own pulses. In the next century, Lydgate also states, in a typical disclaimer, the unity of affect that the poet of love must share with lovers:

> *For vnto wo accordeth compleynyng*
> *And delful chere vnto heuynesse:*
> *To sorow also, sighing and wepyng*
> *And pitous mournyng vnto drerynesse;*
> *And whoso that shal writen of distresse*
> *In party nedeth to know felyngly*
> *Cause and rote of al such malady.*
>
> *But I, alas, that am of wit but dulle*
> *And no knowyng haue of such mater*
> *For to discryve and writen at the fulle*
> *The wofull compleynt which that ye shul here,*
> *But euen like as doth a skryuener*
> *That can no more what that he shal write*
> *But as his maister beside doth endyte:*
>
> *Ryght so fare I, that of no sentement*
> *Sey ryght noght, as in conclusion,*
> *But as I herde when I was present.*
> *(Complaynt of a Loveres Lyfe, 183–99)*

The opening lines of this passage repeat the teaching of the manuals of rhetoric on the proper conduct of the orator in treating a doleful subject, but from line 187 onwards Lydgate's reference is to the courtly assumption that the love poet must actually participate in the feelings of his subject. The presupposition is quite alien to that of Latin learned poetry, of which Curtius said that the critic should ask himself not what experience the poet was seeking to describe, but rather which theme he had set himself to treat.[13] Whatever the realities of their poetic practice, courtly poets like Machaut and Deschamps professed to write from experience and from feeling.[14] Lydgate, however, denies that he shares feeling to any great extent with the complainant in his poem, and that he is writing simply as a copyist lacking in emotional identification. In this, and in the words he chooses to express it in line 197, he is imitating Chaucer. For although Chaucer's understanding of the feelings of lovers was celebrated in his own time, it is a persistent claim of his narrator that he cannot participate in their emotional world. In the opening of the *Parliament of Fowls*, in the *Legend of Good Women*, and especially in the *Troilus*, he emphasizes his separateness from the lovers for whom his poems are written and whose adventures they relate. He is merely a functionary, a servant of the servants of Love, under whose correction his verses must stand. At the beginning of *Troilus and Criseyde* he denies that it is worth his while to pray for help to the God of Love, since he is so obviously

162

unsuited to such a pastime, but he willingly helps to promote the ideals of *gentillesse,* calling upon lovers 'if any drope of pyte in yow be', to recall their own sufferings and by their analogy to envisage those of Troilus. Here he even goes so far as to say that he will pray for lovers, chronicle their ills, hold them in charity and compassion, though without himself being one of their company. At the beginning of Book Two he repeats that he writes of love 'unfelyngly' and 'of no sentement', then again in Book Three, he prays to Venus:

> techeth me devyse
> Som joye of that is felt in thi servyse.
>
> Ye in my naked herte sentement
> Inhielde.
>
> (41–44)

This refusal to admit community of feeling with lovers has a number of purposes, from the traditional didactic device of the dull dreamer to the avoidance of responsibility for his poetic productions. Most important, however, is the implicit refusal to be counted as a full member of the world of this narrower kind of *gentillesse.* The attitude might have been a tactful one for a servant of the court who was of *bourgeois* origin. It tacitly admitted the superiority of the courtiers with their refined feelings, and it also lent subtle flattery when the recognition of situations and emotions allegedly faithfully recorded by an uninvolved character would testify to the *gentillesse* of their own hearts. But most of all, perhaps, it genuinely represents Chaucer's reservations about the tenets of the courtly ethic. The distancing enables him to submit it to comparison with the other ethics which we have discussed; it permits him to adopt an ironic perspective. For although Chaucer was among the first to use the words *felyng* and *sentement* in English in their emotional senses, and is perhaps the subtlest courtly psychologist of the Middle Ages, he always approaches love and *gentillesse* in a spirit of enquiry rather than participation. He is a privileged observer in the paradisal park rather than an inhabitant.

If Chaucer chose to hold himself aloof from the ideal which placed poetry as one of the accomplishments of the *gentil* superman, other social types were excluded by their very nature. We have seen that these included the aged and the poor, but it also included the *vileyn.* Now, although this, in practice, would mean men of a low social status, in theory, *gentillesse* might include people of all social levels who possessed the appropriate virtues. Especially in later romances, for example, we hear of *curteis* bourgeois.[15] The *vileyn* or *cherle,* however, represented a moral type just as much as the *gentil* – and he was his opposite. The opposition could be made in terms of physical appearance, when the churl was ugly, snub-nosed, dark and disproportionate, or it could be made in terms of his graceless behaviour; but essentially it was made in terms of his brute insensitivity. 'Hard is the hert that loveth nought in May,' sang Guillaime de Lorris; yet there were those to whom this season meant nothing, those churls who 'can not of lovyng' (*RR*. 2333). Instead of going forth rejoicing with the birds, they go with nets to trap them (*LGW* (F) 136). The churl's heart is hardened to love and the Spring, as it is to his fellow man. His condition, like that of the *gentil*, is defined by aspects of his personality and by actions rather than birth. In the morality of the *Romaunt of the Rose*, echoed by the Wife of Bath:

> *A cherl is demed by his dede,*
> *Of hie and low, as we may see,*
> *Or of what kynrede that he bee.*
> (*RR*. 2200–2202)

Pitee and *frendshipe* are associated with *gentillesse*, whilst *hardnesse*, *danger*, and *mysseiyng* are features of *vilanye*. So powerful is this association between *pitee* and *gentillesse* that we find a curious semantic development of the word *cruel* as its reflection. *Cruel* of course is in opposition to *pitous* in the popular representation of the judicial situation. However, in terms of the capacity for compassion (i.e. sharing emotions), *pitous* is opposed by *hard*. It is not uncommon, however, to find *cruel* extended to uses where its sense is the affective one, 'unfeeling', associated with *hard*:

> *In al this world ther nys so cruel herte*
> *That hire hadde herd compleynen in hire sorwe,*
> *That nolde han wepen for hire peynes smerte,*
> *So tendrely she wepte.*
> (*TC*. V, 722–5)

Once *cruel* has adopted the sense 'unfeeling', its symmetrical opposition to *pitee* means that it is associated with *vilanye* in the same way as *pitee* is with *gentillesse*. Thus we find Sir Kay contrasted with Sir Gawain as respectively the epitomes of *vylanye* and *curteisie*. Kay is *Mysseiyng*, and 'of word dispitous and cruell.' More strikingly, in the *Tale of Melibee* we are told that it is a sign of the *gentil* that he protects his good reputation. His opposite is 'he that trusteth hym so muchel in his goode conscience / that he displeseth, and setteth at noght his goode name or loos, and rekketh noght though he kepe nat his goode name, nys but a crueel cherl' (VII, 1646–7).[16] That a churl can be called *cruel* for his disregard of the virtues of *gentillesse*, that, like the churl Danger in the *Romaunt of the Rose*, he can be disfigured by *ire* and *woodnesse*, points the way to a further contrast with the *gentil*. Indeed, except in social status the churl is identical with the tyrant, and as moral symbols both are the antithesis of the

164

gentil. It is an antithesis maintained in terms of affectivity; both lack the *pitee*, the sensitivity of the *gentil* man.

But the contrast between them might be maintained in a different way, in terms of the contrast between *mesure* and excess, for although *gentillesse* and its ideals are built upon the originally Christian concept of unity of affect among the converted, the ethic did adopt certain rationalistic ideals also. Most notable is that of *mesure*. As an ideal it was adopted with a hearty regard for its situational aspects – an understanding that it meant appropriateness to circumstances and situation. It becomes, indeed, a social virtue, often directed more towards manners than morals. It may connote the self-restraint which enables a hero of romance to enter a crowded and censorious hall, conducting himself and speaking with poise and decorum. In this it contrasts with the outrageous man who rides fully armed on horseback into the hall, boasting of his martial exploits. *Mesure*, in fact, is the ability, an effect of practical prudence, to adapt one's speech and manners to the required situation. Chrétien de Troyes, indeed, implies that *curteisie* consists essentially in *mesure* (*Perceval*, 8124–34).[17] Defined rationally, then, *gentillesse is mesure* in behaviour; defined affectively, it is sensitivity of soul. All in all, the ideals of *gentillesse*, where it endeavours to maintain a balance between emotionalism and rationality, were well in tune with orthodox medieval morality. The rationalist philosopher might criticize it for excessive emphasis upon the emotions; the Churchman for its exclusiveness and materialism. But although the esteem in which worldly goods were held would lead to its condemnation by both, the basic ethic of *gentillesse* was sufficiently acceptable to be considered perfectable either in a religious or philosophic manner. After all it was, in a sense, no more than a deviation from the other two ethical systems which might easily be corrected. It is when we turn to discuss ends that *gentillesse* comes into conflict with the Christian ethic, for the end of Christian ethics was eventual union with God, whilst *gentillesse* had no clearly formulated end outside the achievement of secular courtly perfection. This purposelessness was seized upon by early critics of *curteisie:* William of Malmesbury accuses the troubadour William of Aquitaine of living a life of careless self-indulgence, as though the universe ran by chance and was not governed by a divine providence.[18] The only criticism which the Clerk can level at the young marquis of his tale is that, virtuous as he was, 'he considered noght / In tyme comynge what myghte hym bityde,/ But on his lust present was al his thoght.' (IV, 78–80).

A purpose was given to the *gentil* man, however, when he fell in love, and here we should remember how the life of the foolish young Troilus, or that of the Man in Black, was polarized by the first glimpse of their ladies. Aimlessness is now replaced by burning commitment, and it is in this that the *gentil herte* is most likely to come into conflict with Christian ethics. For the dominating purpose of the courtly lover is union with his lady, and in his devotion there is a clear parallel with the Christian ethic of love whose end is in God. Poets and their medieval audience were well aware of this parallel, and it was exploited for every kind of literary and witty effect. Exploitation of the parallel is a manoeuvre particularly dear to Chaucer, and one in which he was an innovator in English poetry. Its moral significance is dauntingly difficult to identify, and indeed it is best to admit that no unqualified ruling on it is possible. At its gravest the deliberate confusion of the theology of Christian religion with the courtly doctrine of love might represent blasphemy and sin. To deliberately turn from God to a lesser goal was a definition of sin. If no turning away were involved, it was at least error in mistaking a lesser good for perfect felicity. But numerous passages by men who were no doubt devout Christians – Lydgate was a monk – suggest that the Christian analogy was not treated with universal horror by all right-thinking men. A man is not a Sunday-citizen every day of the week, and it must be that the courtly wit relating theology and love was an admired literary device. That the same man may on different occasions adopt different postures is illustrated by Chaucer himself. There is the Chaucer of the *Retractions*, the Chaucer of *Troilus and Criseyde*, and the Chaucer of *Womanly Noblesse*. Attitudes to love and *gentillesse* are different in each, yet all are of the same man. The lesson is that in reading Chaucer we must read closely but also flexibly. Typical Chaucerian attitudes and beliefs may emerge, but nothing is more destructive than a programmatic approach which imposes one unchanging moral perspective upon a man so various in his knowledge and interests.

Within Chaucer's works, and within those of his contemporaries, the attitude to love among *gentil* folk was not a settled one. It was rather a kind of running battle between reason and emotion. Although the contrast between the Christian and courtly love ethics is always implicit, it is rarely expressed as an opposition, whilst the conflict between Reason and Love has formed part of literary convention. It surfaces in one form in the practical prudence of Criseyde considering whether or not to fall in love with Troilus, in another in Troilus's sense of responsibility to his country in Book Four. Yet again, it is found in the narrator's exhortation of the Man in Black to have patience in suffering. A reconciliation with rational values is found in the essential stability in love of the *gentil*: constancy is the first requirement of the lover. But perhaps it is a constancy which has more in common with the fixity in faith of the saint than the *securitas* of the philosopher. There is a tendency, indeed, for the lover to reject the rational virtues in *gentillesse* and abandon himself to his passion, and although the lover is then at odds even with the narrower ideals of worldly

166

gentillesse, there is a further tendency to admire this heroic devotion to passion which contravenes all kinds of morality, sacrificing *mesure* to intensity of feeling.

Although never seriously justified, it is this total devotion which is the mirror-image of Christian devotion, and which borrows a pseudo-justification from theology. To participate in this kind of love a man must have a *gentil herte* for it is only the sensitive man who is so affected as to achieve the necessary intensity and purity of commitment to love. Love becomes the sole motivating force in the lover's life; all his acts are directed to achieving union with his lady. His intentions are therefore pure in the sense that they are unmixed with any other purpose. Literary references to *fine amor* have more relevance to this unity of intention than any implication of the platonic purity of the passion.[19]

As in Christian theology, devotion alone, perhaps supplemented by the knowledge of frustrated suffering, is considered to evoke the *pitee* and the *grace* of the lady. Chaucer often employs the theological commonplace that this is undeserved, depending rather upon the goodness of the giver and the faithful service of the recipient. A striking example of this is Troilus's prayer to Love:

> *For noldestow of bownte hem socouren*
> *That serven best and most alwey labouren,*
> *Yet were al lost, that dar I wel seyn certes,*
> *But if thi grace passed oure desertes.*
>
> *And for thow me, that leest koude disserve*
> *Of hem that noumbred ben unto thi grace,*
> *Hast holpen.*
> *(TC.* III, 1264–70)

An alternative to the theological example of *grace* is the image, drawn from feudal or divine justice, of *mercy* or *pitee* extended beyond the proper limits of reason:

> *Here may men seen that mercy passeth right;*
> *Th' experience of that is felt in me,*
> *That am unworthi to so swete a wight.*
> *(TC.* III, 1282–4)

The essential feature of both images is that of a relationship dominated directly by shared feeling and renouncing rational restrictions. Such lovers are indeed united in feeling as they are in will, so that a relationship of equality is established in which neither adopts the rational role as guide and adviser of the other. The parallels with the monastic ideals of *amicitia* are recognizable, and indeed it is not unusual to regard lovers as belonging to a quasi-monastic order.[20] But the 'frendshipe' of lovers lacks the transcendental end of *amicitia*. Just as in Christian theology, however,

167

the recipient of grace employs it to perform good deeds which in due course add to his virtue. Troilus, we are told, fortified by his love for Criseyde, works wonders on the battlefield, and exchanges vices for virtue. When at last they are united, the joy of the lovers in their earthly paradise is parallel to that of the saints in heaven, and their tranquillity of soul equal to that of the philosopher.

This, then, is the theology of love as it was considered to be manifest among people of *gentil herte*. But that it was more a literary manoeuvre, a game of wit parasitic on Christian religion rather than a serious and stable doctrine in itself, is indicated by at least one common self-contradiction. The rhyme *serve: deserve* is very common in reference to the love situation in the works of Chaucer. In fact, occurring at the line-end, rhymes of either of these words with anything but the other are extremely rare. There is, then, a very close association between service and deserts in the Chaucerian representation of love. In many of these uses, Chaucer's view is 'orthodox', and the word is used to deny that *grace* is merited; but in only slightly fewer numbers there is an implication that *grace* can in fact be deserved by service or good qualities: a kind of Pelagian heresy within the love theology. It has always been a problem in Christian theology to remember that good works in themselves bear no merit, and in the treatment of love this provision is often forgotten:

> *He lay and thoughte how that he myghte serve*
> *His lady best, hire thonk for to deserve.*[21]
> (*TC.* III, 440–1)

Troilus's rationality strengthens his *gentillesse*, supporting his *mesure*, and winning the esteem of the populace and Criseyde alike, but it is his weakness as a lover, for he constantly attributes to the God of Love a quality which experience proves not to be his: the rational and just treatment of his dependents. Even in his very last words on earth, Troilus has not learnt this basic truth. Instead of acknowledging that the lover deserts the reason which moderates *gentillesse*, and steps voluntarily upon Fortune's wheel,[22] he is still reproaching Criseyde for a supposed injustice:

> *But trewely, Criseyde, swete may,*
> *Whom I have ay with al my myght yserved,*
> *That ye thus doon, I have it nat deserved.*
> (*TC.* V, 1720–22)

The tragic irrelevancy of this complaint is not revealed to him until after his death when his rational soul, rising to the eighth sphere, untrammeled by lower appetites, can directly perceive the truth.

But although Troilus is in error, he is not a fool. His predicament is that into which his *gentillesse* might lead any young man. His constitution combines in extremes the good qualities of all human beings. He is supremely susceptible to love and emotion, and at the same time of fine intellect and idealizing soul. A Stoic renunciation of love as a sickness of the soul would seem to him dehumanising, just as subjection to the passion of lust would seem demeaning. The answer is a kind of rationalization of his passion, and the presentation of it as an ideal in itself. This is the inevitable reaction of the *gentil herte* in love. Mature reflection, which is impossible for the youthful pagan, would have shown him the insecure basis of his idealization and counselled a less whole-hearted commitment, but his behaviour was not so foolish that it might not have been emulated, Chaucer suggests, by many a fourteenth-century Christian courtier. And in bleak reality, the affective ethic of courtly love was a dangerously amoral one, renouncing the rational *mesure* from which virtue sprang, directing quasi-religious feelings towards a transient object, submerging individual responsibility in union of will, and advocating an unconsidered currency of love which was proper only to a Christian context:

> *... best is*
> *That ye hym love ayeyn for his lovynge,*
> *As love for love is skilful guerdonynge.*
> (*TC.* II, 390–92)

Too hasty participation in such exchanges, without prudent consideration, was the cause of many tragedies and the subject of many poems. The intentions of one who declares love are difficult enough to determine even with reasoned analysis, but simple trust in the good faith of another lover is a recipe for chaos, and the *Legend of Good Women,* or the story of Dido and Aeneas, retold in the *House of Fame,* are evidence of it. Indeed the moral implications of the more exaggerated love ethic are so horrendous in the context of medieval ethics in general, that this alone is sufficient evidence to suggest that it was not regarded with the high seriousness that we are sometimes in danger of granting it; otherwise we should expect condemnation to have been longer and louder. Although there were no doubt many who took advantage of the ethic of courtly love, and invited condemnation for treachery, lechery and pride, there must have been few indeed who would embark upon such a potentially disastrous road in real earnest.

The ideals of *gentillesse* in its broader sense, however, were a different matter, and could be discussed with some seriousness. In its balance of superhuman sensitivity with rational moderation it presented both a possible ideal of conduct and an image in hyperbolic terms of the condition of mankind as a whole, divided as he was into sensitive and rational natures. The balance at the best of times between these is an unstable equilibrium, and it is the more so in the *gentil* man, both in view of his natural constitution and the fact of his lack of ultimate purpose. In the *gentil* man, then, we have the spectacle of a moral ideal insecurely founded and perpetually poised on the edge of chaos. The tyrant and the churl, the saint, the philosopher and the just king were all in their own ways static and invariable symbols of moral good or evil according to the estimation of one ethical system or another, but the *gentil* man was a dynamic symbol poised between the tyrant and the philosopher, and as such closer to human nature as it was ordinarily experienced. The story of Troilus is *par excellence* the story of such a *gentil* man. In his strengths and in his weaknesses, in his dependence on ethical concepts of an entirely secular kind, and hence in his catastrophe, he treads paths open to the fourteenth-century courtier who would espouse the ideals of *gentil-lesse* and then pass on to the narrower dedication to love. *Troilus and Criseyde* presents this process and criticizes Troilus's course both from the perspective of Christian and of rationalistic morality, but although it comes to a polemic conclusion addressed to its own age, just as in the *Parliament of Fowls*, Chaucer offers us no satisfying answers to the problem of the reconciliation between God, reason, and humanity.

Notes

INTRODUCTION

1 The word 'usage' refers to the customary employment of language items or combinations of items in fulfilling the functions of language in society. It is related to 'performance' rather than 'competence' and to acceptability and appropriateness in situation rather than to linguistic 'well-formedness.'

2 The term 'architecture' is derived from an article by L. Flydal, 'Remarques sur certains rapports entre le style et l'état de langage,' *Norsk Tidsskrift for Sprogvidenskap*, 16 (1951), 240–57. It was adopted by E. Coseriu in his article 'Lexical Structure and the Teaching of Vocabulary' in *Linguistic Theories and their Application*, A.I.D.E.L.A., Council of Europe (London, 1967), pp. 9–90.

3 G. N. Leech, *Towards a Semantic Description of English* (London, 1969), pp. 83–5.

4 The fullest attempt to classify stylistic variety in English is that of D. Crystal and D. Davy, *Investigating English Style* (London, 1969).

5 J. R. Firth, *Papers in Linguistics, 1934–51* (London, 1957), p. 44.

6 D. Hymes, *On Communicative Competence* (Philadelphia, 1971). Also the discussion of this topic by John Lyons, *Semantics*, 2 vols (Cambridge, 1977), Vol. II, pp. 570–91.

7 A discussion of the non-linguistic aspects of establishing the validity of a reading is to be found in E. D. Hirsch, *Validity in Interpretation* (New Haven, 1967), pp. 164ff.

8 H. S. Bennett, *Chaucer and the Fifteenth Century* (Oxford, 1948), pp. 82–5. A similar, although much more judiciously qualified, view is held by N. F. Blake, *The English Language in Medieval Literature* (London, 1977), pp. 8off.

9 The term *diglossia* is used to refer to the circumstance in which two languages co-exist in the same community in a relationship of unequal prestige, one being regarded as culturally superior to the other. The relationship between

French and English in England passed through stages of bilingualism, *diglossia* and bilingualism together, and by Chaucer's day had reached the stage of *diglossia* alone. C. A. Ferguson, 'Diglossia', *Word*, 15 (1959), 325–40; also Roger T. Bell, *Sociolinguistics* (London, 1976), pp. 116–44.

10 In the early fourteenth century, fellows of Merton College spoke English at table, wore 'dishonest boots', and even married. C. E. Mallet, *A History of the University of Oxford*, 3 vols (London, 1924–27), Vol. I, 118. See further A. C. Baugh, *A History of the English Language*, Second Edition (London, 1959), pp. 165–6.

11 Attempts to demonstrate continuity of poetic and prose tradition in terms of general, and often impressionistic, stylistic connections are unconvincing. The attempt to link the *Ancrene Riwle* to fifteenth-century successors like *The Orchard of Syon* in terms of their purpose and audience is made more successfully by N. F. Blake, 'Middle English Prose and its Audience,' *Anglia*, 90 (1972), 437–55. In more general terms, the survival of stylistic devices in early Middle English literature is unrelated to the art of prose or verse, but is a function of the devotional purpose of the literature.

12 *King Alisaunder*, edited by G. V. Smithers, 2 vols, E.E.T.S. O.S. 227, 237 (London, 1952, 1957), Vol. II, pp. 28–40. The author of *King Alisaunder* may also have been responsible for the versions of *Of Arthour and of Merlin*, *The Seven Sages of Rome*, and *Richard Coer de Lion* which are preserved in the Auchinleck MS. (*ibid.*, p. 41).

13 Otto Jespersen, *Growth and Structure of the English Language*, Ninth Edition (Oxford, 1962), p. 87.

14 Linguistic borrowing is discussed as a process of importation of foreign linguistic patterns, followed by the substitution of native forms into those patterns, in E. Haugen, 'The Analysis of Linguistic Borrowing,' *Language*, 26 (1950), pp. 210–31; reprinted in *Approaches to English Historical Linguistics*, edited by R. Lass (New York and London, 1969), pp. 58–81.

15 The 'style curial' was a style which had been developed in the papal *curia*, but which, by the mid-fourteenth century, had become extended to provincial chancelleries also. Jens Rasmussen, *La prose narrative française du xivᵉ siècle* (Copenhagen, 1958), pp. 32–33. An analysis of the style of Chaucer's *Melibee* in these terms may be found in Diane Bornstein, 'French Influence on Fifteenth-Century English Prose as Exemplified by the Translation of Christine de Pisan's *Livre du Corps de Policie,' Mediaeval Studies*, 39 (1977), 369–86.

16 The relish for dialectic in courtly poetry derived originally from the schools, whilst its psychological subtlety derives equally from Aristotle and the penitential tradition. Many of the topics and motifs of courtly verse may be sought in the Latin authors of antiquity as well as more recent curriculum authors.

17 'Verbal repertoire' is 'the totality of linguistic forms regularly employed in the course of socially significant interaction' and is considered to extend beyond traditional language boundaries. J. J. Gumperz, 'Linguistic and Social Interaction in Two Communities,' *American Anthropologist*, 66.6, Part II (1964), 137–63. Reprinted in *Language in Social Groups*, edited by Anwar S. Dil (Stanford, 1971), pp. 151–76.

18 In his *Balades*, Gower repeatedly uses the phrase *fin amour* together with a

whole range of courtly motifs and diction associated with it. The phrase does not occur in his English works, either as borrowing or loan translation. It is apparent that the sensibility of the courtly lyric, and the courtly love situation, was associated by Gower with the French language. His choice of the language here is a literary stylistic one.

19 E. Ekwall, *Studies on the Population of Medieval London* (Stockholm, 1956), p. lxii.

20 Some account of this audience may be found in Derek Pearsall, *Old English and Middle English Poetry* (London, 1977), pp. 194–7. See further Derek Pearsall, 'The Troilus Frontispiece and Chaucer's Audience,' *Yearbook of English Studies*, 7 (1977), 68–74. Also, D. W. Robertson, jr., *Chaucer's London* (New York and London, 1968), pp. 200–13.

1. THE TYRANT

1 For the chronology of these alterations, see *The Works of John Gower*, edited by G. C. Macaulay (Oxford, 1899–1902), Vol. IV, *Latin Works*, pp. xxx–xxxii, and Vol. II, *English Works*, pp. xxi–xxviii. Also, J. H. Fisher, *John Gower: Moral Philosopher and Friend of Chaucer* (London, 1965), pp. 116–27. Dates are necessarily speculative, and doubt has been cast upon the traditional assumption of three recensions. It may be that a new collation of the MSS of *CA.* is necessary. N. F. Blake, 'Caxton's Copytext of Gower's *Confessio Amantis*,' *Anglia*, 85 (1967), pp. 282–93.

Unless otherwise stated all translations of Gower's Latin are from *The Major Latin Works of John Gower*, translated by Eric W. Stockton (Seattle, 1962).

2 George R. Coffman, 'John Gower, Mentor for Royalty: Richard II,' *PMLA*, 69 (1954), pp. 953–64. See also Maria Wickert, *Studien zu John Gower* (Köln, 1953), pp. 110–40. The anonymous author of *Mum and the Sothsegger* took it upon himself to offer advice to Henry IV, and even Chaucer's own tale of Melibee might be considered to have relevance to contemporary royalty.

3 The traditional concept of the *magister principis* is well illustrated in James Yonge's (1442) translation of Jofroi de Waterford's French text of the *Secreta Secretorum*: 'and therefor had this olde Pryncis wyth ham hare maistris, as Alexander, arystotle; Nero, Seneca; and Troiane, Plutark' (p. 150). *Secreta Secretorum*, edited by Robert Steele, E.E.T.S., Extra Series 74 (London, 1898).

4 The possibility of a merchant bearing gold unmolested across a kingdom is a favourite symbol of the effective jurisdiction of its king. Bede uses it to illustrate the peace of King Edwin of Northumbria (*Historia Ecclesiastica*, II, xvi), and the Peterborough chronicler of William the Conqueror (*Peterborough Chronicle*, edited by Cecily Clark, Second Edition (Oxford, 1970), p. 12). It finds its way into romance in *Havelok the Dane*, 45–50. An interesting account of the weak and pusillanimous ruler, *le roi fainéant*, is to be found in Edward Peters, *The Shadow King: Rex inutilis in Medieval Law and Literature, 751–1327* (New Haven and London, 1970).

5 *The Parisiana Poetria of John of Garlande*, edited and translated by Traugott Lawler, Yale Studies in English, 182 (New Haven and London, 1974), pp. 10–11. This advice is found in John's section on *inventio*, which is the term given by rhetoricians to the process of selection of tractable material suitable for literary elaboration. That John is in fact describing as much as prescribing can be seen from historical works like the *Gesta Stephani*, edited by K. R. Potter and R. H. C. Davis (Oxford, 1976), where the dichotomy is maintained between Stephen and his adversaries. The former is *pius, benignus, humilis, semper compassionis et pietatis abundans* (p. 207); the latter are *tyrannus* and *furibundus*.

6 The tradition that Seneca acted at Nero's *magister* and a restraint on his tyranny derives from the dedication of the *De Clementia* and from a brief reference in Jerome's *De Viris Illustribus*, xii, 851; *PL*. 23, 629.

7 Barnabò Visconti, Lord of Milan, died, reputedly by poison, in December 1385. Chaucer himself had visited Milan on diplomatic business in the summer of 1378, and although he may not have become personally acquainted with Visconti, he had probably met other Englishmen who knew him well. A group of Englishmen were at this time in Visconti's service, and it is likely that Chaucer had business with their leader. See R. A. Pratt, 'Geoffrey Chaucer Esq., and Sir John Hawkwood,' *ELH*, 16 (1949), pp. 188–93.

8 This account of the diatribe is based upon that given in A. Oltramare, *Les Origines de la Diatribe romaine* (Lausanne, 1926).

9 R. R. Bezzola quotes Gerald of Wales's claim that Henry II had read *De Clementia. Les Origines et la Formation de la Littérature courtoise en Occident* (Paris, 1958), III, i, 17. In the fourteenth century the better known works of Cicero, Seneca, and Ovid could be obtained 'without much difficulty.' R. R. Bolgar, *The Classical Heritage and its Beneficiaries* (Cambridge, 1954), p. 262.

10 Deschamps refers to Chaucer as a Cicero in rhetoric, an Aulus Gellius in practical sciences (see p. 54 below for the division of *philosophye* into practical and speculative branches), and a Seneca in ethics. Caroline F. E. Spurgeon, *Five Hundred Years of Chaucer Criticism and Allusion*, 5 Parts (London, 1922), Part V, pp. 16–17.

11 Works of guidance for rulers are found in Western Europe from ancient times, and in the Middle Ages are influenced not only by the writings of the Church Fathers, but also from Arabic sources. The greatest development of the *miroir de prince* as a genre took place in Carolingian times, when writers such as pseudo-Cyprian and Jonas of Orleans were influential. John of Salisbury, Vincent of Beauvais, and Giles of Rome contributed to the eventual emergence of works in the vernacular in the fourteenth century. For the historian, the discussion of tyranny which is found in works of this kind is chiefly interesting for its political and legal aspects. The psychological symbol of the tyrant, of course, extends far beyond such technical writings, and indeed it is unlikely that Chaucer and his contemporaries drew their conception of the tyrant directly from specialized *miroir de prince* literature (Wickert, pp. 113–4). An account of the tyrant from the politico-legal point of view can be found in Helen Wieruszowski, 'Roger II of Sicily, *Rex-Tyrannus*, in Medieval Political Thought,' *Speculum*, 38 (1963), pp. 46–78. A useful review of *miroir de prince*

literature is contained in Dora M. Bell, *L'Idéal Éthique de la Royauté en France au Moyen Age* (Paris and Geneva, 1962). See also Bezzola, III, i, 71.

12 Tyrants take delight in cruelty

Cruel and inexorable anger does not become a king

What difference is there between a tyrant and a king . . . except that tyrants are cruel to serve their pleasure, kings only for a reason and by necessity?

13 How great a blessing to escape anger, the greatest of all ills, and along with it madness, ferocity, cruelty, rage, and the other passions that attend anger.

14 The usage of *De Clementia*, in which *rex* and *tyrannus* are placed in opposition, seems to be based upon an earlier Greek distinction between the beneficient ruler (*basileus*) and the tyrant. Compare Isidore of Seville, *Etymologiae*, IX, iii, 18–21.

15 In the table, parentheses around *crudelis* indicate that the word is used in *De Clementia* with a special technical sense which is not directly comparable with Gower's usage. Asterisks indicate words of rare occurrence. The rarity of *crudelis* in the usage of Boethius may indicate that he had some perception of the ameliorative connotations of the term in Seneca's usage, and wished to avoid them with reference to tyrants. In later medieval Latin usage the Senecan distinction is often ignored; but see below Chapter Seven, p. 127.

16 Margaret Schlauch comments upon 'language already hoary from centuries of theoretical debate' in the accusations of tyranny contained in the articles of the deposition of Richard II. 'Chaucer's Doctrine of Kings and Tyrants,' *Speculum*, 20 (1945), pp. 133–56 (p. 155).

17 These are the words in the Latin text which Chaucer renders by the lexeme *wood*.

18 Miriam T. Griffin, *Seneca: A Philosopher in Politics* (Oxford, 1976), pp. 148ff.

19 The popular representation of the tyrant as he appears in romances such as *Havelok* or the Wakefield plays of *Magnus Herodes* or *Coliphizacio* does not exhibit the characteristic vocabulary which we have been discussing. In these popular works he is imperious, abusive, threatening, often carrying his threats into the most direct physical violence, and swearing by *Mahoune*.

20 *Ancrene Wisse*, edited by J. R. R. Tolkien, E.E.T.S., Original Series 249 (London, 1962), p. 108:
Edhalden oðres hure ouer rihte terme. Nis hit strong reaflac hwa se ʒelden hit mei þe is under ʒisceunge?

21 The association between the tyrant and Antichrist is an old one, and in fact forms part of John of Salisbury's justification of tyrannicide.

22 Lactantius, *Divinarum Institutionum*, V, xi; *PL*. 6, col. 585:
What brutality (*feritas*), what fury (*rabies*), what madness (*insania*) to deny light to the living, earth to the dead.
In the *Gesta Stephani*, Geoffrey Talbot unfeelingly (*incompassive*) digs up bodies from the graveyard at Hereford whilst constructing ramparts.

23 The relationship between prowess employed in righting wrongs and *pitee* is discussed and illustrated by Gervase Mathew, *The Court of Richard II* (London, 1968), pp. 120–22.

24 *Parson's Tale*, X, 988–92.

25 R. Neuse has argued that Theseus's character is ironically conceived, that in fact he deliberately adopts the posture of an ideal ruler in order to cover his real injustices. Such a reading is possible, although, in my view, unlikely to be valid. 'The Knight: The First Mover in Chaucer's Human Comedy,' *UTQ*, 31 (1962), pp. 299–315. Reprinted in J. A. Burrow, *Geoffrey Chaucer* (Harmondsworth, 1969), pp. 242–63.

2. THE IMAGE OF THE TYRANT

1 The same expression is used of a lover's fortunes in the *Knight's Tale*, I, 2397; *Complaint unto Pity*, 110; and *Anelida and Arcite*, 182.
2 Of the dozen uses of the word *hyre* by Chaucer, perhaps half imply disreputable gain. The word has very humble social connotations, since it is strongly associated with the wages of a labourer. Although it is not out of place in the *sermo humilis* of Christian moral idealism, its appearance in a courtly context suggests irony. It is notable that Troilus (*TC*. I, 334) employs the term to mock at the uncertain rewards of lovers, but later prefers to refer to *guerdoun* in his own case.
3 That the banners have a symbolic function is not certain, but they are strongly suggestive of balance and excess. In contemporary warfare, a red banner signified war to the death, in which no quarter would be given. This was the significance of the French *Oriflamme*. A white banner indicated truce and conciliation. In heraldry, red signifies cruelty and ferocity 'as of princes at war'. M. H. Keen, *The Laws of War in the Later Middle Ages* (London, 1965), pp. 104–110. Similar associations are found in stage directions in the fifteenth-century *Castle of Perseverence*, where Justice is to be dressed in red, Mercy in white.
4 *Confessio Amantis*, I, 18–24, and Nature's careful dissociation of herself from Reason in *Parliament of Fowls*, 631–7.
5 An account of the orders of the Flower and the Leaf can be found in *The Floure and the Leafe*, edited by D. A. Pearsall (London, 1962), pp. 22–9.
6 See below, Chapter Seven, pp. 127–8.
7 Peter Dronke, *Medieval Latin and the Rise of the European Love Lyric*, Second Edition (Oxford, 1968), p. 10. Professor Dronke is able to quote an example of this *topos* in an Ancient Egyptian papyrus. Medical authorities are cited by John Livingstone Lowes, 'The Loveres Maladye of Hereos,' *MP*, 11 (1913–14), pp. 491–546. In addition, see Roger Boase, *The Origin and Meaning of Courtly Love* (Manchester, 1977), pp. 132–3.
8 The fourteenth-century *Livre du Chevalier de la Tour Landry*, written by the Knight for the instruction of his daughters, was translated into English and printed by Caxton in 1484. *The Book of the Knight of the Tower*, edited by M. Y. Offord, E.E.T.S., SS 2 (London, 1971), p. 164.
9 Jean Seznec, *La Survivance des dieux antiques: essai sur le role de la tradition mythologique dans l'humanisme et dans l'art de la Renaissance*, Studies of the Warburg Institute, XI (London, 1940), pp. 35ff.

10 The tendency to avoid moral responsibility by invoking planetary influences or the intervention of fortune is a theme exemplified in a number of Chaucer's characterizations, notably the Wife of Bath and Criseyde, and it is also found in Gower's condemnation of Richard II, whose fall is explicitly separated from such influences (*Vox Clamantis*, II, 4). St. Thomas Aquinas (*ST*, 1a, 115, 4) makes it quite clear that whilst a man may be affected by the stars, he is not controlled by them. The influence of the stars is upon the lower nature, so that the wise man is master of the stars to the extent that he is master of his own passions.

11 C. S. Lewis, *The Allegory of Love* (reprint New York, 1958), p. 2. For a fuller statement of this usage in Old French, see R. Dragonetti, *La Technique poétique des Trouvères dans la Chanson courtoise* (Bruges, 1960), pp. 61–113.

3. PRACTICAL WISDOM

1 That Theseus's attempts to impose order raise more ethical problems than they solve is argued by Elizabeth Salter, *Chaucer: The Knight's Tale and the Clerk's Tale* (London, 1962). The general view, however, is that, whatever the limits of his power, 'Theseus invokes and represents' a principle of order in the tale. C. Muscatine, *Chaucer and the French Tradition* (Berkeley and Los Angeles, 1964), p. 184. See also the similar assessment by D. W. Robertson jr., *A Preface to Chaucer* (Princeton, 1962), pp. 260–65. A useful summary of critical attitudes to Theseus may be found in J. O. Fichte, 'Man's Free Will and the Poet's Choice: the Creation of Artistic Order in Chaucer's *Knight's Tale*,' *Anglia* 93 (1975), 335–60 (pp. 342–5).

2 John M. Manly and Edith Rickert, *The Text of the Canterbury Tales*, 8 vols (Chicago, 1940), Vol. II, p. 371.

3 Ill-considered speech is castigated by moralists of all kinds. The reproof of it is to be found in sermon material (Alan of Lille, *Summa De Arte Praedicatoria*, XXVI, *PL*. 210, 162), repeated to children in courtesy books (Caxton, *The Book of Curtesye*, edited by F. J. Furnivall, E.E.T.S., Extra Series, 3 (London, 1868), pp. 17 and 29), and in general encyclopaedias (Brunetto Latini, *Li Livres dou Tresor*, edited by F. J. Carmody (Berkeley and Los Angeles, 1948), pp. 236–45). An injunction to prudent silence somewhat reminiscent of that in the *Manciple's Tale* is found in the Prologue of Matthew of Vendôme's *Ars Versificatoria*.

4 Conventional wisdom occasionally receives the support of pastoral counsel, as in Mirk's *Festial*, edited by T. Erbe, E.E.T.S., Extra Series, 96 (London, 1905), p. 290. The context is a sermon on marriage:

Wherefore, os by Goddys ordynaunce, a man schal taken a wyf lyke of age, lyk of condicions, and lyk of burth; for þereos þese ben acordyng, it is lyk to fare wel, and ellys not.

5 *De Officiis*, I, v; and also *De Inventio*, II, liii.

6 See *Beowulf*, 1060, where it is probable that *foreþanc* represents *prudentia*. We may recall that *Beowulf* was placed within the *miroir de prince* tradition by

Levin L. Schücking, 'The Ideal of Kingship in *Beowulf*,' M.H.R.A. *Bulletin*, 3 (1929), 143–54; reprinted in *An Anthology of Beowulf Criticism*, edited by L. E. Nicholson (Notre Dame, 1963), pp. 35–49.

7 *Peter Abelard's Ethics*, edited and translated by D. E. Luscombe (Oxford), 1971), p. 129; *Summa Theologiae*, 2a 2ae, 47, 6. Aquinas tells us (2a 2ae, 50, 1), perhaps recalling Isidore, that Prudence and Justice are the outstanding virtues of a ruler.

8 Reginald Pecock, *The Folewer to the Donet*, edited by Elsie Vaughan Hitchcock, E.E.T.S., Original Series, 164 (London, 1924).

9 The thirteenth-century French adaptation of the *Anticlaudianus* made by one Ellebaut represents one aspect of Prudence operating at this humble level. The personification is described as possessing skill in eloquence and tact in avoiding giving offence to neighbours. *Anticlaudien*, edited by Andrew J. Creighton (Washington, 1944), lines 357–9.

10 J.-A. Weisheipl, 'The Classification of the Sciences in Medieval Thought,' *Mediaeval Studies*, 27 (1965), 54–90.

11 Aquinas (*ST*. 2a 2ae, 55) equates *prudentia carnis*, which is marked by its limited wordly ends, with the *sapientia mundi* of St. Paul: 'sapientia enim hujus mundi stultitia est apud Deum. Scriptum est enim: comprehendam sapientes in astutia eorum.' (I *Cor*. III, 19). In later Latin, Paul's attack on Greek philosophy is often echoed in the contrast maintained between *prudentia* and *astutia*. Gregory complains that the worldly wise, in their turn, regard the wisdom of the just as *fatuitas*, and, speaking in euphemisms, they call perversity of mind *urbanitas*. The worldly accomplishments of courtliness, under the names of *urbanitas* and *curialitas* are forbidden to well-intentioned noblewomen by Vincent of Beauvais, *De Eruditione Filiorum Nobilium*, edited by Arpad Steiner, Medieval Library of America, 32 (Cambridge, Mass., 1938), p. 194.

12 The notion of vices and virtues in gradational rather than opposite relationship is common in both Classical and medieval treatises: Cicero, *Tusc. Disp.*, II, xx, 47; *De Inv.*, II, liii; Augustine, *Contra Julianum*, III, xx, *PL*. 44, 748; Aquinas, *ST*. 2a 2ae, 52. Jill Mann has some interesting critical comments on the satirical value of words denoting ideals, but whose semantic breadth extends into the less than ideal. Unfortunately, she is content to ascribe this as a device to Chaucer's elusiveness, rather than recognize its basis in linguistic usage. *Chaucer and Medieval Estates Satire* (Cambridge, 1973), pp. 195–97.

13 E. T. Donaldson, 'The Idiom of Popular Poetry in the *Miller's Tale*,' *English Institute Essays, 1950*, edited by A. S. Downer (New York, 1950), reprinted in *Speaking of Chaucer* (London, 1970), pp. 13–29.

14 For a similar view expressed in slightly different terms see, V. J. Scattergood, 'The Originality of the Shipman's Tale,' *Chaucer Review*, 11 (1977), 210–31 (especially pp. 225–6).

15 In the ethic of popular romance a positive moral value is frequently placed on productive labour. A similar phrase is used in *Sir Isumbras*, where the hero is forced to earn his living as a miner: 'þay bade hym swynke . . . Hafe we none oþer ploghe' (397).

16 Geoffrey de Vinsauf, *Poetria Nova*, I, 43–8 in E. Faral, *Les Arts poétiques du*

xiie et du xiiie siècle (Paris, 1971), pp. 194–262. In translation in *The Poetria Nova of Geoffrey of Vinsauf*, translated by M. F. Nims (Toronto, 1967), pp. 16–17.

4. THE PHILOSOPHER

1 Seneca alludes to the story in *De Constantia Sapientis*, xviii, 5, but Chaucer's source may have been Jerome's *Adversus Jovinianum*, I, 48, although the parallel is not a close one.

2 John M. Steadman, *Disembodied Laugher: Troilus and the Apotheosis Tradition* (Berkeley, Los Angeles, London, 1972), p. 54; C. S. Lewis, *The Discarded Image* (Cambridge, 1964), pp. 152ff.; W. C. Curry, *Chaucer and the Mediaeval Sciences*, 2nd edition (New York, 1960), pp. 299–315.

3 E. V. Arnold, *Roman Stoicism* (Cambridge, 1911), p. 412.

4 The reference to ship and oar constitutes a common symbol of irrationality, representing a situation in which the vessel is guided by chance rather than the helmsman. The image is common in Stoic writings in which the *principale* is referred to as the 'steersman' of the soul. Peter of Blois, in a letter to Henry II, condemns the illiterate king as a 'ship without an oar, a bird without feathers.' *PL.* 207, 211. Compare *Troilus and Criseyde*, I, 146 and II, 3.

5 Compare *Ep.* xliv, 7; *De Beneficiis*, VII, ii, 3; and Cicero, *De Officiis*, I, xx, 69.

6 Arnold, p. 111.

7 An outstanding feature of Cynic doctrine was their scorn for any participation in public affairs, an attitude which was sometimes carried to a rejection of the conventions and comforts of ordinary society and a reliance upon the simple necessities of life. The ambitious conqueror was therefore the natural opposite of the Cynic philosopher.

8 George Cary, *The Medieval Alexander* (Cambridge, 1956), pp. 83–5 and notes. An English translation of the *Disciplina Clericalis* is now available in *The Disciplina Clericalis of Petrus Alfonsi*, translated and edited by Eberhard Hermes, translated into English by P. R. Quarrie (London, Henley, 1977). The story of Socrates and the king appears on pages 154–5.

9 A similar opposition between a philosopher and a man of affairs is to be found in *De Officiis*, I, xx–xxi.

10 In his discussion of felicity (*Tresor*, xlvii) Brunetto Latini uses a very similar vocabulary: *felicité, souffisance, fermeté et la constance, li sages hom, en pais et en tranquillité.*

11 Sic enim definitur iracundia, ulciscendi libido (*Tusc. Disp.*, III, v, 2).

12 This association is evident in *Piers Plowman*, C-text, I, 117:

God was wel þe wroþer. and tok þe raþere veniaunce.

13 Overtones of social and moral pejoration are inevitably built into the semantic structure of the verb *grucchen*, since it is historically a French borrowing used by the powerful of the resentment of the weak against their rule. It is consequently frequently associated with churls (as in *William of Palerne*, 271) and is often reproved by homilists.

14 Boethius, II, p. x.
15 The value of a fictitious pagan past as a setting for the works of a philosophical poet is noted by Robert B. Burlin, *Chaucerian Fiction* (Princeton, 1977), pp. 98–9.

5. TRANSFORMATIONS OF THE PHILOSOPHER

1 The Latin analogues make overt the reference to constance in her reply: Non est superbia sed constancia (*Legenda Aurea*); Ego constanter locuta sum non superbe (Mombritius).
2 Hagiographic motifs of this sort perhaps preserve the attitudes of an earlier age in which Christian apologetists were at pains to assert the superiority of their system over those of the pagans. Even in the twelfth century, in Abelard's *Dialogus* (*PL*. 176), we find the Christian triumphing in argument over a pagan philosopher. Centuries earlier, Lactantius had called the third book of his *Divinarum Institutionum* by the challenging title 'Concerning the False Wisdom of the Philosophers.'
3 G. H. Gerould, 'The Second Nun's Prologue and Tale,' in *Sources and Analogues of Chaucer's Canterbury Tales* (New York, 1941), pp. 664–84 (p. 670).
4 *De Constantia*, xiv, 1; *Ep*. cxxi, 14; Cicero, *De Finibus*, iii, 20–21. Albertus Magnus, *Quaestiones super de Animalibus* XV, qu.xi refuses to admit the intelligence of women, preferring to ascribe their acumen to *astutia*, with its evil associations, rather than *prudentia*. Aquinas (ST. 2a 2ae, 47, 4) considered reason to exist only as a potential in children. The Stoic view was that reason developed at the age of seven (Arnold, p. 250), which was the age at which the formal education of boys commenced in the Middle Ages also. Nicholas Orme, *English Schools in the Middle Ages* (London, 1973), p. 117.
5 R. Kellogg and R. Scholes, *The Nature of Narrative* (New York, 1966), pp. 93–98.
6 In this poem, *fruyt* refers to the moral benefit to be derived from the work, and is not an echo of the *nucleus-cortex* dichotomy of the exegetes. In fact it is a rendering of the *fructus* or *fructus legentis*, which is in turn the metaphorical title of the final cause or effect of the work, one of the Aristotlean four causes by which works were classified in the *accessus* tradition, which provided introductions to the classics of the past for the use of medieval students. For the use of this phrase, see R. B. C. Huygens, *Accessus ad Auctores*, 2nd edition (Leiden, 1970), p. 78; p. 86; p. 99. Alan of Lille, in his *Distinctiones Dictionum Theologicalium* (*PL*. 210, 799) refers to *fructus* as equivalent to *utilitas*, an expression also used in the *accessus* tradition of the ultimate moral effect of a work of literature.
7 E. R. Curtius, *European Literature and the Latin Middle Ages* (New York, 1953), pp. 98–105. Albertus Magnus, in his *Quaestiones super de Animalibus*, XIII, qu. iii and XV, qu. xi, explains how, on physiological grounds, women

necessarily lack not only prudence but incisive reasoning and moral stability. His arguments would not be accepted by most modern readers.

8 J. B. Severs, *The Literary Relationships of Chaucer's 'Clerkes Tale'* (New Haven, 1942), pp. 229–48. Severs set the tone of later critical comment on Chaucer's treatment of his sources by calling attention to his heightening of the cruelty of Walter and the pathos of Griselda, his sharper realization of setting and his more evocative poetry. The fact that he also expands moral themes and moral psychological analysis receives no notice.

9 The potentially destructive tension existing between traditional literary and philosophical ideas and what she sees as Chaucer's imaginative sympathy with his characters is eloquently presented by Elizabeth Salter in the summation of her essays, *Chaucer: The Knight's Tale and the Clerk's Tale* (London, 1962).

10 Seneca also echoed the diatribe in his distrust of popular opinion. *Ep.* xliv, 6.

11 There is a parallel in his treatment of *Il Filostrato*, which in *Troilus and Criseyde* becomes more philosophically earnest as well as more humane and pathetic. C. S. Lewis, 'What Chaucer Really Did to *Il Filostrato*,' *Essays and Studies*, 17 (1932), 56–75.

12 G. Paré, *Le Roman de la Rose et la Scholastique courtoise* (Paris and Ottawa, 1941).

13 C. S. Lewis, *Studies in Words*, Second Edition (Cambridge, 1967), pp. 165–80.

14 *Peter Abelard's Ethics*, edited with a translation by D. E. Luscombe (Oxford, 1971), p. 55.

15 J. D. Burnley, 'Chaucer's Art of Verbal Allusion: Two Notes,' *Neophilologus*, 56 (1972), 93–99 (95–9).

16 Vincent of Beauvais, *De Eruditione Filiorum Nobilium*, ed. Steiner, p. 194.

17 Criseyde's physical appearance is close to that of a measured ideal, and should therefore, *a priori*, be expected to reflect an ideal moral constitution also. Vincent of Beauvais (quoted above) expected the moral probity and physical appearance and demeanour of his ideal young ladies to reflect each other. But Criseyde's joined eyebrows are an imperfection which Albertus Magnus sees as significant of *femineitas* and *flexibilitas*. For him, feminity is more or less synonymous with moral instability. (*Quaestiones super de Animalibus*, I, qu. xxvi).

18 The word *escoulouriable* 'slippery' is commonly used figuratively in Old French to suggest transience. In moralistic passages, it is often collocated with *vain*, and applied to the instability of worldly things.

19 In his *Summa de Arte Praedicatoria*, the most widely read of the medieval manuals of preaching, Alan of Lille discusses the word *pax*. There are, he says, three grades: that peace associated with the joy of heaven, and two kinds to be found on earth. His discussion of the latter two is worth quoting at some length since his usage coincides closely with that we have been discussing in the last two chapters. The first, *pax pectoris*, proceeds *ex mentis tranquillitate*; it is secure from the transience of worldly things, vice is expelled, and the *sapiens* is content with this alone, desiring no outward goods nor fearing the rage of princes. The parallel with the *tranquillitas* of the philosopher is obvious. The second kind of peace achievable on earth, *pax temporis*, issues from a sense of worldly well-being and is undesirable morally, since it is *fallax . . . lubrica et*

transitoria (*PL.* 210, 156). The *Summa Britonis*, a popular thirteenth-century dictionary, of which more than 130 manuscripts survive, mostly from the fourteenth century, lists as synonyms of *lubricus*: *levis, vitiosus, vanus, frivolus, ineptus, lascivus, luxuriosus, defluens,* and the verb *vacillare. Summa Britonis sive Guillelmi Britonis Expositiones vocabulorum Biblie,* edited by L. W. Daly and B. A. Daly, 2 vols (Padua, 1975).

20 The theme *patientes vincunt* is repeatedly used in *Piers Plowman* to celebrate the power of patience (e.g. C-text, XVI, 157). Alan of Lille also extols the quiet victory of the patient in his *Summa de Arte Praedicatoria:*

> Et philosophus ait: Morum patientia summa, haec est per quam martyr moriendo superat viventem, patiendo triumphat, in tribulatione invenit dulcedinem, in labore quietem.
>
> (PL. 210, 140).

A Latin proverb, *patientia vincit omnia,* is quoted by H. Walther, *Lateinische Sprichwörter und Sentenzen des Mittelalters* (Göttingen, 1965), no. 20833f.

6. THE STATE OF THE HEART

1 'No pity sustained him then whom the envious hand assailed.' *Cronica Tripertita,* II, 37. Stockton (p. 301) renders *pietas* here as 'sense of duty.'
2 Chaucer's allusion to *De Clementia,* I, iii, 3 alters the sense of the Latin. Seneca in fact commends rational *clementia* rather than affective *pietas.* Furthermore, instead of recommending it above all other virtues in a prince, Seneca actually stated that *clementia* becomes no man better than a prince. Chaucer's alteration echoes rather the spirit of Isidore than Seneca:

> Regiae virtutes praecipuae duae: iustitia et pietas. Plus autem in regibus laudatur pietas; nam iustitia per se severa est.
> (*Etymologiae,* IX, iii, 5)

> There are two outstanding virtues of kingship: justice and humanity. And humanity is more to be praised in kings, for justice alone is harsh.

3 The semantic implications of this usage are complex, since hardness of heart in sin implies both a failure to demonstrate contrition and firm resolution on a course of evil. In this latter sense, hardness is paradoxically associated with constancy. Certain writers, for example Brunetto Latini (*Tresor,* II, xlii; lxxxviii, 13) regard constancy as intrinsically more desirable than changeability. Following his source, the *Moralis Philosophia,* perhaps by William of Conches, (*PL.,* 171, 1033), Brunetto points out that constancy in error cannot, however, constitute virtue.
4 Frances A. Yates, *The Art of Memory* (Harmondsworth, 1969), pp. 49–50. The image becomes a commonplace of scholastic psychology.
5 *On the Properties of Things: John Trevisa's translation of Bartholomew Anglicus' De Proprietatibus Rerum: a critical text,* edited by M. C. Seymour and others, 2 vols (Oxford, 1975).

The most influential author pressing the physicians' view was Galen. His attack on the Aristotlean belief that the central organ of sensation was in the heart was based upon the results of dissection experiments. He nevertheless accepted a mechanistic notion of perception which required that the brain cell receiving impressions be of a soft consistency. Owsei Temkin, *Galenism* (Ithaca and London, 1973), pp. 54–55.

6 J. L. Lowes, 'The Loveres Malady of Hereos,' *MP*, 9 (1914), 491–546.

7 The question of where Aristotle placed the central organ of sense is rather a vexed one. In his biological works, it is in the heart, but in *De Anima*, although the heart is considered to be the physiological basis of emotions, it is never explicity identified as the recipient of sense impressions. Stephen R. L. Clark, *Aristotle's Man* (Oxford, 1975), p. 71. T. J. Tracy, S. J. points out that Aristotle was primarily concerned with the soul in the latter work, and probably considered that such questions belonged rather to the physiology of perception. *Physiological Theory and the Doctrine of the Mean in Plato and Aristotle* (The Hague and Paris, 1969), p. 217 n. Whatever the justice in this contention, medieval commentators on *De Anima* were similarly evasive about the location of the central organ of sense, although there seems to have been a widespread assumption that it lay in the heart. By Chaucer's time, however, scientific opinion tended to accept the view of the physicians that sensation was situated in the brain, even in contexts which reveal marked Aristotlean influence in other matters.

8 Yates, p. 74.

9 Thomas Waleys, *De Modo Componendi Sermones*, in Th-M. Charland, *Artes Praedicandi* (Paris and Ottawa, 1936), pp. 396–7.

10 Pecock, *Folewer to the Donet*, p. 25.

11 For example, W. H. Clemen, *Chaucer's Early Poetry* (London, 1963), p. 55 and S. S. Hussey, *Chaucer: An Introduction* (London, 1971), p. 34.

12 A brief account of the theory of memory *loci* is given by Frances Yates (pp. 18–9). She also speculates on how this technique may have affected narrative structures in medieval poetry (p. 90). A somewhat similar application of memory techniques to explain the structure of the *Canterbury Tales* is offered by D. R. Howard, *The Idea of the Canterbury Tales* (Berkeley, Los Angeles, London, 1976), pp. 134–209.

13 *William of Palerne*, re-edited by W. Skeat, E.E.T.S., Extra Series 1 (London, 1867). The effect is mentioned by Plato, *Theaetetus*, 194b, and is widespread in medieval literature from Dante, *Purgatorio*, xvii, 23–4, to Henryson's *Testament of Cresseid*, 499–511.

14 The deliberative and prophetic functions of the imagination have been discussed by Randolph Quirk in 'Vis Imaginativa,' *JEGPh.*, 53 (1954), 81–3, and V. M. Hann, 'Chaucer: "Heigh Imaginacioun",' *MLN*, 69 (1954), 394–5. Professor Quirk's article has been reprinted in *Essays on the English Language Medieval and Modern* (London, 1968), pp. 27–9. Both authors allude to Dante's use of the phrase *alta fantasia, Paradiso*, xxxiii, 142 and *Purgatorio*, xvii, 23–4. Chaucer's use of the phrases *heigh fantasie* and *heigh imaginacioun* may possibly have a similar reference, but the contexts are indecisive, and Chaucer commonly uses the adjective as a kind of intensifier referring to faculties, vices,

and virtues as various as *prudence, malice*, and *cruelte*. On the deliberative function of the imagination, see further P. Michaud-Quantin, *La Psychologie de l'Activité chez Albert le Grand* (Paris, 1966), p. 65.

15 *The Appeal of Thomas Usk*, in *A Book of London English, 1384–1425*, edited by R. W. Chambers and Marjorie Daunt (Oxford repr., 1967), pp. 18–31.

16 Troilus is following to the letter the behaviour of the lover laid down in *The Romaunt of the Rose*, 2806ff.

7. WITHIN REASON

1 Cicero, *De Inventione*, liii, 159.

2 See quotation below, p. 127. Seneca's words are echoed without acknowledgement by Alan of Lille: 'O homo, misericordia secteris in proximo, non intuitu fortunae, sed causae; non aegritudo animi sed charitas Dei clementia excitet,' (*Summa de Arte Praedicatoria*, xviii. *PL*. 210, 148). Despite recasting the idea in Christian terms of reasonable love, Alan agrees with Seneca in disapproving of too easy sympathy. The distinction of vice from virtue on rational grounds is clearly stated also by Cicero, *Tusc. Disp.*, IV, vi and II, xx, 47.

3 Arnold, *Roman Stoicism*, p. 103.

4 A similar view had been expressed in Antiquity by Carneades. See J. M. Rist, *Stoic Philosophy* (Cambridge, 1969), p. 1.

5 Book II of *Troilus and Criseyde*, where Chaucer is writing most freely of his sources, shows the most urbane play with the precepts of rhetoric. Neither this nor his remarks in the *Nun's Priest's Tale* are to be taken as evidence that Chaucer scorned rhetoric in its right place. Brunetto Latini tells us (*Tresor*, III, i, 16) that those with eloquence conferred by rhetoric are the flower of the world, and, borrowing the idea from the opening of *De Inventione*, that their skills are the basis of social cohesion.

6 Cicero, *Tusc. Disp.*, III, viii, 16–18; *De Officiis*, I, xxvii, 94; I, xl, 142; I, xxv, 89.

7 Compare J. D. Burnley, 'Proude Bayard: "Troilus and Criseyde", I. 218,' *NQ*, N.S. 23 (1976), 148–52.

8 Compare *Canterbury Tales*, VII, 2299; X, 465.

9 *Canterbury Tales*, IV, 1678–9; X, 861. See C. E. Shain, 'Pulpit Rhetoric in Three Canterbury Tales,' *MLN*, 70 (1955), 234–45; and also, Siegfried Wenzel, 'Chaucer and the Language of Contemporary Preaching,' *SP* (1976), 138–61.

10 As, for example, *Canterbury Tales*, X, 833–5; *Piers Plowman*, B-text, XIV, 55–81. But see below (page 141) for the conception of the infused virtue of temperance whose measure is differently set from that of the intellectual virtue.

11 C. B. West, *Courtoisie in Anglo-Norman Literature* (Oxford, 1938), p. 1. Also, Jessie Crosland, 'The Conception of *Mesure* in Some Mediaeval Poets,' *MLR*, 21 (1926), 380–84.

12 Comparably equable climates are found in *PF*. 204; *LGW*. 128, and 1483; *RR*. 131.

13 Just as *mekenesse* and *daunger* temper one another in *Romaunt of the Rose*,

3581–2, so in *Confessio Amantis*, III, 235–6, *mercy* is seen as the mutual moderation of *pitee* and *crueltee*.

14 More autem vulgi hoc nomen etiam operibus misericordiae frequentatur. (*De Civitate Dei*, x, 1. *PL*. 41, 279) 'indeed in popular speech this name (*pietas*) is often used of acts of compassion.' Also Alan of Lille: Pietas est virtus qua aliquis misericordia movetur erga aliquem. (*Distinctiones Dictionum Theologicalium, PL*. 210, 901).

15 Evidence for Chaucer's rendition of Latin *clementia* is unfortunately lacking.

16 See above, p. 33.

17 Gower's position seems to be close to the rationalist view of Cicero and, more recently, St. Thomas Aquinas in *ST*. 1a 2ae, 59, 1, where he states that if *misericordia* is considered to be a habit enabling a man to bestow pity according to the judgement of reason, then it may be considered a virtue. This is close to the view of St. Augustine also.

18 Jean Frappier, 'Sur le Mot "Raison" dans le Tristan de Thomas d'Angleterre,' in *Linguistic and Literary Studies in Honor of Helmut A. Hatzfeld*, edited by A. S. Crisafulli (Washington, 1964), p. 176.

19 *Oeuvres de Guillaume de Machaut*, edited by E. Hoepffner, S.A.T.F. 46, 3 vols (Paris, 1908–21), *Le Dit dou Lyon*, 1773–1800. *The Book of the Knight of the Tower*, edited by M. Y. Offord, E.E.T.S., Supplementary Series 2 (London, 1971), pp. 164–7. In the *House of Fame*, 269–72 and 286–92, the problem of discerning the intentions of a lover is expressed by Chaucer in terms critical of Dido. Compare his more sympathetic treatment of her story in the *Legend of Good Women*.

20 J. A. W. Bennett, 'Gower's Honeste Love,' in *Patterns of Love and Courtesy: Essays in Memory of C. S. Lewis*, edited by John Lawlor (London, 1966), pp. 107–21. Bennett defines Gower's conception of *honeste love* as the co-existence of faithful love within marriage and *caritas* within the Christian state.

21 This is the basis of the famous claim by Andreas Capellanus, *De Amore*, vi, 141–2, that love cannot exist within marriage. His definition of love as an inordinate desire to receive a passionate, furtive and hidden embrace is a caricature of scholastic definitions of the passion of love. For a translated version, see Andreas Capellanus, *The Art of Courtly Love*, translated by J. J. Parry, edited and abridged by Frederick W. Lock (New York, 1957), p. 17.

22 See also *Anelida and Arcite*, 112.

8. BEYOND REASON

1 Translations of Lactantius are from *The Works of Lactantius*, translated by William Fletcher, D.D., 2 vols (Edinburgh, 1886).

2 *De Civitate Dei*, xiv, 9; ix, 5.

3 Cicero, *De Officiis*, I, xiv; *Tusc. Disp*. IV, xxvi, 56. Alan of Lille (*PL*. 210, 176) distinguishes three kinds of alms-giving: the first (*frigida*), springing not from

natural sympathy but the desire for worldly glory, is reprehensible; the second (*tepida*) arises from humane sympathy, is possible without Christian belief, and therefore has no merit; and the last (*calida*) is the result of Christian charity and is deserving of glory. A different emphasis is given by Aquinas when he states that a work of charity is more laudable when it arises from rational consideration than from a mere feeling of pity (*ST*. 1a 2ae, 24, 3).

4 References to Love in its manifestation as a cosmological force are quite common in Chaucer's works: *Bo*. II, m.viii; *CT*. I, 2988; *TC*. I, 237; III, 1261.

5 Aquinas (*ST*. 1a 2ae, 26, 3) calls this *dilectio*. *Dilectio* is distinct from *amor* since it implies rational choice – an act of the will. Nevertheless it is regarded as a species of *amor*, and is therefore often called by that name.

6 Peter of Blois, *De Amicitia Christiana* is edited with a French translation by M.-M. Davy, *Un Traité de l'Amour du xiiᵉ siècle* (Paris, 1932). Peter's treatise is heavily dependent upon the earlier work of Ailred of Rievaulx. For the ideal of friendship in secular literature, see Gervase Mathew's essay in *Patterns of Love and Courtesy: Essays in Memory of C. S. Lewis*, edited by John Lawlor (London, 1966), pp. 45–53.

7 Chaucer uses phrases (*love of frendshipe; love of frendes; frendes love*) which may appear to be translations of *amor amicitiae* on five separate occasions, all in *Troilus and Criseyde*. On each of these occasions the reference is simply to friendship. In four of the five uses, *love of frendshipe* is implicitly or explicitly contrasted as a relationship between the sexes with sexual love. Chaucer's usage is quite modern and has a different significance from the Latin usage. *Amor amicitiae* is perhaps better to be associated with Gower's *honeste love*, since the distinction between it and *amor concupiscentiae* is close to that between *honestas* and *utilitas*. (Cicero, *De Inventione*, II, lii, 157–9).

8 Peter of Blois, i, 9; Brunetto Latini, *Tresor*, II, xliii, 6.

9 *ST*. 2a 2ae, 157, 2–3. This distinction between affect and effect is a familiar one in the classification of vices and virtues, and is made by (?) William of Conches in the *Moralis Philosophia*. This work is attributed to Hildebert of Laverdin by Migne, *PL*. 171, 1015. The same distinction is made by Pecock, *Folewer*, p. 81.

10 Amongst the pagans of the later period *humanitas* was an admired virtue. Both Epictetus and Marcus Aurelius, although of Stoic persuasion, speak of the desirability of a willingness to understand and bear with one's fellow man on the grounds of shared humanity. The latter even speaks of 'a sort of sympathetic connexion' between men in the same society (*Meditations*, ix, 9). Aulus Gellius complains that his contemporaries are using the word *humanitas*, which he considers should properly refer to humane studies, to imply nothing more than benevolence (*Noctes Atticae*, XIII, xvii, 1). Pagan authors, however, do not stress the ideal of affective unity so strongly as is presumed by the Christian conception of charity.

11 I *Corinthians*, xii, 26; II *Cor.*, i, 4–7; *Romans*, xii, 15–6; I *Peter*, iii, 8. Also Augustine's definition of *misericordia*:

> Quid est autem misericordia nisi alienae miseriae quaedam in nostro compassio qua utique si possumus subvenire compellimur?
>
> But what is pity except a kind of fellow-feeling in our own hearts for the

sufferings of others that in fact impels us to come to their aid as far as our ability allows?

(*De Civitate Dei*, ix, 5)

12 *Summa Theologiae*, vol. 24 (1a 2ae, 68–70), edited with translation and notes by Edward D. O'Connor, C.S.C. (London, 1974), pp. 80–87.

13 *The Book of Vices and Virtues*, edited by W. Nelson Francis, E.E.T.S., Original Series 217 (London, 1942), p. 117.

14 Compare Alan of Lille: 'Quid incarnavit Christum, nisi misericordia? quid subjecit eum nostrae miseriae, nisi sua clementia: haec est sola via hominis ad Deum, Dei ad hominem.' (*PL*. 210, 147).

15 Uses of the phrase *wepen for pitee*, however, give only an inkling of the ubiquity of the collocation *wepen*, *pitee* and *routhe*.

16 Seneca, for example, became a witness of Christian revelation, and an exchange of letters between him and St. Paul had been forged as early as the fourth century. By the fourteenth century there were those ready to accept him as a convert. L. D. Reynolds, *The Medieval Tradition of Seneca's Letters* (Oxford, 1965), pp. 81–6.

17 Augustine, *De Doctrina Christiana*, iii, 10. It is unfair to convict Augustine of advocating interpretative fantasy, since his advice to seek figurative reconciliation of passages at variance with the doctrine of charity is hedged round by warnings to interpret responsibly, in accordance with literary context. *On Christian Doctrine*, translated by D. W. Robertson jr. (New York, 1958), pp. 78ff.

18 The use of the image of an eye usually implied the perception of prudence, but Abelard (ed. Luscombe, pp. 54–5) speaks of the intention as *oculus cordis*, and the author of the *Pistle of Discrecioun of Stirrings* assures his readers that: 'Iȝen of þe soule þei ben two, reson and love.' Furthermore, he claims, the latter is likely to seek out its end of salvation quicker and more directly than the former. The text appears in *Deonise Hid Diuinite and other treatises on Contemplative Prayer*, edited by Phyllis Hodgson, E.E.T.S., Original Series, 231 (London, 1955), p. 72.

19 *Peter Abelard's Ethics*, ed. Luscombe, pp, 44–5.

20 The author of the *Book of Priue Counseling* goes so far as to reject love as the direct path to God, preferring to hope for communion by a motion of the will acting out of a deliberately emptied consciousness: 'Whan þou comyst bi þi-self þenk not before what þou schalt do after, but forsake as wel good þouȝtes as ieul þouȝtes . . . and loke þat noþing leue in þi worching mynde bot a nakid entent streching into God.' *The Cloud of Unknowing and the Book of Privy Counselling*, edited by Phyllis Hodgson, E.E.T.S., Original Series, 218 (London, 1944), p. 135.

Such mystical pretensions were not acceptable to the author of the short treatise 'Of Angels' Song,' who saw the dangers of attempts at communion with neither the guidance of reason nor a clear object for affection. For him reason and 'burning love' are essential, and he will have no truck with *naked mynde*: 'it suffys to me forto lyfe in trouth principally, and nouȝt in felynge.' *Yorkshire Writers: Richard Rolle and his Followers*, edited by C. Horstmann, 2 vols (London, 1895), I, pp. 181–2.

21 Colin Morris, in his book, *The Discovery of the Individual, 1050–1200* (London, 1972), pp. 96–120, sees a close analogy between the *amicitia* of the monasteries and the ideals of courtesy.

9. THE GENTIL MAN

1 D. S. Brewer gives a valuable account of the associations of courtesy to the *Gawain*-poet in *Patterns of Love and Courtesy*, edited by John Lawlor (London, 1966), pp. 54–85.
2 A good idea of the breadth of application of the terms may be gained from *Romaunt of the Rose*, 2175–2342. See further, D. S. Brewer, 'Class Distinction in Chaucer,' *Speculum*, 43 (1968), 290–305; Nevill Coghill, 'Chaucer's Idea of What is Noble,' Presidential Address to the English Association (London, 1971); W. O. Evans, ' "Cortaysye" in Middle English,' *Med. Studies*, 29 (1967), 143–57; Alan T. Gaylord, '*Gentillesse* in Chaucer's *Troilus*,' *SP*, 61 (1964), 19–34.
3 Compare Dante, *Inferno*, V, 100: 'Amor, ch'al cor gentil ratto s'apprende,' and Guinizzelli: 'Foco d'amore in gentil cor s'aprende.' The idea is a commonplace of courtly poetry.
4 Compare *CT*. II, 615. We may recall that the Wife of Bath laughed at the suffering of her husbands. The idea that guiltless suffering should stimulate pity is as old as Aristotle's *Rhetorica*, ii, 8, and is alluded to by Aquinas, *ST*. 2a 2ae, 30, 1.
5 'La doucor de la melodie/ Me mist el cuer tel reuerdie' *The Romaunt of the Rose and Le Roman de la Rose*, edited by R. Sutherland (Oxford, 1968), lines 707-8. Clearly the English translator perceived the connotations of the original and adopted these rather than the literal colour sense of the phrase.
6 'Kar chant d'oisel e estrument/ Est d'amur an angusement.' Hue de Rotelande, *Ipomedon*, edited by E. Kölbing (reprinted Geneva, 1975), lines 8905–6. The nightingale which sings of love is a popular device of the lyrics of the trouvères. R. Dragonetti, *La Technique poétique des Trouvères dans la Chanson courtoise* (Bruges, 1960), pp. 169ff.
7 The essential condition of mutuality of will, which is seen in the egalitarian marriage of Dorigen and Arveragus, is shared by *amicitia* and by all truly courtly relationships. Such equality is the basis of friendship according to the definition given by Brunetto Latini: 'Et chascuns des amis ayme son bien et li uns fet gueredons a l'autre par sa bone volenté, selonc ygaillance; et cele est vraie amistié.' (*Tresor*, II, xliii, 8). A similar idea is emphasized in *Sir Gawain and the Green Knight*, 1498–1500. Gawain's defensive strategy in this scene is to deny mutuality of will by representing himself as the lady's instrument.
8 *The Awntyrs off Arthure at the Terne Wathelyne*, edited by R. J. Gates (Philadelphia, 1969), line 554. Examples, such as this, of regret at animal suffering should warn us against too easy an assumption of irony at the expense of the Prioresse. Ironic interpretations based upon psychological theory, or any other technical reference, must have firm contextual support.

9 *De Anima*, 421a 23f. In fact Aristotle awarded primacy in various places to the senses of sight and touch. He appears to have regarded the latter as in some way the more basic, since it is associated with the very possession of life itself. He denies, however (*De Sensu*, 442b) as Democritus' folly, the notion that the other senses are built upon touch. Nevertheless, his treatment of them often seems to depend upon an analogy with touch. Aquinas interpreted this as implying that the other senses were eventually dependent upon touch, and thus he makes an association between tactile sensitivity, general sensitivity and subtle intellect. Aristotle had been content to link subtlety of touch directly with that of mind.

10 The Latin is quoted from Sancti Thomae Aquinatis, *In Aristotelis Librum De Anima Commentarium*, edited by P. F. Angeli M. Pirotta, O.P. (Turin, 1959), Book II, Lectio xix, 484 and 485. Translations are by Kenelm Foster, O.P. and Silvester Humphries, O.P., *Aristotle's De Anima in the Version of William of Moerbeke and the Commentary of St. Thomas Aquinas* (London, 1951), p. 304. See further *ST*. Ia, 76, 5. Albertus Magnus also associates soft flesh with superior understanding. This intellectual eminence, he explains, is not to be associated with a superior imagination, as some have mistakenly believed, but with the subtlety of the medium (*spiritus cordis*) which carries impressions from the sense organs to the central organ of sense, apparently the heart. Albertus Magnus, *De Anima*, edited by Clemens Stroick, O.M.I. (Aschendorff, 1968), II, iii, cap. 23.

11 See, for example, *Boece*, III, p. vi. Old French translations of Boethius rendered *nobilitas* either as *noblece* or *gentillece*, and Chaucer simply adopted Jean de Meun's rendering in every case.

12 Consider, for example the purpose of the translations into the vernacular of works like Boethius, the *Rhetorica ad Herennium*, or Brunetto Latini's encyclopaedia, the *Tresor*, which together represent a mere fraction of the didactic, secular literature which appeared in French towards the close of the thirteenth century. Similar works were translated into English within the next century and a half.

13 E. R. Curtius, *European Literature and the Latin Middle Ages*, translated by Willard R. Trask (New York, 1953), p. 158.

14 Glending Olson, 'Deschamps' *Art de Dictier* and Chaucer's Literary Environ-ment,' *Speculum*, 48 (1973), 714–23 (p. 721). Chaucer's denials of feeling underlying his composition of courtly poetry contrasts with the case of lovers in *Legend of Good Women*, 69 and with Chauntecleer who sung everything *of herte* (*CT*. VII, 3303).

15 *Courtois* burgesses are found in French romance at least from the thirteenth century, but do not become usual in English romance before the fifteenth century.

16 Here the sense of *cruel* is in effect a restoration of the etymological sense 'crude, rough' of Latin *crudelis*. The opposition between *cruel* and *gentil* is realized in terms quite peripheral to the more frequent sense of the words.

17 Gawain is asked by a lady whether he is the most esteemed of the Round Table. His moderate reply that he is neither the worst nor the best is praised by the lady as *grant cortoisie*. See also the *mesure* advised by the Scornful Damsel (6684–9),

and the following statement in *Perceforest*, II, 147: 'Courtoisie et mesure est une mesme chose.'

18 William of Malmesbury, *De gestis regum Anglorum*, edited by W. Stubbs, 2 vols, Records Commission IV. 90 (London, 1887–9), vol. II, p. 510.

19 J. D. Burnley, '*Fine Amor*: Its Meaning and Context,' (forthcoming in *The Review of English Studies*).

20 For example, *Troilus and Criseyde*, I, 336; IV, 782.

21 In Old English *þanc* is associated with Latin *gratia*, and contextual synonymy between *thank* and *grace* is common in Chaucer's poetry, especially in the courtly love situation. The evident paradox of the collocation *grace deserve* (e.g. *CT*. I, 1232) is frequently hidden by the substitution of the synonym *thank*. If we consider this synonymy to belong to a different semantic sub-system from the Augustinian definition of grace – one in which *grace/thank* refers to the legitimate reward for service rendered – then the constant use of the Augustinian significance in religious analogies by writers referring to the courtly love situation serves as good evidence of the confusion of any alleged system. The implication is that the religious analogy is one of stylish wit, more or less extended, rather than any serious attempt to work out a consistent philosophy.

22 As in the *Kingis Quair*, edited by John Norton-Smith (Oxford, 1971), line 1193.

Index of Words

In this index the various grammatical forms of each word are represented by a single head word: thus *avisement* stands also for *avys, avysen, avysely,* and *constantia* refers also to the verb *consto.*

Subject Index